DEMOCRACY AGAINST ITSELF

THE FUTURE OF THE DEMOCRATIC IMPULSE

Jean-François Revel

Translated by Roger Kaplan

THE FREE PRESS
A Division of Macmillan, Inc.
NEW YORK

Maxwell Macmillan Canada
TORONTO

Maxwell Macmillan International
NEW YORK   OXFORD   SINGAPORE   SYDNEY

The Free Press
A Division of Macmillan, Inc.
866 Third Avenue, New York, N. Y. 10022

Maxwell Macmillan Canada, Inc.
1200 Eglinton Avenue East
Suite 200
Don Mills, Ontario M3C 3N1

Macmillan, Inc. is part of the Maxwell Communication
Group of Companies.

Printed in the United States of America

printing number
1 2 3 4 5 6 7 8 9 10

Library of Congress Cataloging-in-Publication Data

Revel, Jean-François.
  [Regain démocratique.   English]
  Democracy against itself: the future of the democratic impulse/
Jean-François Revel: translated by Roger Kaplan.
      p.   cm.
    Includes index.
    ISBN 0–02–926387–5
    1. Democracy.   2. Post-communism.   I. Title.
JC423.R45313 1993
321.8—dc20   93-19693
                                                       CIP

TO
BRANKO LAZITCH

CONTENTS

Contents

PREFACE
to the American Edition

DEMOCRACY AGAINST ITSELF is not a book about current affairs, aimed at such recent political events as the end of communism, the failure of socialism in the Third World, or the increased interest in human rights just about everywhere. Rather, this is a book about a timeless problem, the search for the best political system available, or at any rate the least pernicious one—which amounts to the same thing. That system is democracy. And in this regard, I have endeavored to show, by looking at many examples taken from history no less than from today's headlines, that every society which has worked more or less well, which achieved any sort of viability, and which produced civilizations men found tolerable, have been—or are—societies that in some sense are democratic.

To be sure, not all of these societies are democratic by today's standards. All of them are not founded on universal suffrage and representative government. But the important point is that many societies which we call "traditional" include democratic elements. The rulers, even when not chosen by the people, have obligations; and the ruled, even when not considered the source of society's legitimacy, enjoy limited but real liberties, judicial rights, and inviolable laws.

To understand such societies, which are neither democratic nor totalitarian, I have referred in the chapters below to such examples as the Roman Empire—with its very substantial degree of decentralization and local self-government—Europe's medieval cities, Holland in the seventeenth century, and even Mexico in that period. Modern democracy, based on representative government, equality before the law, universal suffrage, and freedom of opinion and information, grew out of elements of democracy, cultural freedom, and individual rights. It is of fundamental importance to recognize how ancient or traditional societies differ in their very essence from totalitarian regimes, or even from those we call modern authoritarian. For the essence of these totalitarian or modern authoritarian regimes is that they destroy an existing democracy, or the conditions that render it possible in a society.

The despotisms of our century, in other words, adopt an attitude of deliberate hostility toward democratic societies, which by contrast coexist peacefully. Ancient societies were not deliberately antidemocratic. They found some sort of internal balance in the context of the rule of law, with all the implications for citizenship and for the development of democratic institutions, which this entails. Moreover, in these regimes what we call today civil society enjoyed a high degree of independence from the political authorities in the conduct of its daily affairs. By contrast, totalitarianism suppresses and ultimately destroys civil society. It can do nothing else to attain and hold on to power.

Thus the meaningful opposition, in political philosophy, is not between democratic and totalitarian societies. It is between normal and abnormal societies. Compared to democracy, totalitarianism is abnormal—but it is abnormal by comparison to all other societies as well. Plenty of societies in history were not democratic in the sense that we understand the term today, but they were not totalitarian and pathological, in the sense that the Hitlerian and Stalinist regimes were. Not all normal system are democratic, even if, for reasons that I shall examine below, the idea that democracy is synonymous with political normality gradually gained universal currency. On the other hand, democratic systems too can be pathological: Chapter 13 examines certain aspects of this problem, which is also the subject of a previous book of mine, *How Democracies Perish*. But this pathology is different from totalitarian pathology. Democracy may suffer from a variety of illnesses, some of which may even be fatal, but it is not the system itself which is intrinsically pathological, one where the regime, to repeat, can maintain itself in power only by utterly extirpating the autonomy of civil society and private individuals. There have been numerous nondemocratic societies in history and they never had to resort to such extremes.

Each chapter in *Democracy Against Itself* represents a step in the development of a theory on what I call the practical necessity of democracy. Democracy's practical superiority derives from the fact that it is the only system which, through trial and error, can become aware of its mistakes and correct them. Totalitarianism cannot correct itself: it is forced to follow its logic until the final catastrophe. Ancient "normal" societies had certain propensities for self-correction, but these were less developed than democracies'—which indeed is why these kinds of societies tended to move toward greater degrees of democracy. This is why the section of this book about the Third World argues that the causes of underdevelopment are essentially political, not economic. Underdevelopment, however, can also have ideological or religious causes; it may be due to a certain worldview, as I try to show in my chapter on Islam.

However, I believe in no such thing as the end of history, nor in the inevitable triumph of liberal democracy. Regression is possible. The human mind is always seeking after new utopias, which cause men to forget the practical criteria required by democracy and which lead to attempts at imposing ideal systems on society. Among their other virtues, democratic systems are useful in that they establish constitutional safeguards, which prevent political fanatics from gaining a monopoly of political power.

This is why I attach a special importance to the section of this book devoted to the collapse of communism and, in particular, the chapter, "How to Get Out of the Consequences of Communism." The key word here is "consequences." For beyond the anecdotal interest of these recent events, there is a question of universal and timeless significance: How can an abnormal society become normal once again? This is entirely different from the issue of how a normal, albeit undemocratic, society becomes democratic. There are many examples in history of this latter process. But building a new civil society, based on freedom, law, and enterprise, and erecting it on the shambles of totalitarianism, represents an entirely new problem, with far graver difficulties. Rather naively, the West believed this would be a relatively easy matter during the early days of Gorbachev's *perestroika*.

Gorbachev's originality—which made him a hero in the West and a knave in the Soviet Union—was that he honestly tried to reform communism. To reform means to change while preserving. It means improving things, replacing a system's details in order to save the whole. This was to the West a reassuring program, for it saw in this idea of decommunized communism a way to rid itself of the totalitarian threat from the inside, while maintaining stability and continuity and without upsetting the international balance. The idea also appealed to the international Left, which saw in Gorbachev the fulfillment of its old dream of a democratic socialism, the celebrated "third way." Thanks to Gorbachev, the Left could say that the collapse of communism was not a refutation of socialism, nor of the Marxist tradition. At the same time, Gorbachev appealed to conservatives such as Margaret Thatcher and George Bush, who were eager to win the Cold War without excessive damage to the existing geopolitical balance.

But Gorbachev was hated in the Soviet Union. There people could see in their daily lives that his efforts to patch up a dead system lengthened their suffering and deepened their misery by pushing back a complete collapse and a reconstruction from scratch. The special and unique value of the Gorbachev era is that it provided empirical evidence for the impossibility of getting out of a totalitarian system other than by destroying it totally, which cannot be done, alas, before it has itself utterly destroyed civil society. It is in the interest of humanity to study this incomparable experiment in great detail, for it may bring us the lessons we need to avoid ever again succumbing to a totalitarian temptation.

There are no general laws of history, which is made entirely by human action. But there are lessons to be learnt from the experiences of the past, and these allow us to avoid making the same mistakes over again. This is what political philosophy is for. And its teaching is that in these closing years of the twentieth century, the only regime that is both legitimate and efficient is democracy.

PART ONE

NONSENSE AND COMMON SENSE ABOUT DEMOCRACY

CHAPTER ONE

THE DEMOCRATIC HIGH

Modern democracy was conceived in the eighteenth century. Put into practice, in a limited way and in very few countries, in the nineteenth century, it was very nearly murdered in the twentieth. Barely saved from the Nazi assault, defended, with great difficulty, against communism, it had remained since 1945 highly vulnerable and widely scorned. And then of a sudden, in the mid-1980s, there occurred a reversal of democracy's fortunes, on the level of ideas no less than in ordinary political practice, at the popular level no less than in elite opinion. How did this happen? And why? Is the change for real? Will it last? Will it lead to a strengthening and spreading of democracy around the world? Is it based on clear ideas that are being put into practice in a serious and honest way, or on vague, incoherent, and false notions that will lead to new deceptions and sufferings?

The importance of liberal democracy was derided, through most of the twentieth century, by those who placed a higher value on other supposedly more concrete priorities, such as poor countries' economic development, social justice, material and cultural equality, "world peace," the fight against "imperialism"—which, since World War II, has been synonymous with American foreign policy for the Left—and against a malevolent capitalism hiding behind the mask of "formal liberties." In this view, human rights were thought to be a juridical abstraction with no substance, a trick to mislead the powerless, the poor, the ignorant; a form of protection of use only to those who benefit from the privileges of wealth and knowledge.

The great renewal of democracy spread, in the eighties, in the three types of society we have known during the past decades: developed democracies, developing nations (among which there is much variety), and communist societies.

In the democracies, the main advance took place in the sense that the democratic principle no longer was challenged from within. Radical revolutionaries simply disappeared from inside these societies, with the exception of terrorists who, to be sure, were able to do a lot of harm but had no chance of seizing power or setting forth a coherent program. The old revolutionary parties became either openly reformist, as occurred in the case of the Italian Communist Party, or increasingly marginal, as in the case of the French Communist Party (CP). This was a profound reversal compared to the preceding decade, during which the general secretary of the French CP terrorized other political leaders and the media to such a degree that to attack him directly invited the wrath not only of the entire Left but of a good part of the Right as well! But now the Left emerged from the great dream of reconciling socialism and liberty. The new general secretary of the Italian Communist Party, Achille Occhetto, stated in 1989: "Our objective is no longer the socialist system achieved by democratic means, but democracy guided by socialist ideals." This is more than a revision—this is a reversal of Marxism. As to the socialist parties, they accepted one after the other not only social democracy, but even economic liberalism or market economics. The French Socialists were the last, in 1981, to still want to change society, rather than certain aspects of it. Their monumental failure, which was obvious by 1983, sobered even them. In 1989, the British Labour Party, tired of losing elections, removed from their program all references to public ownership of the means of production.* "Capitalism" stopped being a dirty word, as the Left recognized the necessity to limit the role of the state in the economy and the media, and even found nice things to say about private enterprise. What we witnessed might be called a "decriminalization of civil society," now viewed as a model for the state, rather than the reverse. But, beyond the arguments over the optimal degree of economic liberty compatible with social justice, what mattered was, precisely, that the discussion was focused only on the degree of intervention: it had become a practical matter not an issue of principle. All political currents, with the exception of the

*The Labour Party lost the 1992 elections.—TRANS.

most marginal ones, now accepted the idea that you had to accord priority to political democracy, individual freedoms, and human rights. After a century and a half of doctrinal conflict between socialists and liberals, the latter could declare victory.

In a still more interesting change, the Third World reached the same conclusion. "Third Worldism" came under increasing criticism in the 1980s. The term had been used, on the one hand, to explain underdevelopment in Marxist terms, as in "rape of the Third World" and "unfair exchanges" by capitalism, and, on the other, to justify "revolutionary" and "socialist" and "progressive" dictatorships as the only way to mobilize poor countries and liberate them from "dependence." Every experiment along these lines ended in sinister failure, deteriorating into misery, famine, corruption, despotism, and sometimes bloodbaths. By contrast, nonsocialist right-wing dictatorships that remained capitalistic seemed able to take off economically and to evolve toward political democracy. Thus, South Korea, the Philippines, Pakistan, and Latin America's noncommunist dictatorships reoriented themselves toward representative government and free elections. A humiliating moment occurred for the Left in October 1988: The same month witnessed a referendum in Chile in which General Pinochet accepted the voters' disavowal, and a massacre by Algeria's progressive, socialist, and revolutionary government of hundreds of adolescents demonstrating peacefully for the work and the food the regime was incapable of providing.

The Third World faced two conclusions: First, political democracy, far from being a luxury for the rich, is a necessity for the poor—a means by which civil society can send messages to the political authorities, rid itself of a corrupt and incompetent government, and invent the tools necessary for economic development. Second, and the past thirty years has demonstrated this repeatedly, it is easier to return to democracy from a fascist military dictatorship than from a socialist-progressive dictatorship, probably because in the latter despotism the state's control over the economy is far more pervasive and profound.

Then in the second half of the decade, the democratic revival reached the very heart of communism. In August 1989, in Warsaw, for the first time in Eastern Europe in forty-three years, a Communist party agreed—without civil war or foreign invasion—to take a minority role in a government led by noncommunists. What we were witnessing throughout Eastern Europe and the Soviet Union was not a reform of communism, as was being said, but the rout of communism. Up till then no reform was found that made it possible for a communist country to emerge from underdevelopment and find a long-term path to economic efficiency in democracy and freedom. What we have been seeing since 1989 is an economic disintegration so advanced that communism had to choose between disappearance and massive and bloody repression, as occurred in China in June 1989. More precisely the question was: Can communism be reformed without destroying itself?

At any rate, whereas only ten years earlier it had been almost impossible to argue, even in the West, that socialism was definitely and irretrievably finished, its failure now proclaimed to the whole world that the liberal democratic model was superior. Nineteen ninety-one saw even the collapse of Sweden's social democratic model, which for a long time was thought to have retained the advantages and jettisoned the liabilities of both systems. Bankrupt, rejected by the voters, Sweden's social democracy made way for a wave of privatizations—as did Zambia once it rid itself of Kaunda. From all sides were heard lyrical praises of democracy—which is very well—but more than this: confident proclamations that the "democratic revolution" would triumph everywhere in all countries and overcome all difficulties. Gorbachev himself, transformed into the benevolevent mentor of the world's oldest democracies, proclaimed at the U.N. on 7 December 1988: "The whole world is becoming democratic." On every continent conferences met to sing praises to the new goddess, whose inexistence it was forbidden to deny: not only democracy, but universal democracy, the complete democratization of the world.

I called this new faith the "democratic euphoria." Is it justified?

CHAPTER TWO

ILLUSIONS AND REALITIES OF THE DEMOCRATIC EUPHORIA

There is no doubt that democracy gained ground in the 1980s, both as an ideal in people's minds and as a reality of political practice. Freedom House, a New York-based human rights organization, publishes an annual report on freedom in the world. In 1986 it said that out of a global population of about 4.8 billion, 1.7 billion lived under democratic regimes, 1.1 lived in partly democratic regimes, and 1.9 billion in unfree societies. Determining these numbers is no easy task, of course. It was based on the painstaking application of a long list of specific criteria that measure different aspects of political, civil, and personal freedoms. In some societies, certain freedoms may be available even as fundamental human rights are violated. In others, the situation may be reversed. Thus, the Freedom House scale is a study in gray areas.

The key point, however, is that on this complex gray scale, freedom has been making steady progress. Since Freedom House published its first report in 1974, the numbers have reflected a very substantial improvement. Thus, in 1986 over 36 percent of the world's population lived in societies that could be termed free against 32 percent in 1973; over 23 percent lived in societies that could be termed partly free (21 percent in 1973); and over 40 percent lived in totally repressive societies (47 percent in 1973).

In the next few years, these improvements accelerated. As the world's population topped five billion souls in 1988, both the absolute numbers and the proportions of people living in freedom increased. Over 38 percent of the world's people lived in freedom that

7

year, the highest percentage since Freedom House began its surveys. Conversely, by 1988 the percentage of the world's population living in completely repressive societies had reached an alltime low of just under 38 percent, and by 1991 it was down to 31 percent.

No classification is perfect, and none can reflect with absolute precision the exact level of human rights in a given society. But Freedom House's is both subtle and realistic, and what it reflects is the undeniable fact that there was, as the last decade of the century began, a generalized global trend toward liberalization. The striking thing about this democratic wave is that the countries it reached were all outside the communist sphere; even those countries that were not in the Soviet orbit, but that had adapted a socialist-totalitarian model, such as Algeria, Benin, or Burma, were left untouched. In Latin America, when an extreme-right dictatorship collapsed, it gave way not to a dictatorship of the extreme left but to a moderate, centrist government. It seemed the Spanish model of "democratic transition," such as had occurred in 1976, was being adopted in Latin America. Whatever else it meant, and whatever backsliding subsequently occurred, this evolution represented an ideological and political victory for liberalism. Communism had not fallen back yet, but it was stopped in its tracks. The Third World no longer viewed communism as a model of rapid development, particularly since it was, at last, evident to all that it was itself a form of underdevelopment. Of all the blows dealt Marxist theory by reality, democracy's social and economic efficiency is probably the most potent. And even as there was a demonstration of the practical value of "formal" democracy for the purpose of reducing social inequalities, it became apparent that the state itself, or more accurately statism, was a drawback on growth. In short, not only political liberalism, but economic liberalism, or the free market, was finally getting its due credit. In 1989, when the Stroessner dictatorship in Paraguay fell and Chile was in the midst of a painfully slow but nonetheless real democratization process, there remained only two despotisms on the American continent: Cuba and Nicaragua, which happened also to be the countries whose economies were the most wretched and whose populations were suffering the hardest deprivations.

These facts might have provided European socialists and American "liberals" some incentive for reflecting upon their own past responsibilities regarding the regimes they had encouraged and those they had

8

scorned. The events of the late 1980s demolished their long-standing arguments for the superiority of "real" over "formal" liberties and gave the lie to their apologies for the left-wing regimes that supposedly promoted economic well-being and social justice, even if they did so at some cost to political democracy. What was evident was that by whatever name they were called, socialist and communist regimes inspired by Marxist progressivism or "Third-Worldism" failed to satisfy any human needs, material or spiritual: neither well-being nor liberty, neither social rights nor political rights, neither human dignity nor economic security, neither culture nor nourishment. Until then, the Left, broadly understood, sometimes granted that "real socialism" might have some defects, but simply refused to admit what should have been clear for decades, namely that it is inherently reactionary and that the real revolution of the twentieth century would be a movement by the world's peoples against communism for the conquest and the preservation of freedom.

Until 1985, communism seemed irreversible. The progress of democracy chronicled by Freedom House and other observers took place entirely outside the communist sphere. As a matter of fact, the latter had expanded after 1945, and even more so after 1975. Democracy might be making progress in the noncommunist world, but this world was itself shrinking in relation to the communist one.

And then from 1985 on, the democratic wave was felt even within the communist universe. Communist leaders had to recognize, as Third World leaders did, that market economics represented their best chance for emerging out of the stagnation of socialism—not that anyone knew how to combine the market with communist political institutions. Already at the end of the seventies, China had preceded the Soviet Union in attempting this bizarre marriage between freedom of enterprise and the collective ownership of the means of production. Countries such as Hungary and Poland studied the problem of the "passage from socialism to capitalism," an expression rich in irony in an intellectual tradition that for a century and a half had sought the secret of the road that went in the other direction. To be sure, communism from the very beginning had adapted its system in order to mitigate its failures and, if nothing else, to convince Westerners that they should bail it out. But with Mikhail Gorbachev ideas for reform were taken much farther. Most significantly, they were enriched by political inferences, by a critical view of recent history, and by a degree of access to information and freedom of expression that undoubtedly went much farther than earlier "thaws," and that produced an unprecedented situation.

In 1987 and 1988, the disappearance of a few third-world dictatorships and the weakening of totalitarianism in a few European communist countries (including the most monstrous of these, the Soviet Union) made such an impression that people began to think of planetary democratization as if it were virtually complete. To question this new dogma was considered a sacrilege. It was as if there were no important differences, no obstacles, no chances for backsliding, between the symptoms and the final (desired) result. From signs that, unquestionably, were positive, some leapt uncritically to the final chapter of history, as if it were already written and was valid for every region in the world.

To take one example among many, Freedom House's normally sober magazine, *Freedom at Issue*, proclaimed in 1989 that the nineties would be "the decade of global democracy." To be sure, the author was offering a program as much as he was predicting the future; still, this represented the kind of language, self-confident to the point of ecstasy, that began to blossom in the media, in scholarly literature, in political conferences. Democracy had won, it was endlessly repeated, and the threats to it either were gone or were on the way out.

When enthusiasm is added to cleverness, there is a risk of mistaking the embryo for the adult, or even the birth announcement for the triumphant step up to the Olympic podium, which the baby is expected to reach. From 1985 on, political analyses seemed to be guided by this sort of cleverness, taking for granted an imagined future.

Foreign affairs provided excellent examples of this sort of wishful thinking. In 1987 Gorbachev stated that he wished to put an end to regional conflicts, so the West leapt to the conclusion that they were resolved already and that democracy had triumphed in such war-torn places as Afghanistan, Angola, Mozambique, Cambodia, and Nicaragua. Five years later, after the departure of Gorbachev, the termination of the Soviet Union, and the evaporation of the "new [foreign policy] thinking," armed communists are still very much there and whatever the optimistic hopes of Western statesmen and commentators, democracy remains, at best, a possible outcome of a drawn-out fight for power.

There is no doubt the collapse of the Soviet Empire, when finally it occurred, opened up prospects of national liberation and political freedom for millions of people. The West's reaction to Gorbachev's promises, however, should be remembered as an example of the democracies' depressing tendency to believe a problem is resolved as soon as the other side promises to resolve it.

Pausing for a moment at the year 1989, we might observe that at that time there were two billion souls living under communist or fellow-traveling regimes, including such paragons of liberalism as Algeria, Romania, Vietnam, and Ethiopia. Mass terror and bloody repression were coming down on the people of China, Cuba, Tibet, Burma. The Soviet Union was still there and was still the world's premier military power. And this was when it was most fashionable to say that communism had disappeared and democracy had triumphed. The failure of communism had at last been understood, but once again theory was being confused with reality and it was as if communist and despotic states, with everything they represented for the people unfortunate enough to live in them, had miraculously disappeared, to be immediately replaced by universal democracy.

This kind of thinking was closer to magic than to historical analysis. To be sure, there was far more reason to be sanguine than ten years earlier. But how were billions of men and women supposed to get out of political systems that remained highly resistant to change and that had no built-in processes of self-amendment? How were billions of individuals to get beyond economic systems so sick no one could figure out either how to keep them going or finish them off? If communism could not be cured, how could one imagine promptly building normal democratic societies on its wreckage? Once again, we were expecting the problem to just go away because we wanted it to, instead of focusing on the task we would need to undertake. The idiotic euphoria with which we in the democracies contemplated the shambles of communism, figuring the answer would come down from heaven, seemed to be the final item on the list of the forms of wilful blindness that I had described in *How Democracies Perish*.

I wrote that book in 1985 and since then it has caused me no end of comments such as, "Now that communism is on the way out, should you not rethink your arguments?" However, the theme of my book was not that the democracies would perish. My book analyzed the illusions about Soviet communism that could prove fatal to the democracies. The excessive optimism about Gorbachev was a perfect illustration of my thesis. The crisis of communism was a fact. But the weakness, the clumsiness, the intellectual laziness, and the passivity of

11

political leadership no less than public opinion in the democracies were facts too. We found it impossible to seize the opportunity, which we had not earned, to hasten the spread of freedom around the world. Our interpretation of the evolution of communism seemed to have one major purpose, namely, to justify our inaction and the continuation of our economic aid to a dying and repressive system, even as our generosity seemed mysteriously to evaporate when confronted with the needs of such countries as Hungary, Czechoslovakia, and Poland, which needed help not to perpetuate communism but to extract themselves from it. Rereading the programs and analyses in the West in the years between 1985 and 1990, you realize they all reached the conclusion that it was imperative to take the communist rulers at their word and give them what they asked for—even the Chinese after the massacres of June 1989 in Tiananmen Square in Beijing.

It was not the West that changed, but rather the aggressive potential of communism. It reached so profound a degree of economic crisis that it could not sustain its expansionary course—but it certainly was not trying to defend us despite ourselves.

In reality, the reversal of the situation to the democracies' relative advantage was due to three factors—which were not the result of anything they did, which contradicted their expectations, and which even, I would argue, disappointed their hopes. The first of these factors was the total, and now irreversible, failure of the communist systems, which took place with a rapidity all the more surprising since the democracies had done all they could in the "détente decade" (1970–80) to shower them with all manners of presents—economic, financial, diplomatic, and strategic. The second factor was that the peoples of the Third World rejected "Third Worldism" and requested capitalism and democracy, against the predictions and the wishes of elite opinion (and left-wing parties) in the U.S. and Europe. The third factor was the vigorous economic upturn in the rich countries and developing countries which rejected socialism.

The irony, in short, is that democracy was saved not so much because it defended itself (except during the first term of Ronald Reagan, which was decisive albeit strongly criticized) but becaue of the unexpected disintegration of the forces that opposed it. To this was added the disappointing discovery that democracy was in better health than the elites thought possible and that capitalism ignored the funeral announcement made by socialists every year with virtuous obstinacy since the middle of the nineteenth century.

The real measure of democracy's capacity to resist subversion is not the disappearance of certain threats—these abated by themselves—but democracy's response to remaining threats and to new ones. To be sure, these are not as deadly as was a nuclear-armed Soviet Union bent on expansion, but is there any reason to take comfort in the frivolous and inconsequential responses of the democracies to international state terrorism, hostage-taking, Islamic fundamentalism, or belligerent dictators like Hafiz al-Assad or Saddam Hussein? The Gulf War of 1991 does not mitigate this analysis. Without doubt the U.S.-led coalition against Saddam was a welcome act of fortitude, all the more so for being so unexpected. But let us not forget that, first of all, this was a threat that the democracies themselves had created and financed, and let us not forget, either, that after their military victory they did not finish the job by putting this threat out of commission for good. Only a few months after his "defeat," Saddam was in a position to get his nuclear- and chemical-weapons program going again, mislead the U.N. inspectors regarding his installations, and oblige the Western powers, in the summer of 1991, to threaten him with aerial bombings if he did not fall in line. After mobilizing half the planet, to have to replay the same act was not exactly a stunning political victory, particularly in relation to the amount of military power deployed in the first place.

Yes, liberal democracy appeared to have won a complete victory at the end of the eighties in the face of the disintegration of the communist economies. But only ten years earlier, let us not forget, the balance of power was just the reverse and communist leaders did not conceal their intention to play their advantage. Never was communism so threatening as in 1980. For in the seventies, international communism had conquered vast territories in Africa and Asia, had gained an ally on the American mainland, had almost pulled off a coup d'état in Portugal, had gained recognition for the first time by the democracies of its 1940 annexations, and by its conquests later in that decade in central and Eastern Europe, had achieved parity, and then superiority, in nuclear armaments, and could expect Communist parties in Italy and France to achieve power shortly, as indeed they did in the latter.

When General Franco died, the Spanish Left looked forward to a period of radicalization and a new civil war, both of which might have taken place had it not been for the political genius of King Juan Carlos. Capitalism was in the midst of a drawn-out, severe recession.

Totalitarian socialism seemed the obvious answer to the Third World, which was copying, or hoping to copy, the original. To be sure, the "original model" was morally discredited in the developed world. But its political and military might were so intimidating that the West scarcely dared criticize it. "Capitalism" was a dirty word, "democracy" an object of scorn. The party of democratic capitalism—which I insist on calling the party of truth and human dignity—was fighting in those years a lonely rearguard action against totalitarianism, a battle of ideas without which the ideological and strategic preponderance of the socialist countries would have been overwhelming. Even in the 1989 edition of Paul Samuelson's *Economics*, probably the most widely used university text in the world, one could still read: "The Soviet economy proves that, contrary to what the Soviets themselves may believe, a centrally planned economy can function and even prosper."

We should remember this, lest the rapidity of communism's disintegration (undercut by its own inefficiencies) blind us to the fact that there always can be new, even absurd, totalitarian temptations. They are more deeply rooted in human nature than changing political circumstances suggest.

I will examine below the case of ordinary dictatorships or sham democracies; let it suffice for now to note that here, too, freedom has progressed since 1980. But let us recognize that this progress is fragile, that there almost surely will be reversals. Cheers for democracy in Haiti when the Duvalier dictatorship collapsed in 1986 were, alas, premature. It is not enough that a dictator fall for a democracy to be born. Many other factors are needed. No doubt, it was encouraging to see the appearance or reappearance of representative regimes in countries as important as the Philippines, Pakistan, South Korea, and most of the nations of Latin America. But simultaneously there was every reason to fear for the survival of democracy in Colombia, torn apart by drug cartels; in the Philippines threatened by anarchy, misery, armed insurrection; in Argentina, overwhelmed by economic mismanagement; in Peru, threatened by the madmen of the *Sendero Luminoso*; in Brazil, become virtually ungovernable due to the stupidity of its new constitution, even though it was adopted by a democratically elected constituent assembly.

There was, in short, cause to rejoice at the end of the eighties, but there was cause also to worry about an overhasty assumption that the movement toward democracy represented a sort of reverse millennium, the arrival of the eternal kingdom of liberty.

This optimistic feeling was expressed most intelligently by an American philosopher, Francis Fukuyama, with whose thesis I am in basic agreement. He argued that we have reached "the end point of mankind's ideological evolution and the universalization of Western liberal democracy as the final form of human government." But I think we are talking more of a moral and potential victory. Fukuyama is right to restore the role of psychology and culture and ideology in the making of history, in contrast to the role of economics which has taken a preponderant place in the historiography of the past century or so. But he does not go far enough, for he fails to note that history is made not only of evolutions and events but of decisions that are taken and applied by human agents, who have the capacity to upset the seemingly irreversible course of things. Human will sometimes defies the best-laid plans of abstract models.

You can dismiss marginal events as the "rearguard" resistance to the inevitable liberal democratic tide, but it is lives and entire generations that get swept up in these supposedly marginal rearguard actions. Added up, you have most of the people alive in our century. After all, you could argue that in view of what was known about democracy, free economies, and humanistic culture already in 1900, communism, fascism, and nazism were merely rearguard actions. They nonetheless poisoned the entire century. For billions of people, that is what history was, nothing else—and still is. For them, "the victory of Western liberal democracy" never had a shred of reality. The interesting question is why such horrors developed on a supposedly enlightened continent. And so long as we do not really understand this, who can say that we are safe from insanities that will have utterly different ideological premises but whose effects will be no less mysterious, ruinous, and bloody? There is no reason why, if the ordered and orderly world of our grandparents could not stop these things, a world that worships at the altar of the Universal Declaration of Human Rights should have better luck. To say that a regression is doomed in advance is true only in pure logic—in real life, it matters.

Thus, backwardness is not merely a gap between the idea of liberal democracy and its application. It would be if we saw a linear development from traditional societies toward democracy. But in fact, what we have seen in the past two centuries, and in particular since the French Revolution, is the constant invention of new forms of anti-democratism. These are motivated by a hatred of liberty more than by the weight of the past, though the two can join, as indeed they did in the Iran of the ayatollahs.

Intellectual generations reproduce themselves far more than they realize. The inadequacy of Marxist theory is acknowledged as a general proposition, yet you find that in specific cases people find it convenient to fall back on it. Thus, in Nicaragua, the Sandinista junta continued to be described as "progressive" not only by the Socialist International—which is supposed to be made up of anticommunist, democratic socialist parties—but by the mainstream media and even the U.S. Congress, while their opponents demanding the restoration of democracy, the end of press censorship, and so forth were described as "right-wing."

I am often told, "You are breaking down open doors; no one is still defending Fidel Castro," to take another example, "or pretending that he has not made a shambles of Cuba's economy." But the fact is that it was only in an August 1988 editorial that the *New York Times* observed that Cuba is indeed a more wretched place than when Castro took over in 1959. Why is it that Spanish Prime Minister Felipe Gonzalez can visit Fidel Castro and his government of torturers, whereas had he gone to see General Pinochet, even after the latter had put the democratization process on track, he would have been reprimanded by the Socialist International (to which Gonzalez belongs)? Somehow the leftist tyrant is more acceptable socially, and no one protests when he is invited to the inauguration of the Mexican president.

When intellectuals revise their views, they do not necessarily get to the bottom of their initial error; but they do get to have clean hands. This is the characteristic feature of intellectual and political revisionism. The public follows along, imitating the fashionable scorn just as earlier it imitated mindless adoration.

A perfect example of this purification process which permits intellectuals to stay on the right side of history and never need to admit they may have been wrong, was the famous meeting in Paris's Théâtre Récamier in 1977 when Jean-Paul Sartre, who supported and acclaimed every totalitarian butcher of the left on the planet, played host to a group of Soviet dissidents. François Furet has observed that this evening marked the moment when French intellectuals not only broke with Marxism-Leninism, but freed themselves of the complex that obliged them to be "anti-anti-communists."

But if this event had marked a real break, the French intellectual left would truly have learned to recognize totalitarianism when it saw it. Nothing of the kind occurred, and in the years following this evening they continued to find new enthusiasms for tyrannical movements from Nicaragua to Iran, even if they no longer repeated the old lies and behaved with the same cravenness about the Soviet Union or China.

Their "break" with the past was superficial, and was not based on any profound understanding of the totalitarian phenomenon, since they could not or would not recognize new manifestations of this phenomenon elsewhere. The Récamier gala's purpose was only to absolve them of past sins, not to root out the causes of their errors. They needed a symbolic ceremony to salvage their reputations and their status from the shambles of the Soviet and Chinese myths. So they shook hands with the victims of executioners whom they had earlier acclaimed. But did they publicly acknowledge they had been deeply mistaken and these dissidents had been right? Far from it; in no time at all they were accusing the likes of Solzhenitsyn, Maximov, Bukovsky, later on Armando Valladares, of being reactionaries.

The European intellectual Left continued to hold these men in contempt, to soil their reputations, to view them virtually as "fascists." For these dissidents were guilty of a crime: they did not want to save or reform socialism; they wanted to get rid of it altogether. The Récamier gala did not mark a fundamental change; it was merely an amnesty that leftist intellectuals granted themselves, with no commitments for future good behaviour. The dissidents temporarily played the role of sorcerers in this magic exorcism; after which, they returned to their role as traitors and reactionaries, while the intellectuals returned to theirs as prophets. Sweet is the way of error and recantation!

Francis Fukuyama is right in pointing out that the model of society represented by liberal democratic capitalism is now a universal reference and goal. But here begins another problem: how to make reality conform with this theoretical goal? There are few concrete cases around the world that could be said to be in conformity with the goal. The totalitarian left may have been routed ideologically; the fact remains that liberal democracy still has many enemies, both outside and inside the West. Consider the ridiculous case of Stanford University trying to substitute in the freshman curriculum junk by Franz Fanon and Che Guevara for great classical authors such as Dante, Shakespeare, Montaigne, or Cervantes. You will always be out of date when you prefer fashion to eternal values, of course, but this does not stop them. Far more tragic is the experience of whole peoples in Africa or the Mideast where misery, political despotism, and cultural barbarism does not look like a step toward the liberal model. It is important to understand that the Mengistus and Khomeinis are "modern," rather than traditional, products of the late twentieth century. They may have been ideologically discredited—and not everywhere— but that did not threaten their hold on power. Only a few weeks before his overthrow, in 1991, Ethiopian dictator Mengistu (who, in proportion to the population at hand had as many victims on his conscience as Stalin) was still lording it over the Organization of African Unity. He was by no means in disfavor with the international community, which was far more interested in chasing down cricket and rugby players who wanted to go to tournaments in South Africa. Nor is this international community in a hurry to see the departure of Algeria's leaders. On the contrary, the latter are hailed for having the kindness to announce reforms—which, however, do not include their own resignations on the grounds of criminal behavior, fraud, and failure.

You cannot dismiss these regimes lightly with the remark that they merely involve a few isolated religious fanatics. These religious fanatics rule over a huge proportion of mankind. One can laugh at "those bizarre ideas that cross the minds of certain persons in Albania or Burkina Faso," but I happen to believe that the inhabitants of these countries were not amused. There were few observers in the West to fully measure the significance of the events in China in June 1989. Instead, they said that sooner or later the students would win. But which ones? Certainly not those who were killed at Tiananmen Square. Sure, in the long term China will probably liberalize. But what good is the long term in politics, compared to the shortness of human life? China in 1989 signified the failure of liberalism, the success of communism. That is the relevant historical fact. Poland's Solidarity failed in 1981, suceeded in 1989. But the Polish liberals who died in between lost. Let us not copy the communist way of thinking—especially now when we say it is overtaken—and justify the present in terms of the future.

18

History is as much or more a story of backsliding than of progress. Without returning to totalitarianism, it is not inconceivable that the Soviet Union may fail to evolve toward liberal democratic capitalism. It could end up in a kind of anarchy, a chaotic return of medieval feudalisms and baronies. But there is no need for gloomy predictions—it is today, in our times, that people are subjected to such regimes as Ceausescu's, Kim Il Sung's, Ne Win's Burma, Ratsiraka's Madagascar, Idi Amin's Uganda, Sekou Toure's Guinea, Saddam Hussein's Iraq— quite good at killing Kurds with chemical weapons—Hafiz al-Assad's Syria, Khomeini's Iran. These are contemporaries of ours, as are the mass murderers in Tibet and Burundi, as are Pol Pot and Qaddafi, as are Fidel Castro and his show trials, Mengistu with his engineered famines, the butchers of Hanoi and their boat people—not to mention the democratic nations that forcibly send those same boat people back to their butchers. What is to assure us these are not representative of the world we live in? Terrorism destroyed democracy in Argentina and Uruguay in the 1970s, and it may destroy democracy in Peru and Colombia in the 90s; does anyone believe an Argentine or a Peruvian will take comfort in the notion that these are merely details, for history has reached a satisfactory end? What about the Turks, whose democracy was swept away by a terrorist cyclone in 1980? And as for signs of the times, who is to deny the efficiency of state terrorism between 1970 and 1990? Should we dismiss it as being more marginal than democratic institutions, including elections, for which citizens appear to have increasing contempt?

"Solutions" to problems seldom are the consequences of rational analyses. The experts who favored "détente" thought communism would soften as Western aid raised living standards in the Soviet Union; in fact, the opposite occurred: the system became more liberal as the economy collapsed beyond all hope, plunging, in the 1980s, into a terminal illness. It is commonly assumed that Soviet leaders came to the rational conclusion their system was absurd. Had that been so, they would have been true reformers. But they had their backs to the wall and lurched into *perestroika*, which merely accelerated the Soviet breakdown. Real reforms lead to beneficial policies— not inept attempts to patch up catastrophes.

Of course Fukuyama is right in asserting that, to be sure, the whole world is aware by now of the superiority of liberal democracy as a political and social system; but this hardly guarantees its planetary triumph, especially if the democracies fail to promote it actively. It is not

19

written anywhere that things always get better. Regression can and often does occur. "Video meliora, proboque, deteriora sequor," said Ovid: "I see the good and I like it, but I do wrong anyway." Unfortunately, this is the way people most often behave, as well as we can understand from studying history. If we want things to change, we must invent a global democratic politics, and it has to be willed and wilful. Frankly, when I look at the passive reaction of the democratic nations to—to take but one dramatic example—the Chinese butchery in June 1989, I must say we have a long way to go. Our great and brilliant statesmen seem to think that the key to political genius is to know how to wait for things to get better. But in politics as in everything else, only men can make things better. There is nothing sacred about history—it is merely the record of human action.

CHAPTER THREE

DEMOCRACY, TOTALITARIANISM, FREEDOM

HOW THE TOTALITARIAN PHENOMENON IN OUR TIMES CAUSED DEMOCRACY TO BE MISUNDERSTOOD AND WHY, IN CONSEQUENCE, WE MUST BEGIN OUR INQUIRY BEFORE THE TOTALITARIAN ERA.

Early in his book on Sor Juana Ines de la Cruz, Octavio Paz shows how the powers of the viceroy in colonial Mexico were limited by the rights people had. Despite his exhalted position, the viceroy simply could not act despotically. The subjects of the king of Spain whom he ruled possessed established channels through which to make known their demands, as well as to resist encroachments on their interests, their liberties, their customs. "It was a system of weights and measures," writes Paz, ". . . no viceroy of New Spain ever had as much power as a president of Mexico has today." This is a striking statement of the problem of democracy—of the relationship between individual liberty and political authority.

Now, to be sure, neither New Spain nor Spain itself in the seventeenth century was a democracy. The system's legitimacy, as we would say today, was not founded in popular sovereignty. The people had no constitutional mechanism for changing their rulers. But there was a crucial difference between this system—which lasted three centuries—and the totalitarian systems of our own times, and this was that it had not abolished all individual liberties, and there were many areas both economic and cultural that the state took little or no interest in. By contrast, the president of Mexico, though elected by universal suffrage (at least in theory), has powers that can directly infringe upon the life of an ordinary citizen in ways that no viceroy would have dreamed possible. The Mexican system has been criticized for habitual fraud at the polls, and for being based on a single party; but my point is that such a presidential system, even if it involved several parties competing in clean elections—which, after all, is the situation in Venezuela and Colombia and, for that matter, France—would give excessive powers to the executive. Free societies—this is a point that has been neglected lately—do not come into being as soon as there is a popular vote. An elected government may be oppressive and arbitrary. A nonelected government may leave large areas of liberty intact.

In France's ancien régime the local *parlements* exercised judicial power independently of the supposedly absolute monarchy. Observing the independence of the Bordeaux parlement's judiciary, Montesquieu got the idea of judicial independence in general, which he transmitted to American constitutionalists through Thomas Jefferson, who was one of his most assiduous readers. But since the Revolution in France, through five republics, two monarchies, and two empires, judicial power has still not recovered the degree of independence from the executive branch that it enjoyed before 1789, at least in practice.

This is but one example underscoring the fact that freedom is not an all-or-nothing proposition. Certain rights, individual and collective, have been guaranteed better by regimes lacking universal suffrage than by modern regimes which derive their legitimacy from it but which then proceed to overwhelm private rights. A right that can be taken away from you by the legislature is not a right—merely a temporary permission.

Communist totalitarianism perverted the very question of democracy in our times. (Nazi and fascist totalitarianism never claimed to be democratic.) For much of this century, it perpetuated the hoax that it was an advanced form of democracy, and even when this notion lost credibility, it was able to identify as "progressive" and as "left" (with the democratic connotations this implies) regimes that oppressed and starved people, while terming "right" liberal regimes that enhanced prosperity and human rights.

For the moment, at any rate, we have generally overcome this perversion of political thought; but totalitarianism also left in its wake a

22

profound misunderstanding of the nature of liberty. It imposed its way of thinking even on its enemies. Thus, the world is divided in two camps, totalitarianism and democracy. The communists, of course, insisted that theirs was the true democratic system, whereas liberal democracy was a sham and little more than a veiled fascist dictatorship. This was accepted by many individuals and parties in the West and the Third World, including member organizations of the Socialist International such as the French Socialist Party between 1971 and 1983. It was this way of thinking that justified terrorism and inspired the so-called Theology of Liberation.

But even those who rejected this perverse analysis unconsciously made use of the global dichotomy that it implies. It has been assumed through most of this century that anything not democratic is totalitarian. If nothing else, this is a gross misunderstanding of history, which teaches that most of humanity has lived, and still lives, in "traditional" societies that are neither democratic nor totalitarian, but in which rights and prerogatives of individuals are protected.

In other words, the problem of democracy is that it has been defined by totalitarianism: on one side fascism, on the other democracy, and nothing in between. A regime is either in one camp or in the other. But this is a misleading notion. What needs to be well understood is that totalitarianism is above all *abnormal*, and what we must restore is the notion that *normal* governments are governments that adapt with greater or lesser success to the requirements of civil society and whose power can to a greater or lesser degree be controlled by this same civil society. There are regimes that surely can be termed "normal" in this sense, without being democratic. But what this in turn means is that any "normal" society contains at least germs of democracy—greater or lesser degrees of popular sovereignty. Whereas, by the same perspective, it is clear that there was never *anything* democratic about communist regimes.

Certain political scientists, to be sure, reacted against this phony dichotomy by insisting on the difference between totalitarian and authoritarian regimes. Simplified, this explains that whereas in totalitarian regimes the state controls all spheres of society, in authoritarian regimes it tends to leave well enough alone so long as its political supremacy remains unchallenged. The principal reward obtained by political scientists who thought this way during the half-century of Marxist ideological preponderance was a catalog of insults: fascist apologists, agents of American imperialism, and so forth. The dominant ideology condemned authoritarian regimes as greedy for power, whereas totalitarian regimes were generous dictatorships whose saving grace was that they promised to make society better, to "liberate" human kind. Even Mao, despite his crimes and the damage he caused and the foolishness he uttered, deserved credit for wanting to redeem society. He had a goal.

Actually, the idea that a political system might be the key to human happiness is recent. It is an illusion originating in the French Revolution, and it cost the twentieth century dear. But professional politicians love it, since it gives them a privileged role in the forging of mankind's destiny. Indeed, it is not surprising that with the exception of libertarian thinkers, politicians have stressed the role of the state, which is to say they have expanded their own job descriptions. Why should they resist giving themselves a greater purpose in life? Thus all that is good and right will be still better if they are involved in it, and the list is naturally endless: economy, education, scientific research, race tracks, media, medicine, opera, theater. That is why all politicians, at bottom, hate and fear "individualism," since properly understood this suggests they are redundant. For them, the word is a nightmare, suggesting as it does there are areas of the human soul or activity that might escape their solicitations.

Now the purpose of a democratic regime is to permit personal freedom to flourish within legal limits, not to tell people what to do. The socialist cliche is that this definition of democracy is nothing but a liberal cliche. Yet the socialists have been responsible, by referring to the contrary definition, for much of what has gone wrong in the past two centuries and what they call a liberal cliche is merely a definition of a normal society, or if you will of the link between society and state (even a nondemocratic state). We must recover this notion of the "normal society," for it is the basis of justice. Democracy improves on it, but only if it respects it. Democracy is not necessarily an improvement, if it merely confers the legitimacy of popular suffrage on a state that devours the private sphere of society.

Observe, moreover, that the expansion of the state's role not only suffocates society, it suffocates the state itself by giving it jobs for which it was not designed. For there are surely areas where the state can play a useful role. In Lee Kuan Yew's Singapore, the state plays a significant economic role, but as servant not master. In the Renaissance, Lorenzo or Jules II used the state to assist art, not to try to set trends. They commissioned works without telling artists how to

24

do their jobs; and they surely did not commission works simply to subsidize mediocre artists whose support they sought.

Of course, any patron of the arts from the fifteenth to the middle of the nineteenth century expected the artist to work within a certain frame of religious or mythological reference, but this was a framework assumed by the artist himself. His style was his own affair. It is striking that societies run by princes and popes encouraged artistic creation, whereas communism inevitably snuffed it out. This is because patrons of the arts did not substitute themselves for artists. In other words, they did not confuse good taste with artistic ideas; they knew the difference between choosing between creative works and prescribing them. And even when they did the latter, for example after the Council of Trent, their prescriptions dealt only with the formal qualities of the commissioned works. In other words, they knew better than to involve themselves in the artistic process itself.

I am insisting on this because underneath the gloss we are living in a deeply anti-individualistic period in artistic creation. Hector Bianciotti, the French literary critic, observes that "all has been put in place to erase the individual—the first and ultimate resource on which culture depends." What could be more ridiculous than "artistic collectives" formed in the post-1968 years with the ostensible aim of fostering creativity?

Now in the same way, when the state tries to do what the private sphere does better, it succeeds only in crippling its own proper mission. Communist and Third World regimes have offered abundant evidence of this. Statism plus interference retards development and even aborts it. This is why so much foreign aid to developing countries is counterproductive—at least where the majority of the people supposedly being aided is concerned—for as to the rulers, they rarely fail to profit handsomely from the West's misguided generosity. And not only are societies paralyzed by this mix of statist authority and unnecessary intervention, it also leads to what could be called the "illegal state." The more the power of the state spreads through society, the less the rule of law is respected. Instead you find ever more fraud and arbitrary decision making. The more state, the less law. This is not good for democracy. The result may not be full-fledged dictatorship, but something halfway there, which twenty years ago I termed "democratorship." The presidential autocracy of France's Fifth Republic is a good example of this pattern. Each of our presidents has taken into his own hands a few more of the prerogatives of the impartial state.

Statists often justify their preference by references to social justice. They claim only statist intervention can rectify the unfairness of the market and overcome poverty. But whatever abstract value this idea may have, it is massively disproven by empirical experience. The entire twentieth century is a demonstration of the fact that the expansion of the role of the state in society has been accompanied by proliferating misery, hunger, inequalities, illegalities, human rights abuses, police repression, frauds, black markets, and profiteering by the rulers at the expense of the ruled. There is not much need for theoretical arguments here, against such a historical record.

You will find normal and pathological elements in most societies. Totalitarianism is thoroughly pathological, but democracy too contains pathological elements, and nondemocratic traditional societies may be quite normal from the point of view of their members. That is why in looking at such societies it is important to distinguish between those that stem from a long custom and those that are the product of violence and are perceived as arbitrary and temporary.

The regimes established by military strongmen like Pinochet in Chile or Franco in Spain arrogated all the political power to themselves but left the rest of society more or less alone. That is why when they leave power or die, there are still functioning societies: more exactly, societies that never ceased functioning. When the Soviet Union or the countries of Eastern Europe left communism, they found no functioning societies at all—societies destroyed by the experience of "real socialism." While Spain's economy was rapidly modernizing from 1960 to Franco's death in 1975, the countries of the east bloc found themselves, when communism collapsed, in a backward situation for which there was no precedent. They were neither underdeveloped in the sense that they had yet to "take off" economically, nor were they, of course, developed in a way remotely comparable to capitalist countries. They were "artificially underdeveloped."

It is worth noting that the fascist and Nazi totalitarianisms, whose ideological focus was not economics, did not destroy their societies in the same way communism did. Even though their material wealth was almost entirely consumed and wrecked by war and defeat at war, they were able to recover in fairly short order, in large measure because their active populations did not lose all practical know-how, whereas under communism even elementary professional skills are subverted.

Another difference between totalitarian and authoritarian regimes is that the latter can liberalize themselves more rapidly than the former, and are overthrown more easily and more often. Most significantly, the liberalization process is steady. Even before their return to democracy, Spain and Chile enjoyed expanding freedoms, particularly in the areas of access to information and freedom of expression. In order to disappear, totalitarian regimes, by contrast, need to be defeated militarily or to reach a degree of economic disintegration which is the equivalent of military rout. This is why it is not erroneous to state, even today, that communism indeed was irreversible. It was irreversible in the sense that it was absolutely unable to change and prepare a democratic transition. Communism cannot be reformed; it can only be replaced with something else. In this regard, it can be said that Lenin succeeded in one thing only: he made it strictly impossible for a socialist economy to ever revert back to capitalism. A system that can "reform" itself only after it has totally destroyed the society in which it is implanted, a system that can be overthrown only after it has fallen to pieces by its own failures, such a system is surely irreversible. It is not indestructible, but that is quite a different matter. It can change only by dying. It can evolve only by disappearing.

We are dealing here with a peculiarly modern problem. If you take a traditional Islamic society, it will seem quite unfree to a Westerner but it will not be considered abnormal by someone who lives in it. But the Khomeini regime in Iran, even though it involved a restoration of traditional Islamic norms, was understood by its partisans no less than by its adversaries as exceptional and altogether abnormal. The same could be said of a Spaniard under Franco or a Russian under Brezhnev, compared to men living under the Spanish monarchy in the eighteenth century or the Russian tsars: they could not fail to be aware that their traditional liberties were snuffed out by political dictatorships.

One way to measure the degree of freedom in a given society is to count the number of individuals who feel more or less autonomous, and the number of areas in which they can act—for example, work or leisure—according to their own initiatives. This is what gives them a sense of having rights and being protected from arbitrary rules on the part of the political authority. Obviously, the ideal situation is when these rights are derived from democratically controlled institutions. But there are many examples in our times and in history that demonstrate that democracy will not necessarily lead to liberty if there are not other guarantees also.

Hong Kong is a case in point. As a British colony (until 1997), under the authority of a government appointed from London, Hong Kong, at least on paper, is no democracy. There are political parties, but the ruling Executive Council is entirely appointed. Of fifty-six members of the Legislative Council, only twenty-four are elected, the others are appointed. So Hong Kong is not a democracy. But it is a much freer place than others where there are elections. The people of Hong Kong are free; they feel free. Why else would they be trying to get out, as many are, prior to 1997, if they did not fear the loss of their freedom when China takes over? Indeed, this had led to a bitter disagreement with Great Britain, which claims it cannot take all the applicants for immigration. In 1989, after the bloody repression in China of the democracy movement, a million of Hong Kong's residents (out of a total of five and a half million, of whom less than two million live in the city proper) took part in demonstrations to express their support for the students in Beijing and to signify their refusal to be ruled by the Chinese Communists. In September 1991, they voted, by a large majority, in favor of a truly representative regime. This vote was clearly directed against Beijing and the transfer of the colony to China in 1997.

This is the behavior of people who are well aware of the meaning of freedom—and know they have it. They are aware not merely of the prosperity that this freedom has fostered, but of the judicial guarantees that frame their daily lives and allow them to go about their business as they see fit.

At the same time, Hong Kong always has been a magnet for political refugees from other countries. They arrive in waves every time freedom is snuffed out somewhere in Asia—in 1938, when the Japanese took Canton; in 1949, when mainland China went communist; between 1965 and 1970, during the reign of terror known as the "cultural revolution"; between 1980 and 1990, when hundreds of thousands of "boat people" risked their lives to escape communist Vietnam.

The distinguished historian Ernest Renan, in *Marcus Aurelius*, refers to the "republican sovereignty under Nerva, Trajan, Hadrian,

Antonin and Marcus Aurelius." The Antonins countered the despotism of the Caesars just as neatly as the king of Spain, Juan Carlos, in "fathering" the democratic transition, countered Francoism from 1976 onward. In his *Thoughts*, Marcus Aurelius addresses himself: "Be careful not to Caesarize yourself," he writes. "The emperor is conscious of his role as a grand civil magistrate," Renan writes. There is nothing in him of the modern military dictator, nor of the absolute monarch of the type that came into being a thousand year later in Europe. In his *History of Rome*, Mommsen writes that imperial authority was based, as a matter of law, on popular sovereignty, as an extension of the older republican authority. It depended, in other words, on the consent of the Roman soldiers and senators, and not on dynastic or feudal prerogatives. To be sure, this is a far cry from real democracy. So is the election of the doges in the aristocratic republic of Venice. The important point here, however, is that the power of the Roman emperor was not his personal property. It was conferred upon him, delegated to him if you will, and, most significantly, it was power that could be used only within a strictly defined legal framework, which could itself be modified only in accordance with prescribed procedures.

The Athenian citizen participated more directly in political power, but he was, in many respects, less free than the Roman subject. Individual and family rights in the Roman Empire were far more secure than they were in Greece. The Empire, moreover, was organized in a decentralized fashion, leaving as much local autonomy as was compatible with general requirements of security, commerce and transportation, and taxation.

In his *Social and Economic History of the Roman Empire*, Rostovtzeff writes that the fundamental reason for the development of industry was the rapid decentralization under the Flavians and the Antonians. He adds that another characteristic of economic life in the Roman provinces was competition. When we know how much industry and commerce were restricted and regulated in later, more liberal societies, we understand better how unevenly liberty progresses, advancing in one area even as it regresses in another.

It is perfectly clear, when we consider that it included slavery, that freedom in Rome was a privilege not a right. But it is also the case that in many slave societies even today, particularly in Africa and the Muslim world, those who are not slaves are not necessarily free, either. Their rights are not protected by law, as they were in Rome, and they do not enjoy economic, cultural, religious, or philosophical freedom. And bear in mind that slavery was regulated by law in Rome and that it evolved. By the second century, Ulpian stated that "under natural law, all men are born free and equal," extraordinary terms that were forgotten for a thousand years until the political philosophers of the eighteenth century rediscovered them as they sought to enunciate a philosophy of human rights.

You can say a lot of things about the Roman Empire, but you cannot say that personal security, and rights and freedoms—even where noncitizens were concerned—were not better protected than they were in the last fifty years of republican Rome, with its incessant civil strife, political executions, arbitrary rules, and senatorial corruption.

Let me insist on this point: There are many societies that are by no means democratic in any relevant modern sense, but in which both private and public freedoms are developed to significant degrees. Private freedoms constitute what we call "civil society." The term comes from Hegel's *Principles of the Philosophy of Law* (published in 1821): "burgerliche Gesellschaft." I define civil society as the citizens of a country acting on their own initiative, outside the rules of the state and not in response to a rule made by the state. As I showed earlier, civil society may well have a large margin of maneuver even in a politically authoritarian system. For all its bullying and censorship, for example, the Second Empire was one of the most creative periods of French painting and literature. The foundations of modern poetry and the novel were laid in these years (1852–1870). Such a flowering is inconceivable under totalitarianism (except, of course, in dissident or "underground" literature). It is worth noting in passing—but it is highly significant—that the France of Napoleon III, unlike the Soviet Union, underwent an economic growth spurt the likes of which France would not see again for a hundred years. It was Napoleon III who, in 1867, put through legislation making it possible to charter corporations without government permission, as was necessary until then. This represented a liberalization of economic policy against which economic policy-makers in the twentieth century would react. Coincidentally, 1867 also was the year in which Karl Marx published *Capital*, which was out of date as soon as it appeared because it was based on the analysis of a purely personal capitalism.

In short, totalitarianism does not help us understand the organic evolution of normal societies toward democracy, nor the reasons why this evolution is sometimes interrupted. In addition to civil liberties, to economic and cultural rights, political freedoms could and did exist in "normal" societies long before they officially proclaimed themselves to be democracies. Though democracy is supposed to have been invented by the English, American, and French Revolutions in the seventeenth and eighteenth centuries, there have been (and are) forms of democracy in non-Western, or premodern societies, as the Filipino statesman and author Raul Manglapus has shown. Popular will can express itself through channels other than universal suffrage.

Democracy requires universal suffrage, with free elections and secret ballots. I did not mean to suggest the authoritarianism of a Napoleon III is admirable in itself: only that the degree of autonomy that civil society enjoyed under his regime suggests that it was much closer to democracy than to totalitarianism.

The French Revolution imposed a Jacobin interpretation of history and from this it was axiomatic that the regime of Louis XVIII (which followed Napoleon's) was reactionary compared to everything since 1789, particularly since it was expressly called a *Restauration*. But in reality, since 1792 France had been ruled by a succession of dictatorships which claimed to incarnate the general will, even though the supposedly sovereign people never had been given a chance to express this will. Since, as the Italian writer Guglielmo Ferrero put it in 1942, the French Revolution could neither put in practice the doctrine of popular sovereignty nor renege on it, it invented the prototype (without coining the term) of the "dictatorship of the proletariat," which boils down to the ultimate paradox of totally eliminating democracy in order to apply it! This is the totalitarian pathology: no freedom in the name of total democracy! Under Louis XVIII, notes Ferrero, the suffrage was restricted. But there was a legislative assembly with a real and effective opposition. The press was not completely free, but it was surely more free than anything that had been known since the days of the Convention in 1792. Referring to reality rather than ideology, one would have to admit that liberty made real progress under the *Restauration*.

In the Republic of Venice, the suffrage was restricted to the nobles. But it was hardly a tyranny. The observations of foreign visitors, of whom there were many over the centuries, confirm that Venetian institutions, though aristocratic, enjoyed popular support. There were two reasons for this. In the first place civil society had a very broad autonomy, with its neighborhood councils, its professional associations, its corporations, its renowned "*scuole*"—foundations that were outside the control of the doges; and in the second place, there was the reality of the state of law and judicial guarantees. In the sixteenth century, for example, Jean Bodin wrote: "If a Venetian nobleman does something wrong to the most lowly inhabitant of the city, it will be punished and the wrong will be set right. All here enjoy the sweetness of liberty, more because of the wide degree of freedom than the aristocratic government." A sixteenth century Venetian, whatever his station in life, and even if he did not belong to the governing elite, knew himself to be protected against arbitrary authority. I am not sure you could say the same of all the citizens of today's democracies, even with their voting rights.

Whereas many nondemocratic societies were "normal," and were perceived as such by their members, there was never a totalitarian society that was considered normal by anyone, not even by its rulers. The Marxist jargon speaks of "formal" liberties, and if the term means anything it is to communist societies that it should be applied, while many nondemocratic societies enjoy liberties that surely must be called real.

How is it that totalitarianism led to such a profound misunderstanding of democracy and liberty? We are talking here about communist—or Jacobinic—totalitarianism. Nazism and fascism too claimed to emanate from the popular will and were violently opposed to liberal democracy and what Lenin called "parliamentary cretinism," but they never claimed to offer all of humanity a message of liberation, if only because of their extreme nationalism. But socialism caricatured representative regimes and was obsessed with the idea that it could make "formal" liberties into "real" liberties. Totalitarian socialism, or communism, claimed to represent the popular will and to be the champion of social justice. Liberal democrats complained that it trampled upon free elections and political pluralism (including freedom of expression). To this the communists replied that as long as there was social injustice in the world the liberals could not complain. The totalitarian logic boxed the liberals into a corner where they were arguing in favor of the real, and profoundly imperfect, world, against the *goal* of a perfect world (with social justice and democracy for all) which the communists had the nerve of claiming they were aiming for.

Communism's only success when you think about it was to convince even its dedicated adversaries to compete politically on these terms, thus dividing the world into two entirely unreal camps. Many liberals and social democrats fell for this thoroughly artificial and abstract way of putting the issue. This had the further effect of distracting people from a certain number of far more significant realities: in particular, it turned people away from the fact that while liberal democracy was certainly imperfect, communism was a total failure, which failed to even approach the ideal it claimed to be fighting for. Another reality was that thousands, indeed millions, of residents of communist societies were willing to flee their homes to go live elsewhere, even in countries that were by no means democratic. By contrast, no one ever saw people moving willingly to communist countries to live.

Now that communism has collapsed, we must escape from the intellectual trap it laid for so long. We must learn to rethink the realities of society, the ways in which liberties are acquired and maintained and evolved. We have wasted nearly a century during which the totalitarian phenomenon, the communist phenomenon in particular, queered the essential political issues, the issues of how liberty relates to democracy. We must take up where we left off, with an honest and realistic reconsideration of what these terms mean.

To conclude the argument so far: prior to totalitarianism, with such rare exceptions as ancient Inca civilization, societies nurtured varying degrees of liberty, from which political democracy slowly developed. Building democracy is a process of making use of these precious foundations, not destroying them. At the very least, it is a process that ought to consist of not destroying them until a better replacement is available.

Communism uproots these foundations of free and democratic societies. In doing this it creates, or created in our times, utterly unprecedented and, as I have argued, abnormal societies. It is therefore misleading and confusing to even compare totalitarian communism to other societies as we try to understand how to achieve successful democracies. Why did we allow ourselves so long to make such misleading comparisons? The original error, which I examine in the following chapter, is to be found in the idea of revolution.

CHAPTER FOUR

REVOLUTION AND THE
TOTALITARIAN LIE

A false idol has dominated politics, and in particular the political culture of the Left, since the late eighteenth century: the idea of revolution. It is difficult to think of other misconceived notions that have caused more harm, and that have done more to retard progress toward democracy and liberty everywhere. It is here that we find the noxious idea that society cannot be improved little by little, that it must, rather, be destroyed and rebuilt from top to bottom. This prejudice produced nothing but contempt for serious and efficient reforms, and it led to nazism and communism. It provided the justification for terrorism.

The idea of revolution depends on the certitude that a solution exists for the unsatisfactory state of things, and that there is only one solution, and that it is radical, immediate, and definitive. This certitude, in turn, depends on the belief that the unsatisfactory state of things has a single, identifiable cause. This radical ill requires radical surgery; then all will be well. Thus to the men of the Convention during the French Revolution, the answer lay in destroying the monarchy. To the *philosophes* of the Encyclopédie, all that was required was the elimination of superstition. Marx thought all would be well as soon as capitalism was replaced with something else; for Rousseau and Proudhon, the source of the evil was in private property. In his *General Theory of Revolution in the 19th Century*, Proudhon wrote (1851): "I want a peaceful revolution, but I want it to be prompt, decisive, and thorough." Which was fraudulent, because no revolution could possibly change the structures of a society in a matter of months without encountering opposition. There never was a revolution that was peaceful as well as thorough. Freedom—other people's—has always been a problem for revolutionists. To be a revolutionist means to believe that ridding society of some poison or other will immediately bring about the good life and society's well-being, justice, and equality. To reach such an exalted goal, no price can be too high, either in human lives or in privations, for a period which in any case is merely a transition.

There might be some truth to this if the revolutionary idea were true. Unfortunately, since it is always untrue and indeed must be since its basic principle is mad, the happy conclusion that will justify the transitory cruelties never arrives. The so-called transition period quickly becomes the only period: an eternal transition. Moreover, through a paradoxical process of imitation, revolutionaries reproduce the very evils they said they would extirpate. The Jacobins wanted to destroy absolutism, and they established a dictatorship compared to which the ancient monarchical order was liberal. The Bolsheviks wanted to end the exploitation of man by man, and they exploited men more ferociously than any previous regime, chaining them to an unworkable economic system to which millions were sacrificed. The radicals of 1968 claimed to be against imperialism, for the flowering of personal liberty, against all forms of repression—and they aimed their attacks at the democracies, taking as their model the senile and bloody totalitarianism of Mao Zedong.

One of the most striking features of the Soviet system is that for seventy years it did the exact opposite of what it claimed it meant to do. Yet this is the very essence of Leninism. Lenin proclaimed that all political power would reside in the workers' councils (the soviets); he then imposed a single party, a political monstrosity for which he deserves full credit: the "proletarian party" which turned into the worst thing that ever happened to the proletariat, treating workers incomparably worse than any boss could.

Lenin was asked once: can the workers run the state? "Any sensible person," he answered, "knows that is a fairy tale." He claimed to respect the will of the "masses" and democracy, but he dissolved the constituent assembly by force in January 1918 because the "masses" had not elected a Bolshevik majority. Those were the first and last free elections, complete with real parties competing for votes, in the Soviet Union. Lenin claimed to speak for the people, and he had them shot. In the name of freedom he created the Cheka, the forerunner of the KGB. State terrorism and concentration camps began with Lenin; Stalin systematized them. Claiming to be the enemy of capitalism, Lenin lived off it as soon as, thanks to his brilliant management, the Soviet economy nearly went belly up. His successors, like him, viewed economic policy as figuring out ways of living off the West. He denounced imperialism, calling it the "last stage of capitalism," at the very moment when the capitalist empires began the process of decolonization. For his part, Lenin was the initiator of the last colonial empire. He preached universalism, but closed the borders of his country. He claimed to be for disarmament, but followed a policy of frenetic overarmament, as did his successors. At the international conference on disarmament in Genoa in 1922, Lenin ordered the chief of the Soviet delegation to propose a vast program of arms reductions. His comrade negotiator, a Bolshevik veteran, did not understand: "I thought we opposed petit bourgeois pacifism," he said, "and now I should promote it?" "Don't worry, comrade," Lenin replied, "we're only doing this to deceive and confuse our bourgeois enemies."

As a politician, Lenin knew how to be pragmatic, to adapt to circumstances. But pragmatism cannot be an excuse for every contradiction, particularly in a man who claimed that his policies sprang from a comprehensive and coherent philosophy. His philosophy, developed in his *Materialism* and *Empiriocriticism* (1909) and the *Philosophical Notebooks* (1914–1916), became official state doctrine, and the basis of all education, in 1931. Which is why Lenin, in addition to everything else, is responsible for the cultural misadventures of the Soviet Union, including specifically the disastrous notion that there is a "bourgeois science" and a "proletarian science," which led directly to Lysenko's biological frauds. Lenin was forever changing course, and he still was able to maintain that Marxism was forged from a single block of steel, from which no essential part could be removed without abandoning its objective truth.

But Lenin's most outrageous incoherence was unquestionably the gap between his theory of the state and the practical use he actually made of it. In August and September 1917, he wrote a short book and told his friends it was a fundamental statement: *State and Revolution*. It is here that he expressed his famous doctrine of the "withering away of the state." After his usual attacks on the various "fakers," "traitors to the proletariat," and social democrats suffering from "parliamentary cretinism," Lenin claims the true Marxist theory of the state has been misrepresented. When he attains power, he says, he will abolish the army and the police and do away with the civil bureaucracy.

Coming from the founder of the most militarized, policed, and bureaucratic state in history, this program, announced scarcely a month prior to the Bolshevik seizure of power, could be viewed as a brilliant joke. For the father of totalitarianism to promote the idea of a minimal state, like the libertarians, should not, however, make us laugh out loud. For this fraud provides a key to one of the fundamental features of communism: the utter dissociation between acts and words.

Gorbachev was mistaken in thinking that he could refer to Lenin to justify *glasnost*, in the sense of freedom of opinion. Lenin had written (in "What Is to Be Done?"), "Freedom of opinion is the freedom of opportunism, freedom to transform the party into a party of democratic reforms, freedom to introduce into socialism the ideas of the bourgeoisie and the bourgeois elements. Freedom of opinion means eclecticism and absence of principles."

Revolutionaries are forever seeking to combine fatalism and free will. If things must happen, why should it require such exertions on the part of revolutionists? Be that as it may, they are forever disappointed. In 1900, Jean Jaures, the great French socialist leader, stated, "We underestimated the chances of survival of the capitalist system." If only he could live again today!

Since they always obtain the opposite result from the one sought, revolutionists must live with a wild contradiction between rhetoric and reality; then, to get off their limbs, they must blame their chronic failure on the "enemies of the revolution." They seek them out first within their own ranks, which is why the history of revolution is the history of purges. The eternal myth of the "revolution betrayed" allows them to look for the cause of failure everywhere but the one place where they will find it: in their own ideas. In any event, the revolution fails and the "masses" grow tired of it. Confusing effects for causes, the revolutionaries blame their failure on the masses, and proceed to massacre them. This script has been followed every time, from Robespierre to Stalin to Mao. While suspecting it may lack popular support, but unwilling to find out by allowing free elections, any revolutionary government worthy of the name sets up a tyranny in the name of some "general will" that would overthrow it if given the chance. Meanwhile, this illegitimate government proclaims lofty principles in order to violate them. That is why, writes Ferrero, "The essence of all revolutionary governments is the overthrow of the democratic process."

Intrinsically totalitarian and congenitally destructive, due to the double absurdity of their teleological reading of history, revolutions claim an internationalist vocation. Indeed, Albert Mathiez, one of the founding fathers of academic history in France, saw this clearly. In his *Bolshevism and Jacobinism*, he writes, "Jacobinism and Bolshevism are both class dictatorships, using the same means: terror, confiscation, taxes. They both aim for the transformation of society—not only Russian society or French society, but universal society."

This universalist messianism is an end that justifies all means. In particular it justifies the suppression of democracy—in the higher interest of democracy, needless to say! An interesting case is cited by Ferrero. During France's 1848 revolution, King Louis-Philippe was overthrown in February and, for the first time, a national assembly was elected by universal male suffrage. But the vote disappointed the extreme left parties—as the Russian vote of January 1918 would disappoint Lenin—because it returned a moderate conservative majority. Anticipating (but without the same success) Lenin, the left sent the usual Paris mobs into the streets with arms, mobs that always are handy for the left's "revolutionary days," but are in no sense representative of the national majority. What followed were the "bloody days of June," a tragedy which French historians like Mathiez present as a repression of the general will led by reactionary forces whereas in truth, of course, the issue—leave aside the means employed—was to defend from a mob the representative government elected by majority vote. The parties of the extreme left, notes Ferrero, saw themselves as the champions of popular sovereignty, but only so long as the people voted for them and their program. Otherwise, they must substitute themselves for the people. This is, ahead of Lenin, already pure Leninism, the revolutionary fallacy.

This sort of thinking was by no means the exclusive property of the extremists, and it sometimes produced farces as well as tragedies like the June Days. For example, in 1891, a left-wing government censored a play by Victorien Sardou, *Thermidor*, on the grounds that it was disrespectful of Robespierre. It did not occur to them that in limiting freedom of expression (even in a publicly subsidized theater, the Comédie Française), they might be trampling on a basic human right the French Revolution was supposed to have conquered for humanity. It was in the course of a wild debate on the merits of the play that Georges Clemenceau, defending the censorious minister, uttered his famous line, "The Revolution is Indivisible!", which nonsense has been echoed by the left down the years all the way to François Mitterrand. It is better, in this way of thinking, to defend the integrity of the Great Revolution than the principles it stood for.

The Revolution is universal. It covers everything and proposes to create a "new man." It goes everywhere. It is valid for the whole planet, and it is pure. It is "indivisible."

Now it is patent that there are other kinds of "revolution," and the word is not restricted to these totalitarian and universalist projects. There are "revolutions" in sexual habits, in art, in communications. And, indeed, there are even political revolutions, in particular the American Revolution and England's Glorious Revolution, that are the consequence of deeper social and economic changes that already have taken place, and not attempts to force society into an utopian future. But in terms of the problem of democracy, the idea of revolution is the one that was invented in the French Revolution, developed during the nineteenth century, and applied catastrophically throughout the twentieth.

It seems to me it only confuses matters to refer to the anticommunist uprisings of 1989 as "revolutions." These great events were not seeking to attain some utopian goal; on the contrary, their whole object was to restore earlier norms and values that had been subverted by political gangsters. Here the word "revolution" is used with reference to "revolt." Fortunately for the people concerned, they are not revolutions. They are returns, or at least attempts to return, to authentic democratic traditions. Superficial iconographies cause us to confuse insurrection with revolution, but a change of regime does not necessarily imply a revolution, and an insurrection may have as its object the winning back of ancient rights that had been removed by totalitarianism. In effect, the anticommunist revolts at the end of the twentieth century were counter-revolutionary wars of liberation. Counter-revolutionary, of course, does not imply reactionary, but progressive. The reactionaries in Europe were or are the defenders of the communist revolution.

Far from a revolution, a plunge into an untried future, the anticommunist rebels look to the past, to the time before they entered the totalitarian tunnel. Communism was to their countries a political ice age. Coming out of the ice, ex-communist societies find themselves confronted with earlier problems exactly the way they were when the revolution froze them in place, including the problems of creating pluralistic democracies with free economies, freedom of information, religious tolerance, and all the rest. Getting out of communism involves making up for a great deal of lost time, and catching up with broken-down equipment and human resources, since the communist experience produced nothing so well as empty lots and mass graves. Getting out of communism is like physical therapy for the severely crippled, not Olympic training for top athletes. In practice, however, the key point is that democracy gives progress a chance; revolution blocks it.

The one benefit to be got from this dreadful experience is that political thinking is freed of its obsession with revolution and can place democracy at the center of reflection. Politics is not a deductive science. Social engineering has led to one disaster after another. Both ways of seeing problems stem from the idea of revolution. But democracy is a process, not a program. It does not claim to offer solutions. It is a way of seeking after solutions.

The issue here is not the classic distinction in political science between social "constructivism" and faith in the "spontaneous order." It is true, I fear, that we will always be tempted to build a new reality, if necessary by destroying the old one violently, on the basis of an idea. However, there will always be a need for ideas; the point of democracy is to define the rules under which they can be tried out. The radicals of the 1960s were opposed to all kinds of authority, but revealed themselves to be authoritarians of the worst kind. This is only a surface paradox. Like all revolutionaries, they oppose the state until they seize it, then they are in favor of total state power. When they fail to attain power, they fall back on terrorism. The difference is that the radicals were antidemocratic from outside the state; the communists were antidemocratic within the state. But to be a revolutionary is always to be a totalitarian.

Democracy does not mean the absence of government. On the contrary, it is the only form of government that is efficient, for it is the only form of government that can both serve civil society and make use of the creative resources of civil society. It is said that anarchy leads to despotism, which is true. What has been said less often is that despotism leads to anarchy, but this is the lesson of these destroyed and disordered societies that have been left in the wake of communism, the goal of the "revolution."

CHAPTER FIVE

USES AND ABUSES OF HUMAN RIGHTS

One sure sign of the advance of the democratic idea since World War II is that human rights have become a universal and permanent issue. Basic freedoms and respect for human beings have become unavoidable criteria for judging states, societies, even religions. This is a new factor in international relations, and it has a real influence on public opinion.

From the constant examination of how well human rights are respected, it has emerged that democracy is the only regime which is bound by its very nature to human rights, the only regime in which people can expect that human rights abuses will be redressed. By its very nature, moreover, democracy implies freedom of information, and this in turn means that the media in democratic societies are forever investigating human rights issues in nondemocratic countries. This forces dictatorial regimes to either improve their human rights record or to face international ostracism. In short, human rights policies would seem to have been good for democracy.

However, this is true only in theory. Unfortunately, this is one area which as well as any other demonstrates that the importance placed on a given issue by the media and public opinion seldom bears any relation to its importance in real life. Human rights may have been a big issue since 1945, yet there have been few half centuries during which men have been so badly treated. This is true not only because there are so many more people in the world today. It is also true in terms of the percentage of the world's population abused. While it is true that it is inappropriate to compare different historical periods, which we approach with different criteria and different sources of information, it is legitimate to judge a civilization in accordance with its own standards. When Scylla had thousands of his political adversaries in Rome executed, he did not claim to be a champion of human rights. He did not kill people in secret; on the contrary, he publicized his deeds. He had not signed the Universal Declaration of Human Rights and did not have a seat at the United Nations and a vote there with which to condemn other states' violations of human rights. He did not fail any human rights test, as we can say of many regimes in our own time.

Just look at the 1980s, known—not incorrectly—as a decade of democratic renewal. In this decade the Soviet Union waged total war against the people of Afghanistan, reducing the population of that country by half in eight years through the combined effects of massacres and flight. In Iran there was the homicidal mania of Islamic fundamentalists. There were the crimes of Vietnamese communism—the executions, the deaths from exhaustion in labor camps, the boat people, more of whom died at sea than made it to unsafe havens (for they were often sent back). There were hundreds of thousands of Ethiopian corpses due to famines deliberately provoked by the regime in place and the forced movements of people. The Tibetan genocide, begun in 1959, continued. There was the continuing elimination of the Khmer people by Vietnam's occupation army, continuing the work of the Khmer Rouge which it supposedly had put an end to. There were intertribal massacres in Burundi. There were Saddam Hussein's massacres of his own people, before and after the Gulf War of 1990–91.

And here I am cataloging only "mass murder-one," so to speak: clear cases of crimes against humanity. Only our age's taste for political euphemism allows us to use the same term for these crimes—which we call gently "human rights abuses"—as we use when we say that a democracy fails to grant its citizens their "right to rest and leisure" (Article 24 of the Universal Declaration of Human Rights) or their "right to take part in cultural life" (Article 27). It has to be admitted that certain governments and nongovernmental organizations manage quite a feat in scolding certain countries for "violations" of rights such as these while closing their eyes to the destruction of countless human lives in other countries! Western governments did not support Médecins sans Frontières when the latter denounced the Ethiopian regime when it would not give Western food aid to its starving population on the pretext that humanitarian nongovernmental organizations should not be involved in politics. And others have simply said nothing for thirty years while the Chinese communists have very nearly annihilated the people of Tibet and their civilization. When the Dalai Lama came to France to receive an award on December 4, 1989, there was not a single French official to receive him. Danielle Mitterrand, wife of the president of the Republic, who was scheduled to make the award, was asked by the government to avoid the ceremony: negotiations were taking place regarding the building of a French automobile assembly plant in China. Moreover, the Vietnamese were widely approved and applauded for decimating and enslaving the Cambodian people, for surely this represented progress compared to the bloodbath that took place under the Khmer Rouge (a true revolution, that)—a bloodbath, incidentally, that no one in the civilized world tried to prevent. What is certain about the collapse of totalitarian regimes and other dictatorships in the 1980s is that they did not collapse because of any human-rights campaigns by the democracies, whose role remained declaratory and commemorative.

In short, even if we have begun to discuss a "right of interference" in other countries' affairs on human rights grounds (I will return to this later), there has been, since 1945, a contradiction between the stated importance of human rights and the demonstrable ineffectiveness of human rights policies. Why?

The first reason resides in the confusion between rights and aims. Aims that are really political in nature, or economic, social, indeed cultural, aesthetic, moral, and intellectual, have been confused with basic human rights. Take Articles 27 and 29 of the Universal Declaration of Human Rights: "each person's right to human fulfillment." Who can possibly say when such fulfillment has been attained? Must UNESCO organize a commission in which there would be Socrates, Saint Augustine, Goethe, Montaigne, Confucius, and the Buddha? And if they fail to pass someone, where will he complain, or go to collect his compensation?

The first twenty articles of the Universal Declaration list rights that could be applied immediately, everywhere, for they bear no relation to given levels of development. They include protection from arbitrary arrest and detention and forced emigration. They prohibit slavery and torture. They protect private property and insist on fair trials. They condemn execution or imprisonment for one's opinions; they insist on the right to travel freely and to choose one's place of residence. They condemn discrimination. They state the right of association, as well as the right not to join an association as a condition for employment.

No nation needs a bank loan to begin applying these basic rights. They should belong, in every known society, to rich and poor alike, to peasants and city-dwellers, to men and women, to the uneducated and the sophisticated. These are rights which, since they concern private persons, do not strictly speaking require the existence of political democracy. Indeed, as I noted in an earlier chapter, some or all of them were often found in predemocratic societies of the past.

It therefore would have been realistic for the United Nations and the international community to focus their human rights policies on these rights. For no state could have claimed economic reasons prevented it from applying these rights. They have nothing to do with financial resources. Even an authoritarian political tradition would be a weak excuse. The U.N. could have said that respecting these rights was a condition of membership, failure to respect them a cause for expulsion. After all, the Declaration states in its preamble, "The member-states are committed to insure, in cooperation with the U.N., the universal and effective respect for human rights and fundamental liberties." Surely a country can refer to the right of noninterference in its internal affairs to refuse to answer questions on its human rights record. But then, such a country also ought to refuse to sign the Declaration and thereby lose the advantages of U.N.-membership. A member ought to be excluded if it violates rights repeatedly. However, only a vote in the General Assembly can cause a member to be excluded. But since most member states abuse human rights and even routinely engage in crimes against humanity, why should they vote against their own standards of behavior? As a matter of fact, one of the nice things about the U.N. is that it permits many governments to enjoy democracy in their international relations, even as they deny democracy to their own subjects.

It is true that the Universal Declaration of Human Rights, which was adopted in 1948, is not obligatory. It is only a broader interpretation of the U.N. Charter, which was adopted in 1945. But if it was intended to be voluntary, it should not have been necessary to sign the Declaration to join the U.N. It should not have been allowable to sign it with the intention of violating it. The U.N. then would have included two kinds of members, those who had signed the

Declaration and those who had not. The latter would not have taken part in debates and votes on matters of human rights. This would have made things more honest. But even this subterfuge should not have been necessary: for the Charter itself is obligatory, and the Charter, though it does not go into the matter in such detail as the Universal Declaration, is founded on human rights—more specifically, the elementary rights I just mentioned. As soon as the United Nations, in the name of the international community, accepted that the majority of its members violated these rights, not by mistake but as a matter of deliberate and consistent policy, it was clear there could be no viable international human rights policy.

In order to hide this failure, the debate was transferred from rights to goals, and goals came to be called rights. In other words, if you cannot get less, pretend that you are trying to get more. The economic, social, and cultural goals enunciated were those that were sure to be the most difficult to reach, at least by proclamations. As to the political goals, they were avoided along with basic human rights. Yet, Article 21 of the Declaration stipulates unambiguously that "the will of the people is the foundation of public authorities," and this will "can be expressed only by universal suffrage with secret ballots."

This is not surprising, for the heart of the U.N. Charter and its reason for being was the goal of a democratic world. However, the organization evolved into a forum of nondemocratic nations before which are condemned, for the most part, the democratic nations, which are in the minority. The fight for peoples' political rights was abandoned as promptly as had been the fight for the fundamental human rights of individuals.

Is progress in the areas of social welfare, economic well-being, and culture a matter of rights? This is an old question. Should the complete equality between the citizens of a given country, or for that matter among all men everywhere, be discussed on the same level, and viewed as having the same quality and urgency, as the right to move around freely, to express one's opinions, to have a say in one's country's budget by way of representative institutions? Early in the history of reflection on human rights—specifically from the time of the French Declaration on the Rights of Man in 1789—it seemed logical to view social rights as the next step after individual and political rights. It is not by mistake that democratic nations have put into practice increasingly elaborate, and ever more costly, social policies which were designed to promote equality, in fact as well as in law—

or, at least, to lessen inequalities. But it is still the case that there must be a qualitative difference between rights that can be put into practice without delay, and objectives which, whatever you think of them on their merit, require a certain level of material development if they are to be attained. To speak of a "right to housing," in a city that has just been wiped out by an earthquake, means, in fact, to define an obligation of government, in the name of national solidarity, to take care of homeless people, which implies having the financial means of doing so. If the government lacks these means because it has conducted an inept economic policy for decades, as was the case of the government of the Soviet Union at the time of the Armenian earthquake in December 1988, its own proclaimed "right to housing" is pure fiction. In the same way, the right to free medical care has a concrete meaning only in a country that has enough competent doctors and medical supplies. The same goes for education. These things cannot be decreed abstractly, but require a certain economic and cultural development founded on the accumulation of many specific conditions. These are not things that can take place right away, as can real human and political rights.

Or take the "right to work" enshrined in Article 23 of the Universal Declaration. The only way it can mean anything is in reference to the labor market, which must bear some relation to the real world. However, Article 25 states that "everyone has a right to an adequate standard of living." This, in turn, is completely meaningless. An adequate standard of living for an African peasant is unspeakable misery for an unemployed worker in the West. To be realistic, a goal of rising standards of living must be based on policy choices that have much to do with political and economic choices, but not fundamental rights.

Moreover, it needs reminding, even if it should be obvious, that many rights are not human rights. They are practices that grow out of legislation. For instance, the right to retirement at age 60, or the right to a seventh week of paid leave, are gains, or acquired rights. They were won through legislative action. They are not rights that are inherent to human beings and valid for all eternity. To promulgate such rights is meaningful only if a society has the resources to pay for them and the organizational know-how to make them possible in practice. They had no meaning whatsoever for Europe only a few generations ago, when all known societies were predominantly rural, with economies not based primarily on money, and where life expectancy peaked at about age 30. The right to lower fares on public transportation for senior citizens or students (or at the movies) requires that there be public transportation and a film industry, first, and, second, that society should be wealthy enough to subsidize their use by certain of its members. The "right to quiet" means anything only if society passes a law prohibiting nocturnal noise or the use of car horns. But like many others, this is a "right" which requires an adequate police force to make it effective. These kinds of rights were created by the evolution of a society's idea of the good life and the growth of its ability to attain it for ever greater numbers of its members. But human rights are not created. They existed prior to any legislation, and no legislation can take them away. A government can only insure that they are respected—or it can violate them.

According to Jean-Jacques Rousseau, the ideal citizen is a willing slave. Citizenship is defined as that human condition wherein men make a contract to give up their personal rights and individual freedoms, because they have become parts of the "general will." This definition is favored by all professional politicians, for it allows them to exercise power in the name of democracy. For them, man is nothing but a citizen—the "free slave" who owes them allegiance because he elected them. To politicians all that is not political in man is hateful.

The Rousseau and Jacobin traditions hold that an elected assembly has full powers, since it is the incarnation of the general will. Specifically, it has the power to destroy and redesign human rights as it sees fit. In this case, democracy can become a threat to basic freedoms. This is the heart of the Jacobin or Bolshevik contradiction, which, in Ferrero's words, "uses the democratic principle to justify an absolute and uncontrollable government."

Democracy means "the people rule." This usually has been held to be synonymous with freedom because, usually, the people took power away from monarchs or dictators or oligarchs or bureaucrats. But the concept of democracy, on its own terms, is not identical to the concept of liberty, respect for the rights of man, or the human conscience. Something more is needed: a guarantee that democratic power will not violate the fundamental rights of individuals. That is why it is so important to make clear what these intangible human rights are.

Law is not the source, but the codification of human rights. A legislator cannot invent human rights as he sees fit, for real human rights precede legislation. Law can neither create them nor destroy them.

You see human rights, writes Bertrand de Jouvenel in *On Power*; you do not invent them. Above and beyond human rights, societies can use legislation to define plenty of rights: these are artificial and contractual. The work of constitutions and legislation is to create citizens' rights, not human rights.

The great fallacy in this area, in our times, has been to mistake goals for rights. This has caused us to neglect real rights and to do what could have been done, and could be done, right away and in the real world, to insure that they be respected. The dominant ideology of our times, in the mainstream churches no less than in the social democratic Socialist International, has been oriented toward Marxism and "third worldism." This ideology was based on two fallacies, the first of which was that the real way to support human rights is to abolish poverty, including differences between underdeveloped and developed nations. The second fallacy, which flowed from the first, was that differences in wealth are caused by democratic capitalism, which, therefore, must be abolished. It was under the influence of this view of the world that opinion leaders in the West took it upon themselves—indeed, they saw it as a moral duty—to downplay or even hide human rights violations in communist and Third World countries (especially Third World countries with a "socialist" orientation). Instead, they concentrated their criticism on democracies, on right-wing dictatorships, and on countries with traditional forms of government, neither fully democratic nor wholly despotic but guilty, almost always, of being aligned with the West diplomatically. Because of this double standard, the fight for human rights and liberty was shot through with hypocrisy. In losing its strongest characteristic, namely its universality, it lost all efficiency.

For if the fight for human rights or the spread of democracy in the world is undertaken with a hidden (or explicit) ideological agenda, then it is anything but a fight for human rights or democracy. It becomes a political weapon, an instrument of propaganda, which we use only when it serves our side or our point of view. Even if the rights violations that we then denounce are real, we undermine the moral power—and the practical effectiveness—of our outrage by having interested motives. This does great harm to the cause we think or claim to be advancing, for we are using it for mere tactical advantage. With most states, nongovernmental organizations, and religious authorities giving a bad example by using, or rather abusing, the cause of human rights in this way, it is little wonder that no one feels obliged to take human rights policies seriously, for it is clear that the rights of politics are given precedence over the rights of man.

This is nothing less than moral pollution. This is much worse than "selective indignation," which is transparently opportunistic. Here we are dealing with an emasculation of the very concept of human rights, making it that much more difficult to promote them subsequently in a consequential way. When François Mitterrand praises Sekou Toure as a great statesman, when in fact he is the butcher of the Guinean people, he is undercutting a policy of human rights France ostensibly follows in its dealings with foreign states. The Vatican undercuts its moral credibility when, returning from a visit to Cuba in January 1989, Cardinal Etchegaray speaks of the "uncommon joy" of meeting Fidel Castro, adding: "We share a passion for mankind, for man's dignity and liberty." These are but two enormities from a sadly thick anthology. The point is that the president and the cardinal are not, by any measure, men of a totalitarian temper; and they were not engaged in superficial diplomatic protocol. They were supposed to be talking about human rights and, somehow, they found themselves praising dictators guilty of monstrous crimes against humanity.

However, by 1989 a number of events had made it possible to put the cause of human rights back on firm ground. There was the collapse of communism in Europe; there was the ferocious Chinese repression of democratic aspirations; there was the demonstrable failure of "Third Worldism" and its "liberation theology" offshoot to do anything positive for the Third World; and there was the failure of Marxism itself. Whereupon a new question came up: Can there be a global policy of human rights? Does it mean anything to speak of the "international community"? At the end of this century during which there surely was a need for one, can there be, is there, a real community of nations that could, through a delegated institution, protect and promote human rights? Of course there is the United Nations Organization—but its record is one of reflecting, even encouraging, human rights violations, not doing anything about them. Just consider: as late as December 1989, one of the vice-presidencies of the U.N. Commission on Human Rights was chaired by Ceausescu's Romania! The principle of noninterference in a nation's internal affairs is an obstacle to human rights policy. Yet, if the international community is a myth, international law is not. There is no legal basis for intervening militarily—often the only chance for being effective—

in a state to protect the victims of a repressive state or whatever party or person is in charge of it. In other words, international law protects states, not people. When a state attacks another, that is a violation of international law. But when a state attacks its citizens, even if it kills them all, it is not. International law is at about the same stage of criminal law when a father had the right of life and death over his children.

Can it be changed? Under what conditions would preventive or corrective action be legitimate? It will be feasible when it is acknowledged that only democratic governments are legitimate. It is only on the basis of a clear and uncontroversial principle of legitimacy that a despotic regime can be prevented from obtaining international recognition merely on the strength of its ability to stay in power. This is not a utopian principle. It is realistic to foresee—I expect it—a kind of international democratic police.

Sooner or later, governments that are not democratic by the standards of the international community will be viewed as illegitimate. Their power over a given population will not be tolerated. Restraining them will not be seen as interference, any more so than it is considered trespassing to forcibly enter a home where a hoodlum has taken hostages, be they his own family.

Speaking of hoodlums, some of the reactions to the American intervention in Panama in December 1989 showed that some of the worst "leftist," "anti-imperialist" reflexes were still at work. If anyone fulfilled all the criteria for an operation aiming to restore democracy, it was General Noriega. If one thinks he did not, then gangsterism may as well be defined as the first principle of constitutional law. Yet "progressive" newspapers—the *Guardian* and the *Observer*, to take two British examples—covered the event as if it were Hitler's invasion of Belgium in 1940. *Le Monde* in France attacked the U.S. in an editorial on January 5. And the U.N. disgraced itself once again by voting to condemn the U.S., though "only" by 70 votes. With the U.N.'s democratic minority voting against the motion to condemn the U.S., and several Third World countries abstaining, there was some progress. Unfortunately, several Latin American countries, though lately returned to democracy, gave vent to a disturbing "anti-gringo" reflex. Nonetheless, there was an international consensus of sorts to approve an operation which had no basis in international law. A similar consensus was beginning to emerge to prevent the return of the Khmer Rouge to power in Cambodia, though with no clear sense of how to do it in practice.

Further encouragement to the idea of a "right of interference" or of a "right of rescue" for threatened people, was the shame caused by the fall of the Romanian Communist leader Ceausescu during these same last weeks of 1989. The degree to which the democracies had cooperated and aided this barbaric regime was revealed—or rather, recalled, after the facts were known. To be sure, as the Cuban and Chinese cases show, a degree of complicity with communist regimes continued. Nonetheless, the idea that it should be possible to prevent governments from torturing and massacring their populations began to make some headway.

As Michael Novak showed forcefully in his *Human Rights and the New Realism* (1986), a foreign policy truly based on human rights could not promise "peace." For such a policy is bound to conflict not only with the violently repressive totalitarian governments, but with numbers of traditional regimes as well. Some of these traditional societies are characterized by fanaticism and intolerance that are not acceptable in the modern world. On the other hand, certain societies contain a degree of respect for human dignity, and these, Novak points out, should be encouraged to move toward democracy with circumspection, lest a brutal push open the way for a modern despotic regime to take over. At any rate, writes Novak, "A human rights policy is subversive; it implies a restructuring of world order. This may be desirable; it is also inherently conflictual. Willy nilly, this conflict has been thrust upon us."

Without accepting a naive "globalism," it has to be recognized that rights and liberties will be guaranteed only with the disappearance of a certain old-fashioned concept of sovereignty. Can this be reconciled with the diversity of the world's cultures? I will return to this issue at the end of this book. Some of these cultures—for example, the Islamic culture in its fundamentalist version since the Iranian revolution of 1979—intrinsically imply the violation of human rights, as well as institutionalized inequalities and international terrorism. These practices, undoubtedly, reflect the sincerity of the faith of the people who live in such countries. But to recognize its sincerity does not oblige us to approve it or to recognize it for what it is. The misunderstanding about whether and how to respect cultural diversity stems from the confusion between acceptance and approval.

Can a single standard of human rights, a single principle of the legitimacy of political authority, be set for all of humanity without destroying traditional cultures? Just asking the question tells us how

51

far we are from answering it, how much, indeed, this represents a goal which in the foreseeable future is unattainable. But for our own mental clarity and political well-being, we should guard against making lofty "universal" declarations on human rights so long as we are not prepared to enforce them.

PART TWO

THE COLLAPSE OF COMMUNISM

CHAPTER SIX

FORESEEABLE AND
UNEXPECTED

It is a truism to say that no one expected the collapse of the Communist regimes that took place from 1985 on. But to say this, as if to acknowledge an error of foresight, is itself a fresh error, indeed a whole series of new errors. Of which the first consists of saying: "We told you communism was nothing to get alarmed about."

The fact is that despite its subsequent enervation, warrior communism never posed a greater threat than during the period between 1970 and 1985. Had we heeded the advice of all those, ranging from pacifists to the partisans of "détente," who said communism could be appeased if it were not resisted, it would have lasted longer, thanks to bountiful victories in foreign policy, even if it could not, by definition, overcome its internal contradictions. After all, this was like saying there was no cause to be so alarmed by Napoleon in 1805, since he ended up on Saint Helena in 1815. He found himself on Saint Helena in 1815 because a certain number of leaders and peoples did certain things which led to the given conclusion, not because he was not dangerous for Europe in 1805, or represented a danger that was bound to evaporate by itself. As Mario Vargas Llosa said during a conference on liberty in Lima in 1990, every victory against communism, internationally and internally, was earned the hard way. To be sure, real socialism—as the communists quite accurately described their regimes—fell primarily because it simply is not viable and destroys the very societies it claims to organize beneficially. But this fall would have occurred either much sooner or much later, according to the policies chosen by the democracies. Let there be no mistake: men make history, not the opposite.

Already in the nineteenth century, Kierkegaard had ridiculed—and refuted—the "world-historical slaughterhouses" of Hegelianism, in his *Postscriptum to Philosophical Pieces*, an attack that was taken up, and deepened, by Karl Popper in our own time, in his *Poverty of Historicism*. But the "world-historical" habit is still in good shape. Its basis is the idea that what happened had to happen. The practical consequence is that you do not have to do anything, or think anything, or foresee anything. Hegelianism and its child, Marxism, may be out of fashion today, plenty of intelligent people nevertheless continue to view history as a series of necessary, and impersonal, causes and effects, whose outcome can be predicted once it is understood how the machine works. But history is made by individuals. Its course is set by the degree of success and failure of their efforts, which often produce unanticipated consequences. None of these efforts, nor their consequences, can be predicted with any kind of assurance. And when they make mistakes, people like to believe everyone else was in error.

Another reason why it is a mistake to say that no one predicted what would happen is that it is not true. You cannot predict the presence at the right time and place of a leader or a group of leaders who will do certain things, or being in a position to act, will do nothing. On the other hand, it was quite possible to foresee that the people of the German Democratic Republic were so miserable under the Communist regime that they would overthrow it at the first opportunity. The issue was not predicting what would happen, but understanding the situation and how people felt about it. And that is precisely the point: numerous were those in the West—and in particular the West German Social Democratic Party—whose ideas or ideology made them unable to see this.

Nor was the attitude of the West Germans by any means exceptional or even new. From the earliest years of the Bolshevik regime, information about its true nature was available in the West. It was not difficult to know empirically that the Soviet system simply did not work and that it was destroying the economic and social fabric of the country without offering a viable replacement. Throughout the following years, before World War II and after, one report, study, and testimony after another showed, with all the necessary supporting factual evidence, that the system was, inherently, a failure, and that it held up only due to one of the fiercest and best organized police states in all history. But, as we know, this literature until very recently was subjected to an endless barrage of scorn and denial, and not only from the official Communist organizations in the West. It was dismissed with such epithets as "fanatical anti-Communist," which in turn was said to spring from extreme right-wing prejudices or the envy of "renegade" emigres or ex-Communists. Nonetheless, the literature existed; indeed, it was bountiful. Studying it, it was possible to understand that communism was able to create a powerful state, with mighty armed forces and police apparatuses; but it could not create a society good to live in. Why was so little attention paid to this literature, and not only by those in the Communist movement or even on the left, but by journalists, intellectuals, political leaders, American and European Sovietologists? I have often asked myself this question, I have tried to answer it in some of my books. However, the point here is that there is an important difference between lack of foresight and wilful refusal to foresee, just as there is a difference between real darkness and wilful refusal to see.

A third error consists of calling foresight that which is little more than acknowledgement of current news, while neglecting foresight based on real analysis of a system's underlying problems and structures. The issue was not to know when the system would collapse, for that depended on countless specific factors, which combined in different ways in different communist countries. But this was not the real reason there was little foresight regarding communism's fate. The real reason was the inability to agree on the basic diagnosis, namely that it was fundamentally awful and untenable. Every population upon whom it was imposed rejected it when it could. Yet the "experts" and their journalistic acolytes and the politicians who listened to them found it possible to believe that there were "positive sides" to communism, that, for example, East Germany was an economic success story that had satisfied most of its people's needs. If you pointed out that the most anodyne trip to one of these countries revealed that this was nonsense and that these regimes stayed in place only because the Red Army was backing them up, you were accused of being a right-wing warmonger. Well, as soon as Gorbachev decided he would not use force to maintain these regimes, it took three months, not a day more, for them to be swept out of Eastern Europe. Western observers were astonished in direct proportion to their earlier inability to see the real nature of real socialism. Just as they were astonished to see the Nicaraguan Sandinistas go down in defeat in a free election in February 1990, after nearly all the world's media had predicted they would win. The only way it was possible to imagine this was to really believe—contrary to all verifiable evidence—that the Sandinistas were making the Nicaraguan people happy.

This is why I think that to state the West "won the Cold War," which has become the conventional wisdom since 1985, is to display a poor understanding of the crisis that brought on the collapse of communism. Even assuming there really was a Cold War, which I disbelieve, it is a diplomatic and strategic notion. And the failure of communism is surely not due to the foreign policy or policies of the West. On the contrary, this was one area where the Soviets usually played a finer hand, winning some rounds even when they were wildly inferior in strength to the Free World, which either did not know how to press its advantages or did not want to. Indeed, the strategic timidity of the democracies lasted until the very end. For example, in March and April 1990, under Gorbachev, the Baltic states of Lithuania, Estonia, and Latvia proclaimed their independence, which was entirely legitimate under international law, and the West would not support them.

The decisive collapse of communism came from its internal failure—in economics primarily, but going well beyond the economy. Now the fact is that the West refused to believe in this failure, though it was evident for a long time, and it concluded several times that it was in its own interest to repair the Soviet economy. It is altogether conceivable that had it not been for the West's economic help and for its acceptance of communism's atrocious political repression—the collapse of these systems might have taken place much sooner.

On the contrary, the prevailing opinion in the West, even among conservatives, almost always saw matters from the other end: In order to go from communism to democracy, it was necessary to artificially increase the prosperity of the socialist countries by pumping them up with financial credits, investments, and technology transfers that would allow them to "modernize." For this illusion to persist, it was necessary to believe that a socialist economy is fundamentally viable, albeit temporarily stuck. This illusion, in turn, required a faith in statistics that were provided by the interested party. Even when these numbers were evaluated downward by Western "specialists," they were three or four times greater than the reality, but they were authoritative for decades in innumerable scholarly works, school textbooks, newspaper articles. Anyway, thanks to *glasnost* we saw that it was not by getting richer that communist societies would change: it was when they were faced with total disaster on the economic front that they started moving in a liberal direction—which is to say toward their own self-destruction. The Soviet lesson did not take very well, however: witness the calls, once again, to help China "modernize" itself with Western aid and credits, even after the repression of 1989. This would help it move toward "democracy." (The same mechanical logic was applied to Vietnam as well, and the Western powers even agreed to repatriate the unfortunate boat people.) China in 1992 has concentration camps that are just as atrocious as the Soviet ones under Stalin and Brezhnev, and the West is just as quiet about them.

In short, the collapse owes very little to intellectual lucidity in the West, even less to its policy initiatives. Had attention been paid to the correct analyses early on, not years but decades would have been shaved off the world's appalling experience with communism.

And, I have to insist on this, it is not as if no one was paying attention. In 1976 a 25-year-old historian named Emmanuel Todd published a book called *The Final Collapse.* Its subtitle was as refreshingly clear as it was scandalous in the context of the prevailing ideas of the time about the Soviet Union: *A Study of the Disintegration of the Soviet Sphere.* Trained in demography, young Todd did not know Russian and was anything but a Sovietologist. His only direct experience of the Soviet system had been a brief trip to Hungary, "the merriest cell-block in the prison," as it was described in those days, underscoring that it was not the most representative part of the "sphere." Once again, the modest equipment with which the author undertook to write on so difficult a subject shows that the problem was not lack of information, but wisdom in making use of it. Armed with a critical mind, one could use the information openly available to make an accurate diagnosis of what was going on. Armed with prejudices, generations of Sovietologists, fluent in Russian and frequent visitors to the Soviet Union, had managed, since 1917, to produce tons of nonsense, as did the Sinologists who "studied" Mao's China after 1949. Obviously I am not talking about Communist scholars (a contradiction in terms, anyway), who were bound to follow the party line; I mean those who claimed to be scholars with scientific criteria of investigation.

Todd had reached five basic conclusions: (1) By 1975, the Soviet economy was stagnant, though military expenditures prevented this from being readily apparent. Living standards were beginning to fall; (2) The Western economies, by continuing to grow, represented an intolerable contrast to the Soviet people; (3) Information about the West was entering the "sphere" through the satellite nations of Eastern Europe; (4) The ruling class, or *nomenklatura*, became aware that it must reform the centralized command economy or risk a social explosion; (5) But any reform of the centralized communist system would bring with it the disunity of the Soviet empire.

In short, Todd had described *perestroika* ten years before Gorbachev.

Todd's demographic training allowed him to notice a "leading indicator" of fundamental importance: the rising rate of infant mortality and the lowering of life expectancy since 1971. This was absolutely extraordinary, for even the most underdeveloped countries, while certainly they have high rates of infant mortality and low life expectancies, are constantly, if too slowly, improving in these key areas. The communists, alone, had produced a literally sick and sickly system, where these areas were getting worse. And, I insist once more, these data were in the public domain. If no one wanted to draw the obvious conclusions, it was because they contradicted the gospel of détente, whereby the Soviets were "liberalizing," "converging" with the West, "modernizing," or whatever laughable nonsense their apologists in the West wanted to believe.

Todd's book was, in fact, well received by critics who were impressed by its intellectual rigor tempered by good humor, but it had no influence. It provoked the same sort of interest, I think, as did Andre Amalrik's *Will the Soviet Union Survive Until 1984?* six years earlier: clever, but not to be taken too seriously. The opinion-forming and political elites were taking a different view in these years. The fashion was to say the Soviet system was not so bad after all. Even— indeed, especially—the leaders of West European social democracy, which traditionally had been fiercely anticommunist, wanted good relations with the communists. Stars of the Socialist International, such as Germany's Willy Brandt and Sweden's Olof Palme, turned themselves into Soviet public relations agents. Portugal's Mario Soares was a notable exception to this rule, as were Spain's Felipe Gonzalez and France's François Mitterrand on a personal level, but within his Socialist Party many of his top lieutenants were championing the Soviet Union.

For example, in 1977, Pierre Mauroy, soon to be France's prime minister and later first secretary of the Socialist Party, wrote a book called *Inheritors of the Future,* of which it is well worth quoting a few lines to recall how, only a few years ago, some of our foremost leaders saw things. "In 1975 I went to the Soviet Union and in Kharkov, Kiev and elsewhere I always found the same vitality. In elementary schools, in high schools, I found the faith and the enthusiasm which had characterized the schools of the Third Republic.* They had made astounding economic gains; their victories in the field of technology are victories for all the people . . ." and more like this. This was the man who would be in charge of France between 1981 and 1984 and what he found in the Soviet Union was public satisfaction, technological breakthroughs, economic victories. And bear in mind that 1975, when he made his trip, was the worst year for Soviet agriculture since World War II.

But forgive him: This was the time when the Soviet model was spreading in the Third World and the hated word "capitalism" was never uttered unaccompanied by the word "crisis." I recall how in 1976 and 1977 when I stated, in books and articles, that Soviet agriculture was probably in an insurmountable crisis, all I got was sarcasm and scorn. Yet the statistics of Soviet agricultural imports, which told the story, were there for anyone to see. Instead, "specialists" in the West were applauding the economic dynamism of Hungary under Janos Kadar, Poland under Edward Gierek, East Germany under Erich Honecker—all of which were doing only marginally better than the Soviet Union. Meanwhile, French Socialists gave their blessing to the Communist Party with their offer to fight for a "common program," and the Italians did the same for their Communists with the "historical compromise." French Socialism became increasingly Marxist and excommunicated social democracy, the traditional enemy of Marxian socialism. And they were cheering the bloodsoaked and appalling revolutions in Ethiopia, Angola, Mozambique, Nicaragua, El Salvador.

Now it is true that from 1980 on, the Soviet Union was out of fashion, but not because of its internal disasters. The reason was that

---

*During the Third Republic (1879–1940), French Socialists used the public school system far more than the labor movement to spread their ideas. Men like Pierre Mauroy have an almost religious attachment to public schools, unlike François Mitterand, who was educated in Catholic schools.—TRANS.

the invasion of Afghanistan and the repression in Poland put it in bad odor. Due to the darkening climate in international relations, it was possible to write that perhaps all was not well in the Soviet economy and that as a model for Third World countries it left much to be desired since it was destroying them instead of helping them take off. Which did not prevent Western observers from going gaga over the new Soviet leader, Yuri Andropov, when he took over from Brezhnev in 1982.

The point, finally, is that the crisis of communism was foreseeable since it was foreseen. More: what needs to be understood is that the analyses of Todd and others were correct even if the predictions implied by their analyses had not come to pass. An analysis can be sound, but you still need historical agents: individuals. In 1914 you would have been correct to say that Russia could look forward to a future of growth and liberalization. Then came the war and the Bolsheviks, who queered everything.

In 1953, certain actions by the Western democracies could have liberated East Germany from the Soviet grasp. All the conditions were available, the new Eisenhower administration, the death of Stalin, the announcement by Beria that he would accept a reunified neutral Germany, and the revolt of the East Germans themselves. They were ready for their freedom; the Western leaders were not.

Same sort of thing in 1956: it would have been altogether possible to get Hungary out of the Soviet prison and into a neutral status such as Austria's. The Soviets were prepared to accept this, until they realized the West would not help the Hungarians. It is not an exaggeration to say the democracies pushed Hungary back into slavery. In 1961, we know that Khrushchev had ordered the East Germans to take down the Berlin Wall in the event of a military intervention by the Allies. The experts who marvelled at the sudden "unexpected" sight of central Europe's collapsing communist regimes forgot that had the right actions been taken at the right time, these "unexpected" events in 1989 would have been ancient history. As for real-life history, it instructs us that the peoples of central Europe scarcely owe their freedom to Western policies, and the same holds for the independence, in the early 1990s, of the captive nations such as the Baltic states, Georgia, and so forth. Of course we cannot know what would have happened had the democracies taken more activist lines at other times. What is certain is that passivity too is a form of action, and Western passivity in 1990 had the effect of influencing events in anything but a positive direction. For example, it allowed Moscow to crush the Balts for another year. When you consider that as early as 1988, in the thinking of this so-called new thinking, Gorbachev had proclaimed from the podium at the U.N. that democracy was universal. The least the West could have done was to read his speech back to him and demand that he practice what he preached. They did nothing of the kind. Their desire to "help Gorbachev," on the grounds that he was a "reformer," did not flag even when he turned into a conservative. As in the past, the West adopted the Soviet point of view as their own in 1990–91 and tried to preserve the untenable "Union."

Moreover, as regards the Balts, seceding from the Union of Soviet Socialist Republics did not involve a constitutional problem, since they had entered the union unconstitutionally. They had signed no contract, never voted, entered no agreement. The referendum on the union, which the Kremlin organized for the other republics in 1991, did not affect the Balts. "Why a referendum?" asked an Estonian deputy in 1991. "We are an occupied country." The only reason for the West to take the Russian side in this affair, or in the case of the Moldavians who desired to be reunited with Romania, was that we might respect Hitler: after all it was he who had allowed Stalin to annex these countries.

But let us return to the month of March of 1990. Lithuania declares itself independent. Unable to grasp that Baltic independence is unavoidable and that the Soviets and the Balts will never see eye to eye on this, the West declares that it respects the Balts but does not mean to oppose Gorbachev, either. In practice, of course, this amounts to taking the Soviet side. Bush, Thatcher, Mitterrand, Kohl—all "showed understanding" for Gorbachev's "difficult position" and showed nothing but blindness for the more important fact, which was that the Soviet empire was already in an advanced state of disintegration and nothing could save it (in fact trying to save it prolonged the suffering of the captives inside).

In the case of the Balts, forcibly Russified and communized on the basis of a secret agreement between Hitler and Stalin in 1939, the Western leaders committed the same mistake their countries had been making since 1945 regarding central Europe. Whether not to upset the international balance or to cause trouble to a so-called communist reformer, every time the people rose against the communists, we sided with the states against civil society, with the governments against the people. We always were catching up with change instead of leading the way, which meant turning our backs on freedom fighters. Even as the Berlin Wall was coming down and the Germans were voting with their feet for unity, President Mitterrand was declaring (15 November 1989): "Reunification? In a few weeks it will be forgotten." Not that numerous experts did not agree with him. "Reunify Germany? Pure fantasy!" said Alfred Grosser at this time. And when the U.S. ambassador to Germany, Vernon Walters, said on the record that reunification was "certain," the secretary of state, James Baker, reprimanded him.

The West would have done a great deed by recognizing the independence of Lithuania, Latvia, and Estonia in 1990. Such an act would have made the inescapable decolonization of the Soviet Union a far more peaceful affair than it turned out to be. At the very least the West could have suggested the three Baltic republics get a seat at the U.N. After all, Ukraine and Belorussia each had such a seat (a gift from the Allies to Stalin after World War II). This might have satisfied both sides, at least temporarily, and how Gorbachev responded to such a proposal would have been an interesting test of his good will. Instead we did nothing. The Balts got their independence in the wake of the August 1991 coup, which Gorbachev's own government tried to stage against him. By following instead of leading, the West's leaders saved neither their own honor nor Gorbachev's job, for he came out of it all politically weakened.

Fortunately, the men who led the West by their deeds or ideas have not all been blind or inert. Their acts and theses were not always meant to slow down the collapse of communism, rather than accelerate it or at least let it happen by itself. Let us not overlook that even though it can and should be argued that communism might have reached its end (in Europe) sooner, it might also have lasted longer, had it not been for the assertion of certain ideas about communism, until then quite unfashionable, from about 1980.

Political action is the transformation of basic structures into events. As a structural system, the Soviet Union stopped being viable almost from the word go. It survived only by monstrous assaults on society. But by eliminating problems instead of seeking solutions to them, socialism became its own greatest problem. However, for its programmed failure to turn into a given series of terminal events, there was a need for specific human actions based on available short-term factors. It is on this—on human will—that depends the moment when factors permitting change can actually produce change. There is, clearly, a vast amount of possible variety here. Todd is right, historical foresight is possible at the structural level; but Sir Karl is right too when he says it is impossible to know what will happen in the short term. When predictions are right on the dot—which occurs sometimes—this is more like a roll of the dice than a scientific prediction.

As I mentioned earlier, since 1985 readers have been telling me that I erred in saying communism was indestructible and that democracy was doomed. By contrast, other readers approve me for having argued consistently that communism was incurable and incompatible in its very essence with democratic civilization and that it was essential to stand firmly against its demands. Its collapse must show how inane the policies of compromise were that aimed for ideological and geopolitical coexistence. In fact, the two reactions to my work are not mutually exclusive. But since they appear to contradict each other, perhaps I ought briefly to say a few words about the arguments of my earlier books on politics. These have always been concerned with the question of whether it is possible to organize human society on the basis of something other than violence and deceit. And this implies the no less real question of whether men really desire to organize their societies on such a basis.

In *Neither Marx nor Jesus*, which I wrote in 1970, I argued that democratic capitalism was superior to socialism. The critics saw in this book mainly a testimonial to the U.S., which seemed to them paradoxical at the moment when, caught up in the Vietnam war, the U.S. was portrayed as a bastion of reaction, racism, and imperialism. But I was simply pointing out that the communist countries had demonstrably failed and that there was something odd about the fact that so many people—including such conservatives as the soon-to-be president of France, Valéry Giscard d'Estaing—referred, for example, to Mao (recently deceased) as a "beacon of human thought."

I pointed out, moreover, that socialism would only retard the economic and social take-off of underdeveloped countries, which many thought heretical in these years when Castro and Guevara were widely admired. And it did not help that I said that for a country like France to go socialist—just when the Socialist Party was turning left—would be a regression, not progress. What I said was that it was no use looking for a "socialism with a human face": the choice was between many variants of liberalism (including social democracy, which France's socialists despised) and socialism. Against leftist fash-

65

ion, I said that in fact liberalism was more capable of adapting to progress than socialism—and I used as examples the then-new movements for increased women's rights, minority rights, a foreign policy based on human rights, and many more.

In short—and this won me no end of opprobrium—the U.S., with all its faults, was, I maintained, the society most likely to find ways of correcting those faults and advancing toward a freer and better society. Which in turn suggested that the real revolution the world needed was not the Marxist one, as my critics said, and which I said was doomed, but the liberal democratic revolution that had started in the United States in the eighteenth century.

In *The Totalitarian Temptation* (1976), I asked myself why so many in the West took a conciliatory and even obsequious attitude toward the communist systems. How could applied Marxism still win any support, and who would want to destroy comparatively free and prosperous societies in favor of such monstrosities? It takes an effort, but it can be recalled that this was the period during which Marxism was riding high throughout Europe, when otherwise intelligent people were apologizing for extreme-left terrorists, when the Socialist International was cozying up to Moscow, when Italy's Christian Democrats were playing footsie with the Communist Party, when a Communist coup very nearly succeeded in Portugal, when South Vietnam fell (April 1975), and when the liberals in the West were applauding the victory of Pol Pot in Cambodia ("For Most, a Better Life" went the *New York Times* headline that will remain a classic in the genre). I defended capitalism at a time when even partisans of free economies shied away from the term. And I claimed to be writing from the Left—if by this term was meant an increase in the human chances for liberty. Some years later, the same people who assailed me as a crypto-fascist called "left" those Russians who were aiming to liberalize their economy, and "right" (or conservative) the diehards of socialism.

The noncommunist left claimed it had broken once and for all with totalitarianism; in fact, however, it took criticism of communism as attacks upon itself and could not abide me for stating that communism had definitively failed. They wanted to believe that communism, for all its faults, could be reformed and in its essence was better than democratic capitalism. I said it could be neither reformed nor democratized, and they could not forgive me for saying this.

The New Censorship (1977) was a collection of documents with my commentaries which described how *The Totalitarian Temptation* had been received by the critics. I think future generations will find this book valuable for the portrait it gives of the noncommunist Left in the seventies and the climate of intolerance that it created. They denied that Castro had created a gulag in Cuba. They denied that the communists had set up a network of "reeducation" in Vietnam after Saigon fell. And they had the nerve to claim they represented the hope for freedom in the world. They were, on the contrary, trying to "cover up" for the totalitarian Left. But this was so ridiculous, since it was by then clear many times over what the totalitarian Left represented, that I had to conclude they were not doing this merely for a tactical reason (which would have been bad enough), i.e., to convince voters in the democracies that it was okay to elect them. Something deeper had to be at work here. There must be some inclination toward totalitarianism in human nature, and I saw that it was all the more dangerous in that it could manifest itself through movements that were not themselves totalitarian. The creation and maintenance of institutions that would protect liberty became all the more important, as it was obvious that mere rational arguments were insufficient.

Nevertheless, I found it strange that despite the glaring failure of communism, Western leaders remained ideologically complacent and diplomatically and strategically weak. Why were the democracies not tougher in facing down (and hastening the collapse) of their enemies? These were the questions that led me to write *How Democracies Perish* in 1983. Once again, my subject matter was less totalitarianism as it was democratic civilization's attitude to totalitarianism. This time I looked not so much at ideology and culture as at foreign policy where, again, the side that was demonstrably more vigorous acted as if it felt itself inferior next to the Marxist wreck and adopted a position of weakness when it engaged in negotiations.

The idea that was most commented on by reviewers was that communism is irreversible. I discussed this notion earlier and suffice it to say here that until the Soviet withdrawal from Afghanistan (which by no means precipitated the immediate disappearance of the Communist regime in Kabul) and the cascade of revolutions of 1989 in central Europe, it was an absolutely factual observation that there had never, anywhere, been a change of regime once communists had come to power, nor had there ever been a retreat from territory conquered by communists. Without exception, all the other political systems in the twentieth century had undergone changes or had lost territories, colonies, zones of influence. Until then, the Communist regimes were the only ones to which this had never happened.

What needed to be said, I thought, was that there was something outrageous and historically unprecedented in the utter contrast between communism's internal decrepitude and its successful imperialism. And why were the democracies so intent on helping their most mortal enemy not only to survive but to threaten them ever more credibly by helping it achieve military and even strategic nuclear parity and then superiority?

After *The Totalitarian Temptation* and *How Democracies Perish*, I often heard myself accused of excessive pessimism. At the beginning of every interview and following every lecture I was asked, "Are you not too pessimistic?" The fact is that had I been a pessimist I would not have written these two books. I wrote them because I could make a modest contribution to turning the situation around by having some influence on public opinion, which would then demand policies opposed to the ones I feared. I am not a speculative writer. My books are arms, warnings.

Now, of course, a polemical style depends on evidence. It is an aggressive form, but it must be a demonstration too, or it has no effect. A pamphlet that is all flash will not last. It may amuse or annoy, but it can neither instruct nor persuade. From Protagoras to Swift's *Modest Proposal*, the polemical style, when it is concerned with ideas and values, is, before anything else, an exercise in logic, but at a white heat. The reader is forced to face up to the most extreme consequences that might result from certain actions or ideas which, in and of themselves, may seem harmless. The whole point, of course, is to urge the readers to beware and take action that will prevent the undesired results. For example, when I wrote at the end of *The Totalitarian Temptation* that I had thought of calling the book "On the Inevitable Progress of Stalinism in the World and the Vain Efforts to Oppose It," I gave the reader enough credit to realize that I was making this confession tongue in cheek. It is a way of suggesting what could happen in the future if the world continued along the path set in 1975, which was indeed alarming, with communism advancing around Africa and southeast Asia. With the Helsinki Accords Soviet diplomacy achieved a goal it had sought since 1954, namely the ratification of its hold on the satellite nations. In Western Europe the Communist Parties were making progress. The noncommunist Left was returning to an illiberal "smash capitalism" ideology. Through the "theology of liberation" significant numbers of Protestant and Catholic clergymen in Western Europe and North and South America were adopting a Marxist outlook. I meant to alert the reader as to what would happen if all these trends continued to their logical conclusion.

In the same way, to call a book *How Democracies Perish* is not to make a prediction, for then the title should have been, *How Democracies Will Perish*, but to indicate which policies should be discontinued. If you call a book, *How to Lose Money in the Stock Market*, you are assuming the reader understands you want to give him advice on how not to lose money in the stock market. I hope I will be forgiven for making so heavy-handed a point, but we live in a culture where "communication" has replaced rhetoric, and we are forgetting how to take irony for what it is.

When I described communism as a political system that is irreversible, I meant that a communist system either is immune to its own failures or disintegrates completely. But it cannot adapt. It can stand neither reforms nor changes. The Marxist-Leninist argument, "Capitalism is incapable of reform, only revolution can really change things," applies to communism far more than to capitalism. The question was always how long could political oppression be used to impose an inefficient economic system. Soon after Andropov came to power in the Soviet Union, I wrote, "The Soviet economy is so enfeebled that knowledgeable Sovietologists believe that Brezhnev's successor will have to choose between the collapse of the economic system and a bold reform." But in fact "Reform Is Impossible," as the title of my article proclaimed. The only way out is revolution, that is the complete suppression of communism. A totalitarian system either is totally suppressed, or not at all.

Why did the anticommunist revolution begin to succeed for the first time in 1985, in central Europe and then in the Soviet Union? The emergence of so abnormal a regime as communism, "that banal, terrifying, and ridiculous historical construction," as Emmanuel Todd puts it (though I would question "banal"), that regime that is so contrary to man's interests and needs and dignity, cannot be explained by socioeconomic or political or cultural determinism. Neither can its fall. From the start, its fall was inevitable. The question was how to make the inevitable happen. How and why did the inevitable become possible?

Well, the major factors that made it possible for the Soviet system to meet its fate are known. From 1980 there was a turning away in the West of the ideas that had led to complacency. It became more widely understood that socialism was a dead end. The primary importance of political democracy became clearer to people, and human rights, albeit in a confused way, acquired greater status. A handful of writers began to turn around the sense of alienation from democracy the intellectual classes had felt, with such deleterious effects on their cultures. A few political leaders eschewed the disastrous assumptions that had produced détente, and replaced them with a diplomacy of firmness that put an end to the practice of making unilateral concessions.

Had the West had not deployed the Pershing IIs in 1983, the so-called Euromissiles, with some help from France's Socialist president, who had the intelligence to stand up to Germany's socialists; if Ronald Reagan had not launched his SDI, while at the same time providing the Afghan freedom fighters with Stingers that were effective against Soviet aircraft; if the U.S. had not reduced its economic and technological aid to the Soviet Union; if these things had not happened, it is quite conceivable that the foundations of Soviet power would not have cracked. And in the East, had it not been for Solidarity, for Charter 77, for Andrei Sakharov, had not discouragement and doubts as to the viability of communism finally penetrated certain levels of the Soviet leadership, it is likely the revolutionary momentum might have missed its mark, or been stopped, or slowed down. Translating communism's economic disaster into a political disaster required translators. Who were they and what did they do?

CHAPTER SEVEN

REVOLUTIONS AGAINST THE REVOLUTION

A system can be brought low by its own weaknesses only if someone takes advantage of them, shows them up through oppositional activity and publicity about a radically different system, lets them run their damaging course by refusing to help remedy their consequences. This "someone," who of course is not a single individual (but specific individuals are needed), acts on the system either from the inside or from the outside or, most likely, both. This is precisely what communism always did in its war against capitalism. There were numerous partisans of communism within the democracies and they were backed up by its expansionist momentum, which itself was strengthened by its ever-growing military power.

Although it was an article of faith with them that capitalism would collapse due to its own contradictions, the communists (inside and outside democratic societies) never tired of playing an active role in hastening its downfall. The idea never occurred to them that, in the interest of world peace, they ought to help capitalism overcome its problems. By contrast, the democracies often helped communism overcome its problems, from the days of the New Economic Policy after World War I until the last gasps of *perestroika*, from the days of China's Cultural Revolution to the ones following the repression of democracy at Tiananmen Square. Apart from the fact that the democracies had virtually no means for putting pressure on the communist systems from the inside, they seldom made use of the available possibilities for action from the outside. Even so trivial a decision as the refusal to take part in the Moscow Olympic Games in 1980, following the invasion of Afghanistan, was taken only by some within the democratic camp. Others (including France) viewed it as if it were an aggression. Due to this sort of timidity, the liberation of the countries of central Europe owes virtually nothing to us; it was due mainly to changes inside the Soviet sphere. Still, some things were done in the West that hastened these changes. In any event, the surprising effectiveness of our rare moments of firmness proves that communism would have fallen much sooner had we not so often propped it up.

Among the external factors that provoked the beginning of the end of the Soviet sphere (not communism generally) in 1989 were the support of John Paul II and the U.S., though not Western Europe, for the Polish revolt in 1980. Crucial, too, was continuing American and papal support for Solidarity (with its exceptionally shrewd leader) after it was driven underground by the imposition of martial law in December 1981. The Stinger ground-to-air portable missiles which the Reagan administration provided the Afghan resistance prevented the Soviets from winning the war against the Afghan people. The same American leadership, as well as others, notably Costa Rica's president Oscar Arias, intervened to block a Soviet-Cuban takeover of El Salvador and helped roll it back in Nicaragua. Last and perhaps most importantly, the Reagan administration's SDI was of fundamental importance in that it showed the Soviet leadership that it could never compete in the technological race with the U.S.

There were other factors too, such as the work of writers and human rights activists in the West such as Doctors Without Borders, who showed by words and deeds that neither socialism nor the Soviet Union had anything to offer the poorer countries. All these causes led to another cause: Mikhail Gorbachev. The new general secretary realized that the usual short-term repairs of the Soviet system, even with the West's assistance, were losing their effectiveness. He chose to reform the system's foundations and, since he did not know they were unreformable, he brought about the series of catastrophes that led to its disappearance.

Another significant factor in the crack-up of the Soviet system occurred when certain Western leaders decided to proceed with the long-planned deployment of the Euromissiles in 1983, despite threats from the Soviets and pacifist campaigns against NATO. These virulent campaigns, which were supported by the Soviets, were led not only by pacifists and Greens but also by some of the mainstream political parties, such as the British Labour Party and the German

Social Democrats (SPD). The German chancellor, Helmut Schmidt, who persevered in his arguments for deployment against the majority line in his own party and in the Socialist International, is a good example of the key role an individual can play at a historical turning point. A moment of comparable importance occurred when France's François Mitterrand attacked German pacifism at the Bundestag in January 1983.

Alone, however, these European leaders would have been unable to resist the Soviets and Western unilateral disarmers, had not Ronald Reagan reversed what had been the main line of U.S. policy toward the Soviets since FDR. Like Margaret Thatcher, Britain's prime minister since 1979, he understood that the Soviets never give anyone credit for concessions. Had it not been for this conjunction of circumstances, or rather, for this handful of individuals, among whom we would also include Helmut Kohl, who took over from Schmidt as German chancellor in October 1982, the Soviet Union most likely would have notched up another one of the victories it was accustomed to. Thanks to its SS20 missiles, deployed in 1977, it would have maintained military superiority in the European theater and would have parlayed this into political domination and economic extortions, which would have allowed it to survive for another two decades. In this regard, it is worth recalling how easily President Jimmy Carter in 1978 caved in to Soviet pressure, reinforced by its Western accomplices, and signed away the "neutron bomb" program, which could have provided a counterweight to Warsaw Pact tank superiority. Had the neutron bomb program gone forward, who knows but that the Soviet crisis might not have begun sooner, since at that time it already could not keep up in the arms race? Perhaps, in the face of this Western resolve, the Brezhnev-Gromyko team would not have dared to invade Afghanistan in 1979.

Between the missile crisis of 1962 and NATO's "dual-track" decision regarding the deployment of the Pershing IIs in 1983, the Soviets had always succeeded in forcing the West to retreat, gaining an uninterrupted series of diplomatic, political, strategic, and territorial victories in Asia, Africa, and Central America. When military defeat in Afghanistan reversed this trend, undermining the confidence of the Soviet leadership, it was due to the steadfastness of one individual, Ronald Reagan, without whose active support the Afghan resistance could not have won. The French and German leaders were at first inclined to look the other way and write off the invasion of

Afghanistan, which India, though a democracy, cynically approved. Reagan was the first American president who, for years, refused summit conferences with the Soviet leadership, meeting with Gorbachev in Geneva in 1985 only after clear signs of change. He refused to give any ground on the SDI, and did not apply the usual Western method of giving something for nothing other than a media event that is supposed to "help you domestically."

In an insightful article written in 1980, Emmanuel Todd analyzed the invasion of Afghanistan as caused by an economic, demographic, and ideological crisis in the Soviet system, a symptom of weakness more than an expression of strength. It is true it could be interpreted this way, as a counterweight to the Soviets' economic and demographic decline and a preemptive strike against a possible future source of Islamic fundamentalism that could spread to the Soviet Union's Muslim populations. But then, symptoms of weakness seemed to be proliferating that year, in Angola, Mozambique, Ethiopia, Nicaragua, El Salvador, Cambodia, Vietnam—where they were making use of the giant base at Cam Ranh Bay), and even the South Pacific. As the democracies were refraining from doing anything to stand in their way, the Soviet "weakness" was showing an alarming tendency to look like "strength." Compensating for internal weaknesses with external conquests has often succeeded in history. Moreover, the Soviet Union was by then an essentially military empire. Gaining control of so many strategic points around the planet allowed the Soviet Union to reap a rich harvest of diplomatic assets that could be used for economic extortion.

You have to keep in mind that what we are looking at here is not a geological shift but human action. Suppose the U.S. had not reacted to the invasion of Afghanistan, which might well have been the case had it occurred four years earlier, just after the fall of South Vietnam. Then the Soviet Union could have not only conquered Afghanistan but, with India's diplomatic connivance and indeed its military assistance, it could have "Finlandized" Pakistan. Todd is right to argue that in the long run this would not have reversed the Soviet Union's systemic decay. But the two or three decades of oxygen that it would have gained through such a victory would have cost the democracies plenty. In his article, Todd thought that because Afghanistan is an Islamic nation, the Soviets would have refrained from applying the genocidal policy that the Vietnamese applied in Cambodia. Yet they did just that. In order to cut off the freedom fighters from their bases and supplies, the Soviets either massacred or provoked the flight of the civilian populations, destroying villages and crops, littering the countryside with mines, parachuting camouflaged toys, which concealed small bombs that exploded when children picked them up. The war killed between a-million-and-a-quarter and a-million-and-a-half on the Afghan side, of whom 80 percent were civilians. Five million fled to Pakistan, two million to Iran. The U.N. High Commissioner for Refugees estimated in 1988 that one out of two refugees in the world was an Afghan. Between 1979 and 1989 the country's population was halved. The Soviet leadership did not fail for lack of trying. It failed because of Ronald Reagan, who, of course, could not have done anything without the heroism of the resistance. Jean-François Deniau, a former minister under Valéry Giscard d'Estaing, became after 1981 a courageous observer of the world's freedom fighters, risking his life several times in Afghanistan and elsewhere. He observed: "When the resistance got adequate anti-aircraft equipment, it brought down twenty to forty Soviet planes and helicopters per month. To win, the Red Army, which had counted on total mastery of the air, now had to deploy far greater numbers of infantry. This was a political, as well as a military decision."

With their massive financial and military aid, as well as diplomatic support, the Americans also protected Pakistan against the Soviets and against India, all the while providing the Afghan resistance an indispensable sanctuary. A high Soviet official told Deniau that if the U.S. had followed the other Western powers in doing nothing, "In three months, no one will be talking about Afghanistan"—the Soviets not only would have gained advantages that would have buttressed them for a long time, but especially they would have avoided the quadruple catastrophe (military, political, economic, and moral) that brought about the failure of its central system. As Deniau says: "The [Soviet] failure in Afghanistan put into question a whole strategy of intervention in other theaters, where the 'Cuban legions' had provided until then positive results." Which in turn put into question as well the costly regime in Cuba.

Nonetheless, the democracies never went so far as to help people rise up against Communist regimes that were in place. That was forbidden by the very concepts on which the "Cold War" was based, concepts that have been used in such divergent ways, particularly in speaking of the "end" of the Cold War or the "recurrence" of the Cold War, that it has lost all useful meaning. To understand the reasons for the success of (some of) the anticommunist revolutions of 1989, it is useful to recall what the Cold War really was, if only to understand better what was détente and then how the end of détente, due to Reagan, was one of the causes of Gorbachevism.

The Cold War started in 1947, following Stalin's imprisonment of central Europe behind the Iron Curtain, when the West realized it had to prevent him from grabbing Western Europe as well. The free nations, during the Cold War, restricted themselves to blocking all new territorial advances by the Soviet Union and the installation of new Communist regimes. The democracies never conceived of the Cold War as a means of winning back the countries that became Soviet satellites after the Second World War, nor of overthrowing their Communist regimes by instigating or supporting insurrections. It was designed to contain, not roll back, communism. Until the administration of Richard Nixon in 1969, this policy was followed literally: Berlin, Korea, Cuba, Latin America, Congo, Vietnam. The U.S. and its allies, on the other hand, made no effort to attack the Soviet empire on its frontiers of 1947, directly or indirectly. They did not encourage the peoples who rose against their oppression. They regularly abandoned them to Soviet reprisals, even when it was evident that Moscow, panicked, was prepared to compromise; though, of course, to get compromises out of Moscow it would have been necessary to ask for them in the first place. This the West never did at any of the crises that shook the Soviet system: East Berlin in 1953 and 1961; Hungary in 1956; Czechoslovakia in 1968; Poland in 1980.

Richard Nixon and Henry Kissinger began to put the policy of détente in place in 1969, though to be sure it had been invented earlier by Charles de Gaulle and Willy Brandt with his *Ostpolitik*. Détente maintained the Western side of the Cold War bargain, which forbade the democracies from rolling back communism (they went so far as to guarantee the borders that resulted from World War II), but it abandoned the idea that they should block further Soviet expansion. In effect, détente was the abandonment of the Truman Doctrine, which Kennedy had reaffirmed in 1961. Truman had said in March 1947: "It must be the policy of the United States to support free people who are resisting attempted subjugation by armed minorities or outside pressure."

Thus from 1970 on the Soviets were able to send their surrogates forth without encountering serious Western opposition, and they installed regimes that were beholden to them in several countries of

Africa and even on the continent of the Western Hemisphere. They violated the 1973 Paris Accords that were supposed to have put an end to the Vietnam war; they invaded Afghanistan after organizing several coups there. It was during these years that it became fashionable to call any suggestion that the West ought to oppose these warlike actions (or even interrupt the economic aid and the strategic concessions being granted the Communist world in this same period) a "return to the Cold War." Even the attempted Communist coup in Portugal in 1975 almost succeeded, and had considerable support in Western Europe. That was the year of the signing of the Helsinki Final Act, a central aim of Soviet foreign policy since 1954. Henceforth, "Cold War" became a pejorative term used to heap scorn on the idea of resisting Soviet expansion, which was based on the greatest peacetime military build-up in the history of the world. Even suggesting it might be wise to delay constructing a gas pipeline for the Soviets after the declaration of martial law in Poland in December 1981; or that there might be good reasons not to finance Gorbachev's *perestroika* a few years later; or that following the bloody repression at Tiananmen Square, China ought to lose its most favored nation status—all these were denounced as acts of "Cold War." The West Europeans were still saying this at the G-7 Summit in the summer of 1989, even as all of central Europe was openly in revolt against communism.

Then it happened again in June 1990 when Gorbachev and Bush met in Washington. Just as he had six months earlier at Malta, the American president, who had so well interiorized the Soviet view that any disagreement with what they wanted signalled the "return of the Cold War," agreed in advance not to discuss certain key points Gorbachev had warned he would not give in on. The Bush-Gorbachev meeting in Washington in June 1990 repeated the pattern set six months earlier at Malta. Cowed by the notion that a public dispute on important issues would have signaled a "return of the Cold War," the American President agreed in advance not to bring up certain items the Soviet leader did not want to discuss. But since the event would have appeared irrelevant if the two world leaders met to talk about the weather, Bush proceeded to volunteer concessions on other issues. Characteristically, Gorbachev had exhorted members of Congress a day earlier to "end the Cold War." The Soviets needed the Cold War in order to always have the opportunity to blame it on Western governments.

Bearing this tradition in mind, what could it possibly mean to say the Soviet Union lost the Cold War? How can you lose a war no one is waging against you? In fact, what was being displayed was the "détente spirit" of the seventies, interrupted for a few years, and the foundation of the democracies' diplomacy again after 1985. The essence of the spirit of détente was to blame the West for Soviet policies as well as its own. If the Soviet Union under Brezhnev grew increasingly weak inside and aggressive outside, it was the West that had not given enough time for its concessions and aid to bear the desired fruit. By this way of thinking, the democracies suppressed the notion that the first requirement of their policy ought to have been to defend their own interests. Better yet, Gorbachev, as soon as he came to power, succeeded in persuading them that the defense of their interests began with the defense of his own. Brezhnev had not been able to get this idea across fully. But in 1990, the democracies had to sacrifice Lithuania on the altar of *perestroika*, just as in 1968 they had sacrificed Czechoslovakia for peace or, in 1980, Afghanistan and Poland for détente.

Gorbachev's special skill consisted of turning the West into a partner in his *perestroika* enterprise. The more *perestroika* failed, the more the West was convinced that its fate was bound to *perestroika*'s. Which meant that to go against Gorbachev meant to go against themselves. New threats to Gorbachev kept cropping up with endless inventiveness. After the "conservatives" and the rebellious generals, the West found itself worrying about disorder and anarchy, as if it was responsible. Gorbachev compared his situation to Weimar Germany, with the implication that if the West did not pay his bills it could expect a Soviet Hitler. As late as September 1991, a month after the failed putsch, the mayor of St. Petersburg, one of the most liberal Soviet leaders, warned of a "Nazi danger" if sufficient Western financial aid was not forthcoming. But the list of dangers to *perestroika* never included *perestroika* itself even though it was clear this contradictory "market socialism," this illegitimate offspring of Marx and capitalism, could not possibly work.

In short, it is fair to say that from 1985 on, the elites of the democracies took up where détente had left off. They allowed Gorbachev to set the agenda and entered into his game. When the West thought for itself, as in 1980–85, it contributed to the crisis of communism. The crisis occurred because the "bipolar" politics of the Cold War forced the Soviet Union into an exhausting economic competition that it lost. But in 1985, the West returned to a conciliatory attitude, taking Gorbachev at face value the way it earlier had taken Brezhnev. Though the former certainly was preferable, the point is that it seldom occurred to anyone in the free world to question whether his premises—that it was somehow possible to avoid the disadvantages of communism without abandoning the communist system!—might be wrong. It did not occur to them, either, that there might be some way forward for the nations of central Europe other than servile imitation of *perestroika* or "enlightened communism." That is why the democracies disapproved of independence movements in the East and helped Gorbachev put them down. There was some argument about whether or not Gorbachev's chances of success were as good or bad as he himself claimed, but practically no suggestions were made that there might be other ways than his to look at the situation.

The real credit for the collapse of communism belongs to the people who rebelled against it. Now earlier insurrections had failed. How is it the revolutions against The Revolution in 1989 were successful in certain countries? Here the credit definitely belongs to Gorbachev. Not that he was in favor of all that happened. But what he did want made the rest possible and perhaps even in a certain sense inevitable. The consequences of his actions went way beyond his intentions. At first Gorbachev appears to have meant to replace the old Brezhnevite leadership in the satellites with Communist reformers who would pursue local versions of his own *perestroika*. This policy of liberalization in the satellites, however, implied giving up or at least suspending the "Brezhnev Doctrine," which called for using force to defend "fraternal" socialist regimes against any popular attempt to get rid of them. Giving up this prerogative was necessary if the West was to be approached (again) for economic help, in the Soviet Union as well as in central Europe.

The West's good will had been obtained through a brilliant seduction campaign and was by then a key element in Gorbachev's political strategy. He probably underestimated the West's tolerance for repression, which after all came down hard on the Lithuanians in the form of a blockade and several armed interventions. But it is probably true that a direct intervention in central Europe, recalling Prague 1968, or even an indirect repression such as the one in Poland in 1981 would have been too much. This would have wrecked Gorbachev's plans for a "common European home," with the reduction in defense spending and the economic cooperation that the

Soviet Union needed for its survival. The Soviet president still saw a way to maintain the Warsaw Pact, albeit with some autonomy for the "fraternal" regimes. At any rate the Western leadership was itself, in 1989, still insisting that any changes should be made "in respect for present alliances and existing frontiers."

Fortunately for them and unfortunately for Gorbachev, the peoples of central Europe thought otherwise. As soon as they realized they did not face the prospect of bloody police or military repression, they saw no need to accept the meagre fare of limited liberty and moderate socialism that the reform Communists had concocted. Gorbachevism worked for a time in Romania and Bulgaria, where the communists were able to rid themselves of the old tyrants and put less monstrous leaders in place. They changed their name and managed to win elections. However, the Romanian president, Ion Iliescu, was clumsy enough to win an election in May 1990 with 95 percent of the votes, which no one thought credible. A month later the Bulgarian communists put on a more credible show, but, anyway, these communist hold-outs had little time left. Elsewhere in Europe, things were changing already by 1989. The "modern" communists whom Gorbachev had nurtured to take the place of the overthrown Brezhnevite shipwrecks were in their turn swept away in a matter of weeks by the popular torrent, to be replaced by new men who came out of noncommunist, or even anticommunist, currents. More: to the bitter regret of Western socialist parties, voters in the East turned down social-democratic candidates, expressing thereby an unexpected dislike for any form of socialism, even in a country such as Poland where it seemed sensible to go in for a temporary alliance with the Communists.

Moreover, even in countries where they remained powerful because Gorbachev's strategy had worked, the former Communist Parties sensed the need to change their name and go before the voters (even where they rigged the elections) under other labels, as political transvestites. The anticommunist tide revealed the inanity of the idea, which for decades had won favor in the West on the Right no less than on the Left, that in the last analysis the peoples of central Europe had come to terms with the regimes imposed on them by force and really wanted to make a few changes in order to preserve their "positive" aspects. This fraud pleased the European Left, always searching for the mirage of a "mixed economy." At the same time it pleased the Right, concerned about maintaining the stability of states and alliances. The real-life behavior of people proved the only thing that had kept them in communism was terror. As soon as terror disappeared, they had every intention of making communism disappear as well. Though he imagined he had found a "third way," Gorbachev demonstrated unwittingly that if it is not totalitarian, a Communist Regime cannot survive.

This was a point Brezhnev had understood when he used tanks to put an end to the Prague spring. He knew there is no such thing as "socialism with a human face," and that any real reform would bring about the end of socialism. Trying to save socialism by reforming it, Gorbachev killed it. Giving up police terror (at which Andropov was a masterful practitioner) and armed repression, at least in central Europe, he removed the only roadblock on the road out of socialism. But in a country like China, where the repressive apparatus was maintained, the process of economic reform was halted brutally as soon as it reached the natural point of requiring its complement of political reforms in a democratic direction. Which incidentally showed the degree to which public opinion in the democracies remained deaf and blind to reality in 1989, since we were celebrating the "end" of communism at the very time when the Chinese tyrants were once again bringing down the night on a population nearly four times as big as those of central Europe and the Soviet Union together. The Tiananmen massacre and the increasingly ferocious crushing of dissent in Tibet was in a sense a reverse proof of Gorbachevism. It showed that socialism cannot reform itself economically without accepting the political and police norms that are proper to democratic capitalism. The Chinese could not accept this since it meant giving up their power. The Romanian Communists, seeing what was coming, were, as we now know, prepared to drown the anticommunist revolution in blood had it not been for the move by the *"perestroikists,"* aided by the Soviets, against Ceausescu.

It is clear that Gorbachev was forced into reforms by the horrendous economic and social situation inside the Soviet Union. But it was not written anywhere that his attempted reforms had to be accompanied by *glasnost*. It is clear, too, that *perestroika* made matters worse instead of better; Gorbachev did not program his own failure, nor did he foresee that his loss would be democracy's gain. But in order to get help for his reforms he decided that people should know how bad it really was; in permitting information and the criticism that came with it, he was also making way for the system's destruction. But ending the terror while authorizing *glasnost* was not the only policy he could have followed. In Romania, as in Cuba and Vietnam, the terror continued; in the latter two countries they continue still and there is no doubt Fidel Castro would have been overthrown a long time ago if he had renounced the use of terror.

There was during the Gorbachev period an understandable confusion in the West which could be seen in the large number of people who declared themselves in favor of *perestroika* yet also announced that communism was finished. They failed to see that as it was originally conceived, the aim of *perestroika* was not to bury communism but on the contrary to save it. Which is why to help Gorbachev meant to delay the breakdown of communism. This misapprehension queered the entire debate about the policies to adopt toward the Soviet Union in this period, and it is likely that Gorbachev played his cards accordingly.

For example, Gorbachev told *Time* on June 4, 1990, that he was still a Communist and in the same breath announced a vast program of dismantling of the state-run sector of the economy, letting prices be set by the market, and ruble convertibility. As usual, he also mentioned that he would not apply the program just yet. Gorbachev's program consisted of incoherent announcements, half-measures, cancelled decisions, procrastinations. This is understandable, since one cannot pursue policies that are bound to destroy communism while not wanting to destroy communism! However, Gorbachev's hesitations hastened the system's downfall. As Vladimir Bukovsky put it, "The original idea had three elements, *perestroika* (reform), *uskorenie* (acceleration), and *glasnost* (openness). We got acceleration all right, but reforms could not get off the ground. But we got openess." Which is why the situation was so explosive. The Soviet "conservatives" were quite right to say that trying to make the system more efficient would irreparably damage it. Trying to make an animal run that cannot even walk is bound to kill it.

Far be it from me to suggest Gorbachev was playing at the sorcerer's apprentice, whose experiments carried him away. No. There had been forever, on the Left, and even within the Soviet sphere, the notion that you could have a form of socialism that was flexible in its economics and open in its politics. The communist tradition produced and then crushed reformers, such as Imre Nagy in Hungary, Alexander Dubcek in Czechoslovakia, even—to a lesser degree— Nikita Khrushchev. All of them were sincere in their loyalty to socialism and their assurances that their intention was not to return to ordinary capitalism and a multiparty, "bourgeois" democracy. Indeed, they sought to give authority to their ideas and policies by saying they were "returning to Lenin," as Gorbachev himself claimed at first. The implication here, false of course, was that Lenin had been "betrayed" by Stalin et al. As to the Western democratic left, it filled entire libraries with books and articles demonstrating in theory how to get rid of "unbridled capitalism" while maintaining efficient economic conditions and political liberties. In other words, Gorbachev was in good company, even if it is certain that within the Soviet sphere this rich tradition of searching for a "socialism with a human face" had always been in the minority, its representatives having been kept on the margins when they were not shot. In effect, what happened in 1985 was that for the first time since 1917 the Mensheviks took over from the Bolsheviks in the Soviet Union.

Gorbachev's problem, therefore, was not that he was playing sorcerer's apprentice; his problem was that the "Menshevik tradition" (the word means minority in Russian), though the source of discussions and reflections for most of a century (the Russian social democratic party split into Bolshevik and Menshevik factions in 1903), had never been tested in practice. With a very few exceptions outside the Soviet sphere, such as the Allende experiment in Chile, the "third way" only lived on paper. With Gorbachev, it was given an empirical test on a large scale.

The experiment in China under the leadership of Deng Ziaoping was a less significant test, because it was limited to the economic sphere. It made no attempt to democratize political and cultural life. Gorbachev attempted to move on both fronts, as logic required him to do. Even the conservatives in the West thought this third way was possible, since Reagan, Bush, Kohl, Andreotti, and Thatcher were among the new general secretary's warmest supporters. As late as July 1991, in the draft program of the Soviet Communist Party—which the West interpreted as a "break with Marxism"—Gorbachev wrote, "Our tragedy is to have deformed the building of socialism by establishing a totalitarian system." This vision of a socialism betrayed is one of the oldest ideas on the Left. In July 1991 it is not news, even if, to be sure, Gorbachev liquidated Leninist tenets in favor of basic liberties that are incompatible with communism. Still, it remained a reform project, not a rejection of a failed tradition, and for Gorbachev to speak of "a humanistic democratic socialism" did not exactly put him in the vanguard of leftist thinking. Because he suggested jettisoning the class struggle, it was said he was breaking with Marxism. But the notion of class struggle was developed by the great liberal thinker François Guizot in 1828 (when Marx was ten), and in any event the class struggle is a reality, though not the mystical force that it became in Marxism.

There are three broad currents in the history of socialism: totalitarian communism, antitotalitarian socialism, which remains committed to the idea of nationalizing the commanding heights of the economy, and social democracy. With his suggestions that he could aim for a mixed economy, Gorbachev seemed to be opting for the second variety, which combines parliamentary democracy with statist control of the economy—at great cost to society. Gorbachev, who in the book he wrote following the failed putsch of August 1991, still professed to believe in "Marxism-Leninism" and the October Revolution (betrayed by Stalin), seems never to have been able to make up his mind.

In sum, the rapid collapse of communism was the consequence of the conjunction of three causal factors. First, there was the failure of the central system. Second, the democratic countries firmly refused, from 1980 to 1985, to provide the means whereby communism could overcome this failure. Finally, a number of Communist leaders tried to reform the system and believed they could do this without abolishing it.

Without the second and third factors, the effect of the first one would have been exceedingly slow. Whenever the democracies' resolve flagged, communism got a reprieve. This was underscored one last time in June 1990 when after a three-month blockade imposed by Gorbachev and tacitly supported by the West, Lithuania temporarily withdrew its declaration of independence. This would not have occurred had the West supported the Balts. And if the Balts had prevailed at this point, the Soviet Union would have had to be revised, which it was anyway. But at the June summit, George Bush "sold the Lithuanians down the river" (as Americans say), which is to say betrayed them in the name of a very shortsighted realpolitik. *Perestroika*, though no one could tell what it had to do with putting down the Balts, required this felony. François Mitterrand and Helmut Kohl had sent a letter to Lithuanian President Landsbergis a month earlier recommending "dialogue" with the Soviets. This was more that a little hypocritical, however, since it was not accompanied by a letter to Gorbachev stressing that the West could not accept (as officially it never had) the secret Hitler–Stalin protocol, which had turned the Balts over to the Soviet Union in the first place. Through their one-sided diplomacy, the Western leaders in effect supported Gorbachev—which he readily grasped, since he strengthened the blockade and broke the Lithuanians' resistance. This is what "helping Gorbachev" always boiled down to: helping the man and not the reforms he supposedly stood for.

Had the West been a little tougher, would some time have been gained in turning the totalitarian Soviet Union into a constellation of democratic republics, or at least of noncommunist independent states? Perhaps. Perhaps not. Many other things could have gone wrong. The point here, however, is that the West helped Gorbachev lengthen an unacceptable situation, in which the national question could not be resolved—and therefore became harder to resolve peacefully, as we are seeing now—and Soviet colonialism persisted to the incoherent and bloody end. If the idea was to avoid chaos, the analysis was faulty indeed, since chaos is what the unfortunate peoples of the East got and are getting. It does no good, in politics or in anything else, to try to maintain something that is impossible, and the Balt tragedy is just one example of how this rule applies to *perestroika*. In helping communism "overcome" its problems, which were in fact crises, we seemed set on making them last for ever.

Every time we in the West took the contrary attitude, we obtained satisfactory results. History is not made of abstract and impersonal forces, but of human action. "The man of action," wrote Max Weber, "is the one who, in a specific situation, makes a choice based on his system of values and thereby introduces a new factor into the deterministic system." In the Balt tragedy, you could say that the American, British, German, and French leaders resolutely chose to go against their own values and introduce no new factors into the given situation. They preferred the old factor: the democracies help the Communist regimes against the people.

And it is clear that it does not help to say that, anyway, the Balts were soon going to be free since the Soviet empire was doomed. Just when freedom comes makes a great deal of difference to the people concerned! This is the whole point also with regard to the policies the West adopted toward China after Tiananmen or toward Vietnam regarding the boat people. The idea that being nice to them and cooperating with them economically would push them toward liberalization has been proven wrong time and time again, which does not seem to prevent it from being tried over and over. Spain, Portugal, and the Latin American countries made the same mistake with Fidel Castro, inviting him to the Hispanic Summit at Guadalajara in July 1991. The arguments are always the same, and they are always weak: a dictator must not be "pushed to the wall"; he must not "lose face"; he must be "given some rope."

Which never works. A dictatorship falls either due to prosperity, or to bankruptcy. Fidel Castro's has been so brutal, and it has kept the Cuban people in such misery, that it is beyond hope. Fidel gave the back of his hand to the advice he received from the heads of state preaching liberalism; it was like suggesting vegetarianism to a crocodile. Another oddity here, incidentally, is that the soft touch with dictators is only applied to left-wingers. No one ever invited Franco or Pinochet to a Hispanic summit, and these were dictators whose economic successes were real and who were demonstrably paving the way to a democratic transition. Inviting Castro is just another case of one of the most sickening political facts of the twentieth century, the double standard with regard to left-wing tyrants, no matter the dimensions of their crimes.

Politics, of course, involves making intelligent—though sometimes inaccurate—calculations, but it also involves emotional symbols. You could not fail to be saddened by pictures in the newspapers showing the king of Spain shaking hands with the Cuban tyrant. Juan Carlos is the man who midwived the first stable democracy in his country; Fidel Castro had organized in 1989 a bloody and gruesome show trial of the kind we thought was no longer possible, and had watched on video the execution of his victims, General Ochoa and his comrades-in-arms. The handshake may have been a matter of protocol, it nevertheless had a moral, or I should say immoral, significance. Castro's presence queered the Guadalajara summit. Latin American democracy in 1991 was far from robust; with Castro there, were people to think their leaders were less serious than they claimed about democracy? To make matters worse, this stupid invitation made the media focus on Fidel Castro instead of the far more important story, which of course was the democratic renewal in Latin America.

Then, when totalitarian regimes which the democracies have kept alive artificially finally collapse, we are told, "We told you so! Why all the fuss?" This is specious and inhuman. What of the extra decades of suffering, the deportations, the famines, the murders, the exterminations? The democracies can hardly evade their responsibilities by saying that suffering always comes to an end in the end! We still must ask whether other policies might not have overturned these tyrannies earlier. The false sophistication of the "long view" is in reality a rationale for blindness and irresponsibility. An astonishing example of this way of thinking occurs in a June 1990 article by Arthur Schlesinger, Jr., which claims with a straight face that "FDR's Vision Is Vindicated by History" as the title has it, as if the fact that Walesa and Havel triumphed in 1990 justified the sufferings of fifty years that were caused by Roosevelt's mistakes at Yalta, when he allowed Stalin to take over central Europe. The object was not to organize a Europe in the year 2000, but to finish the war against Europe by bringing freedom to people in 1945! History must be measured in human terms if it is to mean anything.

You cannot call a foreign policy triumph for America the abandonment of those parts of the Yalta agreement that the Soviets did not like. And despite this, the victims of this betrayal rebelled whenever they could, and their final victory after years of bloody repression proves that the Roosevelt view of the world (which was not only Roosevelt's) was mistaken. A policy of firmness—insisting, for example, that the Soviets respect their side of the Yalta bargain—would have shortened the duration of the Soviet empire and prevented it from expanding into Africa, Asia, and America.

Moreover, the democracies' defeat at Yalta and their subsequent reluctance to support liberation movements in Central Europe had consequences that carried well beyond 1990, when most of these countries were able to free themselves, in part at least, from the communist yoke. Not only did they fall fifty years behind where they might be if they had been liberated in 1945, they found themselves, in a sense, worse off than in 1939. For the nature of communism is such that it not only prevented the development of a modern economy, it destroyed the old one as well, if only by murdering the individuals who knew how to make it function. "Reform" simply does not have the same meaning here as it does when applied to an economic system which, however deep its problems, is more or less functional.

Communist reality is not a developed economy that requires various improvements, it is a gigantic, useless, unfixable mess. It is not even comparable to underdeveloped countries, which at their own low level at least function. Traditional societies have their agriculture, their crafts, their credit and marketing systems, and so forth. They are not highly developed but they have an internal logic, they respond, however poorly, to human needs. They are a base on which something can be built. But as Alain Besancon put it, in communist countries there is nothing there but a spectre, and most of them do not have the good fortune, like the East Germans, of having a billionaire twin who wants to turn the derelict brother into a respectable gentleman. The issue is not to get them out of a malfunctioning economy, it is to get them out of a situation in which there is no economy. It is not a matter of going from stagecoaches to high-speed trains; they cannot even feed their horses.

On top of its destruction of the economy, of society, of culture, and of human beings, communism destroys something even more irreparable in the short term: the environment. The opening of the frontiers between East and West revealed the full extent of the ecological devastation brought on by socialism, even if you exclude the Chernobyl catastrophe, which itself is readily explained by the nature of communism and its built-in irresponsibility. Let us just look at "ordinary" pollution. Poland and Lithuania cause more pollution in a day than do France and Germany in a year. The Soviet "planners" devastated the natural resources of Uzbekistan and killed the Aral Sea, the greatest landlocked sea in the world. They poisoned the soil with pesticides and annihilated their human resources by crippling children with labor. How many decades—or centuries—will it take to repair these horrors? And the West has a large share of responsibility here, with its thoughtless policies of coexistence and détente and status quo for so many years. Our wilful blindness would have been laughable had it not been a case of aiding and abetting crime. Consider the program of the French Socialist Party in 1972 (jointly signed with the Communist Party). In chapter 3 we read: "Water and air pollution are getting worse, and capitalism, not technological progress as such, is responsible for them." Capitalism? What sort of stupid dishonest ideological cretinism was this? I remember asking François Mitterrand about this passage at the time, when he was first secretary of the Socialist Party. He did not believe it—probably he had not read it. Then he grinned and said that surely such nonsense was merely a rhetorical concession to the Communists. Well, the "Socialist Program for the 80s," published in 1980 when the Socialists had (temporarily) broken with their electoral partners, and reissued in June 1981, when François Mitterrand had been elected president of France, said virtually the same thing: only a liberal economy destroys the economy because it is based on commercial gain.

To be free of communism, it is not enough to get out of it: you also have to get out of its consequences. As François Furet has pointed out, revisionism failed as much as did orthodoxy. Non-Marxian dictatorships—Italy, Germany, Japan, Chile, Spain, to name a few—never had to deal with such overwhelming problems, even when their economies were destroyed by war.

In sum, to call the at-last successful rebellions against communism "revolutions" is meaningless. Revolution allied to utopian ideas leads to fanaticism, but at least it produces (if words mean anything) revolutionary change, albeit usually very dangerous change. This is not what happened here. Anticommunist revolts sprang out of societies that were completely and deeply regressed. There is no way to know how and when they will recover and catch up. The "revolutions against the Revolution" took place in an intensive care ward. They are struggles in which severely injured patients are trying to learn how to walk again. It is not exactly athletic training. They must fix the past, then perhaps they can try to build a future. The tragic lesson that we must learn from their dreadful experiences is that there is no measuring the cost of abolishing liberty, if only for just a few decades.

CHAPTER EIGHT

HOW UTOPIAS COME TO AN END

Man so loves truth that even if he loves something else, he wants it to be the truth.

—St. Augustine, *Confessions*, X, 34

The economic and social failure of communism cannot by themselves explain the system's rout, which began around 1985. Tolstoy says that you lose a war not after being beaten a few times, but when you are in your mind convinced you have lost. Communism, as well as the various Marxist-inspired socialisms, had always failed. However, people continued to believe in these causes, just as the atrocities of socialism did not convince believers that it might be inherently immoral. The decisive and original factor in the eighties was that communists lost faith in communism, and the Left in general lost faith in socialism. For three quarters of a century they had believed that the triumphs to come would avenge the ignominies of the present. And then one day they believed it no longer. All that was left was the daily disappointment of what they had done, and it was disastrous, disgusting, and ridiculous. But why stop believing in the future victory? The failures and the crimes were no worse in 1985 than before. If anything they had lessened. To explain this you have to include a role for mental conceptualizations in the making of history—and I mean conceptualizations that do not have their source in reality. Ideas make the world, bad ones in particular. If judgments about reality actually had their sources in reality, and were tested against reality, communism would have lasted less than six weeks. You can explain communism psychologically, but not rationally, and certainly not with the scholarly apparatus of "infrastructures" and "superstructures." You cannot understand Marxism if you use Marxist terms.

Utopias die the same way they are born: for no real cause. When Marx developed his theory, between 1840 and 1850, there was no reason to believe capitalism was entering its final crisis; yet he believed, and so did millions afterwards, that he had shown that this was precisely the case. On the contrary, modern industrial capitalism was only just beginning. The blights that provoked Marx's indignation, the bitterness of working-class existence in particular, would be alleviated eventually—by capitalism. And yet since the middle of the nineteenth century, successive generations of Marxists, witnesses to the astonishing vitality of capitalism, never tired of predicting its collapse. It was forever collapsing from its contradictions. The last time when the Left was sure this would happen was between 1974–82. A recession in the capitalist world took place then even as there was a relative strengthening in the Soviet economy. The latter occurred because of rises in the prices of oil, natural gas, and gold, which provided the Soviets with the hard currency they needed to buy food abroad. Western Europe, Southeast Asia, Central America were turning Left. The economic recovery, when it began in 1983, left the Marxists confused. The lowering of the prices of energy sources forced the Soviets to face once again their fundamental structural inadequacies. The "correlation of forces," which for a while they thought was moving in their favor, was again turning against them. Yet, similar setbacks had occurred often in the past without causing them to lose their faith in the arrival some day of the final triumph of socialism. Why is it that this time, the proof of their chronic inability to catch up with capitalism broke their morale?

Utopians do not lose faith simply because reality contradicts their expectations. An additional factor is needed, one that affects the believer's world view from the inside, revealing the dogma's shallowness. What factor is this? And why should it function at one time rather than another?

A utopia is a mental concept founded on a single idea. Take away the faith in this single idea, and the belief system collapses, since reality is seen for what it is.

Let me explain: apprehending reality realistically is by no means to be taken for granted. History furnishes examples of loss of confidence in social systems that worked well, even brilliantly, an outstanding case being democratic capitalism between 1945 and 1985. Never had so much prosperity and justice been spread so widely, despite all the imperfections of the system, its crises and inequalities. Yet during this whole period democratic capitalism seemed to be on the defensive culturally. Even those who were neither Marxists nor communists nor socialists nor social democrats felt able to offer a strong defense of the system in which they lived. They felt the tide of history was going in the other direction, and even as they rejected Marxism, democrats saw and judged themselves through the eyes of Marxists, all the more so as the latter controlled culture and education to a considerable degree. To say a system that had done more than any other to spread well-being and social justice deserved to die, as did the young rebels of the sixties, was to reveal a profound and thorough gap between reality and the concepts used to apprehend reality. To recall how stupendously large this gulf was, bear in mind that the revolt against democratic capitalism was led by young people in the best universities, who had access to all the information they could ask for. Yet they chose as their political role models men like Fidel Castro, Mao Zedong, and Che Guevara, whose achievements were not in the area of good government but mass terrorism, not social justice but economic incompetence, not the expansion of liberty but criminality. And this sort of inanity, which was at times carried all the way to acts of terrorism (on the theory that to fight injustice you have to kill bankers and politicians), found some support, at least some "understanding" even among the liberals!

Youthful terrorism was an extreme case, but consider also that in the Western scientific community, it became an article of faith to blame the arms race on the West. As late as the 1980s, when the American Strategic Defense Initiative broke the nerve of Soviet warrior communism and therefore deserves to be credited with effectively ending the arms race between the U.S. and the Soviet Union, most of the West's eminent scientists viewed the American effort as warmongering madness. Andrei Sakharov, who was one of the key scientists involved in the Soviet nuclear weapons program and knew what he was talking about, wrote in his memoirs that the Soviet leadership insisted that no opportunities should be missed to overtake American armaments.

Criticism is the engine of democracy, and the rebels of '68 were quite right to focus on the many real defects of their societies. They brought about a loosening of customs, a humanization of social relations, a fresh emphasis on individual freedom, which have had a deep and lasting impact on the way we live. But they spoiled these positive contributions by paradoxally combining them, all too often, with an ideology of destruction and hate aimed at the very existence of democratic civilization.

In July 1990, a Soviet deputy belonging to Sakharov's reform movement said to a Western journalist: "Sometimes I feel the worst enemies of democracy here are democrats in your part of the world. They always are trying to help our dictators." Trying, indeed. Yet, it was not that Western governments were in favor of communism, but rather that they had an inferiority complex about their own civilization. In the late 1980s, with the Soviet Union on its last legs, best-sellers were written about how it was Western civilization that was declining.

To call the Soviet Union the "Evil Empire" was considered to be in bad taste. When, in 1987, Ronald Reagan challenged Gorbachev to pull down the Berlin Wall, he was thought to be senile or reckless. Yet it turned out to be a profound intuition about what would happen within two years. Western foreign policy, and in particular the policy of *Ostpolitik* practiced by the West Germans, constantly aimed to placate the Communist regimes, against the wishes of the people and over their heads. When Erich Honecker made an official trip to West Germany in 1987, that country's Socialists felt compelled to sign a common declaration with the East German Communists which emphasised that the two parties shared a "broad convergence of views."

The SPD, or at least its powerful left wing, and the Greens openly described the East Germans as being "fortunate" for having been spared the horrors of capitalism; and in the summer of 1989 they said the refugees who were streaming out of East Germany by way of Hungary and Czechoslovakia were traitors, maybe even fascists!

After the collapse of the DDR, the West German Left took a different line, no less dishonest. It said the anticommunist revolution of 1989 was made possible by the *Ostpolitik* of the 1970s. In reality, *Ostpolitik* was a policy to support communism. It was an alliance with the communist states against the people oppressed by these states. It was a series of treaties whereby Bonn recognized the status

93

quo in central Europe and gave the existing regimes diplomatic and economic support. The Federal Republic accepted the DDR as being no less legitimate than itself, and opposed any policies that would have supported the desires of the oppressed peoples to rid themselves of their Communist regimes. The reunification of Germany, in this way of thinking, became pure political fiction. This was the line adopted by Willy Brandt, by his SPD successor Helmut Schmidt, and by such left-leaning, mass-circulation, influential papers as *Der Spiegel*, *Stern*, and *Die Zeit*. The day before the Wall came down, Brandt was still arguing in this way. Then, no fool, he changed his tune, went to the east, and accepted the ovations of the very crowds whose oppressors he had supported.

Democratic capitalist societies have never been perfect, indeed they are beset by grave problems. But it is one thing to recognize this and another to argue that society itself deserves destruction. This "revolutionary nihilism" sprang from two misconceptions. The first consisted of grotesquely exaggerating the vices of democratic capitalism. Second, was a failure to understand the degree to which democracy by its very nature is self-correcting. Communism cannot fix itself; democracy can. It is characteristic of Western intellectuals that they project upon democracy the characteristics of totalitarianism, as well as the reverse. Jean-Jacques Rousseau had spotted it quite well: "They deny what exists, explain what doesn't." In September 1977, a panel discussion in Paris discussed psychiatric hospitals in the USSR. Present were Michel Foucault, Raymond Aron, Eugene Ionesco, Vladimir Bukovsky, and myself, among others. At one point, Foucault (much of whose work was concerned with "confinement") lost his nerve and began to argue vehemently that it was not enough to talk about Soviet forms of confinement, we had to organize the "struggle" against the "Western gulag." For "good" taste this was hard to beat, considering we had among us Bukovsky, who had just emerged from the real gulag. He was overcome by uncontrollable laughter, while Ionesco repeatedly asked in a sonorous voice whether he had heard correctly.

Many intellectuals, even non-Marxists, were thinking like Foucault in these years: they criticized Western society on the basis of a socialist model, which they believed could be "detotalitarianized." This is why so many German intellectuals—who were, to be sure, among the last to break out of the old ways of thinking—had such great problems with their own country's reunification. Otto Schily, who had been a radical in the sixties, who as a lawyer had defended terrorists, who had been a parliamentarian as a member of the Green party and was now in the left-wing of the SPD, heaped scorn on the East Germans when, in their first free election, in March 1990, they voted for the Christian Democrats. To Schily, they were voting not for freedom but for bananas (unavailable in the East), and even as he raved on TV he held one in his hand.

Until this fateful election, the DDR represented to the German intellectual left a safe haven from capitalist pollution. Günter Grass saw in the two states a "Hegelian" way of transcending the national question. So, if the East Germans had voted massively against communism, and even against social democracy, it must be that they were a "furious mob doped by the consumer products on display in West Berlin," in the words of Stefan Heym, a supposedly "dissident" communist writer. It is worth noting that Heym expressed his bile in the pages of the powerful West German weekly *Der Spiegel*, which at the time was paying a minimum of 3000 DM (deutsche marks) per article, ten times the monthly salary of an East German worker. The left's entire reading of reality was a falsification. Even Rudolf von Thadden, a historian close to the socialists, wrote that "the left had got into the habit of seeing in the DDR a social alternative to the Federal Republic, or at least a place where some of the defects of Western society had been avoided. Thus, the Western labor unions praise the East for preventing the omnipotence of capital, and the mayor of West Berlin, Walter Momper, denounces Western *Ellenbogengesellschaft* (me-firstism), a vice supposedly unheard of in East Germany. . . ." (*Esprit*, March–April 1990)

This misrepresentation and veneration of the DDR was shared by many in the West, despite the fact that it was a failure and, as we learned in June 1990, a terrorist sanctuary. In a striking example of the degree to which it is possible to resist reality, tens of thousands of West Germans demonstrated at Frankfurt two months following free elections in the East had buried the communist and social-democratic parties to protest the "brutal annexation" of East Germany, which supposedly was losing its independence to the "imperialism of the Deutsche Mark."

To be sure, most evaluations of democratic capitalism did not attain such depths of fraudulence, And of course most Westerners were not, directly or indirectly, aiding totalitarianism. The point, rather, is that even among those who fought hard for liberal democracy, there was often an unstated conviction that Western civilization was on an irreversibly decadent course and that the future belonged to the left, perhaps not in its present form but then surely in some form yet to be invented, perhaps in China or the developing world.

If I may simplify grossly, the irony was that it was during its greatest decades that democratic capitalism was considered doomed, whereas socialism, the top performer in economic catastrophe and political crimes, was seen as the inevitable winner. Then of a sudden, around 1980, the opposite view took over. Evaluations of social systems began to bear some relation to their performances and merits. Where since World War II, and even World War I, the dominant currents of thought had favored socialism, statism, and totalitarianism, now liberalism had the wind in its sails.

Taken at face value, this mental change is mysterious. There had been plenty of evidence earlier of the failure of socialism and the success of liberal democracy, yet there had never been such an ideological shakeup. There had always been individual disillusionments and defections from the "god that failed," but the change in 1980 was different, it was an across-the-board reversal of the ideological hegemony all over the world in favor of liberalism. This occurred when in the West and in the Third World people realized that the communists themselves—for it was not news regarding their subjects—had given up the faith that had sustained them through nearly a century of failure, namely that capitalism was ultimately doomed and the future was theirs.

The Soviet or Maoist leadership was not composed entirely of cynics. No matter how corrupt, they held to the Marxist-Leninist theory of the fatal contractions of communism. When you think this way you can put up with poor results by telling yourself that to work, your system has to be in control everywhere in order to function properly.

George Orwell once asked a Stalinist, "Why all the bloodshed?"

"You cannot make an omelet without breaking a few eggs," came the reply.

"But," replied Orwell, "where is the omelet?"

"Oh, well, it takes some practice to get it right," said the other.

Utopians, in short, can live for a long time in the future; the present does not prove anything to them. In the mid-70s, I was talking to Jacques Attali, later to be a special advisor to President Mitterrand

and, in 1990, president of the European Bank for Reconstruction and Development.

"You socialists," I said, "never compare capitalism as it is with socialism as it is. You compare capitalism as it is with an ideal socialism that, you claim, will be in the future."

"Why not," laughed this brilliant man, "since socialism is the future!"

The revolutionary demands always that he be judged by his aims, not by his acts. The utopian is unassailable in his vision of the noble edifice of the future that escapes realistic outside observers, who cannot see it for the simple reason that it has not been built yet. But it sometimes strikes the utopian that this mysterious part of his edifice cannot be built, ever. Then everything in his mind is reversed and he goes from ideology to fact. How does this happen? This is a secret of the human soul, for which there is no satisfactory explanation. But already in the early nineteenth century, Theodore Jouffroy had remarked in a famous essay, reality is restored as something—exactly what we do not know—in the belief system of the utopian. The mystery is that the loss of ideological blinkers does not take place only because of the accumulation of evidence, though of course this is necessary too.

The growing impotence of the Communist parties of central Europe and the Soviet Union in the middle of the decade culminated, in 1989, in routs, self-dissolutions, sometimes a mere change of labels, and, in July 1990, in the XXVIIIth Congress of the Soviet Communist Party. This historic congress confirmed the separation between the Party and the state; this had been Gorbachev's goal since the extraordinary party conference of 1988, although in contradiction with his own principles—he kept two hats for himself as chief of state and leader of the party. Against Gorbachev's wishes, this congress marked the beginning of the end for the Communist Party, as Boris Yeltsin resigned from it, taking with him the mayors of Moscow and (as it still was) Leningrad and many of the younger party members interested in reform. The message was clear: there are no means of action for the Party, or in the Party, or by using the Party—in other words, if you want to do anything meaningful by way of reforms, you have to leave it. This led to a mass demonstration in Moscow, which, significantly, called for the dissolution of the Communist Party and the restitution of the goods it had stolen from the people. Yeltsin's comment: "The explosion has begun." There is a kind of mass intuition that has a sure sense of when rulers are losing their grip as they sense they have lost their ideological legitimacy. When the masters cannot conceal this loss of faith in themselves, the oppressed feel the time to attack has come.

As usual, at this congress Gorbachev was both ahead of history and behind. He was ahead in taking the state out of the Party, giving the Presidential Council the power previously held by the Politburo, whose system of recruitment he changed to prevent it from turning itself again into the government of the country. But he was behind because, while wanting to separate church and state, he did not want to finish off the church—i.e., the Party—even though its time had come. Not only was popular feeling in favor of dissolving the Communist Party, it was needed to get economic reforms under way, to make effective use of German financial credits, and to clean up the corruption in public affairs. It was impossible to transform, as Gorbachev meant to do, the Communist Party into an ordinary party, first of all because there were not yet any others, and more profoundly because of its role for three quarters of a century. Who could dream of turning the party of Lenin and Stalin into a normal player in the political symphony of a pluralistic democracy? The death of the party-state system signified the end of Leninism, the final collapse of "ideological monarchism." This gigantic social parasite, this machine to squeeze every drop of vital sap out of society, had done its destructive work and no longer had any reason to exist. The model had been designed exclusively to function as a single party in a totalitarian context. To presume to transform it into a normal party in a parliamentary system was a fairy tale. Like many adroit tacticians, Gorbachev lost sight of the bigger picture that even a child could grasp, namely that the complete dissolution of the Communist Party and the dispersal of its members in civil society was an indispensable precondition to getting the Soviet Union on its way to normality. The ordinary party members were the first to see this. The joke at the time of the Congress was: "To have a career in the seventies, you had to enter the Party; to have a career in the nineties, you have to leave the Party."

The following year, during the plenum of the Party Central Committee in July, Gorbachev proposed the same reforms, one of his major skills having always been to give an original twist to reforms that he had announced previously and never implemented. Along with the economic reform plans, the plans to rejuvenate the Communist Party were put forward as the party was declining. In the preceding eighteen months, it had lost a fifth of its members—four million, some of whom are active in the new political scene. It was losing one election after another, most recently in the Russian republic in June. It was losing its grip on society and Yeltsin, against Gorbachev's advice, wanted to weaken it further by banning party cells in the workplace. Gorbachev suggested a name change, and the coup in August was a fearful reaction by his own colleagues to the rapidity of events.

Thus the global rout of the Communist parties was virtually complete by the time international opinion became aware of it. For years already, they had exerted an influence greater than their real electoral weight; by 1985, in the West only the Italian Communists still could exert real influence on their nation's affairs.

At the end of World War II, Western Europe's Communist parties were winning between 10 and 30 percent of the votes, and they entered the governments of ten countries. Forty-five years later, in ten western countries the communists failed to get as much as 1 percent of the votes. The Dutch Communist Party, the oldest in the West, signed its own death notice on 15 June 1991, merging into a convenient "green left," somewhat as the Spanish Communist Party, which joined a "united left" whose 9 percent of the votes in the 1989 legislative elections had given it 17 seats in the Cortes out of 345, oddly presented as a success in the French press. The Spanish Communists could no longer stand up by themselves. Yet as late as 1976 Santiago Carrillo, general secretary of the PCE, was seen in the West as the motivating leader of a future democratic and republican Spain.

The Spanish case is instructive. In July 1976, when the PCE had not yet been legalized, I interviewed King Juan Carlos, who told me, "We shall legalize the party [this was done in December], and you will see, it will get not more than 10 percent of the votes and will drop continuously afterward." Which is what happened; by 1982, it had fallen below 4 percent. Juan Carlos analyzed the situation thusly: "Where is there a communist electoral base? The middle class which has emerged here in the past twenty years will vote on the center and the right. The democratic left will not vote for the party: it remembers the massacres perpetrated on Stalin's orders, by the Communists during the Civil War." The king had the best political head in the country, contrary to the opinion of him held by the left, and François

Mitterrand in particular since the latter wrote shortly before this interview: "I do not believe in this second-rate king who will be drowned in the rising tide." What rising tide? Mitterrand must have had in mind the revolution that every one assumed would sweep Spain after Franco, avenging the defeat of 1939. This was a prejudice that died hard; at the National Assembly the French Socialists vehemently objected to the presence of President Valéry Giscard d'Estaing at the coronation of Juan Carlos in December 1975, viewing the king as a mere continuation of Francoism. They thought Spain should follow their example with a Socialist-Communist union of the left. This was the last thing the Spanish Socialists wanted (the same was true of the Portuguese Socialists), and the decline of communism in their country proved them right.

Throughout Europe the Communist parties were in decline, even in countries like France or Greece where they had been very strong. In Italy, a PCI that had won 34 percent of the votes as late as 1976 fell to 20 percent in 1990, undermined by moral and ideological doubts that forced it to go through with the by-now ritualistic repudiation of Marxism-Leninism, accompanied by a change of name. In 1990, the PCI renamed itself the PDS, Party of the Democratic Left, not to be confused with the PSD, the Social Democratic Party. Thus, although it was not widely understood, communism as an opposition movement in the West was disappearing just as communism was falling apart as a ruling system in the East. This became clear as soon as there were free elections in the Soviet sphere. In Russia's first election with universal suffrage, Boris Yeltsin was elected president with 57 percent of the votes against 17 percent for Nikolai Ryjkov, the former Soviet prime minister and the candidate of the Communist Party. The former interior minister Vadim Bakatine, who was close to Gorbachev, obtained under 4 percent, not a strong sign of confidence in his patron. Wherever voting was held under free conditions, the Communists (by any name) obtained at best between 10 and 15 percent of the votes. In Poland, where the Communists had dissolved themselves in January 1990 to become the "Alliance of the Democratic Left," they did not even field a presidential candidate. There was some talk of a comeback after the October 1991 legislative elections, because their renamed party came in second behind the Democratic Union of Tadeusz Mazowiecki. But this second-place finish was obtained with under 12 percent of the votes; 90 percent of the votes had gone to other parties. The proportional system of voting adopted in Poland produced an atomized Diet in which there sat even the representatives of a "beer-drinkers' party," who had won under 4 percent of the votes.

Actually, the last world Communist Party conference had taken place in 1969, without the pro-Chinese parties. Since this date, Moscow had been unable to put together a coherent international front of Communist parties, though it had put together movements directed at specific targets, such as NATO's decision to deploy a new missile system in Western Europe. It had even been challenged for a few years in the 1970s by "Eurocommunism," before this too fell into irrelevance. The Third International was dead, but in 1980 no one had noticed the obituary.

The outlawing of the Soviet Communist Party following the failed coup of August 1991, and the disbanding of its natural and indispensable support, the KGB, signaled the end of the Soviet Union as well as the Party. Wherever, as the experience of central Europe showed, a Communist Party found itself in normal conditions of political competition, it risked disappearance. Without power and perks, financial and police apparatus, the Soviet Communists disintegrated like their "brothers" in the rest of Europe. Inevitably it headed toward perdition, despite Gorbachev's rearguard action to transform it. To do this, he had built up a complicated institutional structure, in which the party found itself shadowed, but not replaced, by new agencies of the state. At the top, the two came together in his own person. But when Yeltsin forced Gorbachev to give up his position as general secretary of the Communist Party, he struck a mortal blow at the system that, since 1917, had subjected the state to the party.

However, this simultaneously broke the back of the Soviet Union. For it was the Party, through the KGB, that cemented the involuntary "union" of republics. It was no accident that no sooner was Gorbachev's resignation known than most of the republics, beyond the Balts who had made this clear already, indicated they wanted out from the Union—demonstrating the emptiness of the "referendum" on the Union that Gorbachev had organized only months before.

Thus in September 1991, the West found itself face to face with an earthquake it had hoped to avoid by supporting Gorbachev in all his procrastinations. Fearful of the unknown, the West finally jumped right into it, but this time with neither parachute nor net. They never had an alternative to banking on Gorbachev, even when his failure was patent. The principle cause of this was that no one wanted to redraw Europe's borders, even though it should have been plain that you could not bury communism and preserve the Europe Stalin had made. The mistake was made all over again with regard to China and Vietnam: the West still believed Communist parties were the best agents for the destruction of communism, so long as they got a little help! There was here a misunderstanding of how to achieve international stability. Compromising with doomed systems does not bring about stability, it leads to disorder. By doing this, the democracies, once again, did not help their own cause, let alone the cause of the peoples of Eastern Europe, on the contrary. While it may have been prudent to support Gorbachev at first, this could be done only while keeping clearly in mind that nothing constructive could emerge out of communism, even anti-Stalinist revisionism. Democratization could never be achieved through the reform of the Communist Party, as events in the Soviet Union finally proved.

You do not get a chance every year, or even every century, to see the evaporation of an ambitious messianic doctrine, complete with its social doctrine, its scientific pretensions, its millenarian vision, its unshakable confidence in its own inevitable and universal victory! Yet how could the communists not take strength in their faith, seeing millions fall under their control, tremble at their threats—or applaud them from afar?

After the coup d'état of October 1917, Trotsky referred to the provisional government as being consigned to the trash heap of history; in 1956, Khrushchev exclaimed, "We will bury you!" These rhetorical gestures were significant expressions of the regime's unshakable self-confidence, as well as a self-advertisement for its readily available trash removal and mortuary services. Consider also Mao with his Hundred Flowers campaign—surely he meant to use them in funerary processions. What these heros did not realize was that they were predicting their own future, not capitalism's. They began by falling out among themselves, killing off communist comrades, then they massacred the populations under their control. And now their system falls into their beloved trash heaps of history. Lenin deserves full credit for the copyright: Stalin, Brezhnev, Mao, Castro, Ceausescu were mere plagiarists compared to him. For it was Lenin who invented not only the system, but the temporary expedients designed to keep a regime that was finished by 1921 breathing artificially.

Every generation of Soviet leaders has gone through the ritual at some point of "returning to Lenin," the better to denounce whatever happened to be going wrong. The trouble with this is that the crimes and the failures they denounced as being caused by unfaithfulness to Lenin had their sources in the system he invented.

Gorbachev played this game too, but he was after his first years in power the first to try to jettison this heritage. But he encountered the only successful thing about Leninism, namely, the irreversibilty of the Revolution: the persistance of its results. There was never a communist society such as the dreamers imagined it, but Lenin did succeed in rendering a return to capitalism impossible, or at least supremely difficult. The West Germans, in 1990 and 1991, were the first people in the West to get a sense of the full cost of the failure of a communist society, and they got it through the taxes they had to pay to bail out East Germany. Here was a communist country which, by comparison with the others, initiated its conversion in ideal conditions. Contact with one of the strongest free economies in the world had the effect of bringing about its total disintegration. Consider this: it was after seven years of *perestroika* that the Soviet economy took a nose dive into the abyss. For this is the essence of Leninism: communism does not work, but the exit from communism works even less.

Thus "returning to Lenin" never had a chance of doing anything useful for the peoples of the Soviet Union. What was needed was the most complete break possible. No one was betrayed less than Lenin. Communism's failure is his own. The Soviet system, of which Stalinism is the essential part, sprang from his brain. You can find everything in the fifty-five volumes of logorrhea known as the *Complete Works*. Like the "works" of his successors, this is an endless retread caused by the need to constantly justify the inflexible line and its endless variations. As with the work of his disciple Mao, the work of Lenin shows that a man's ideas can influence millions for several generations despite being inherently perverse.

On the practical plane, reconstructing society would be as difficult as its destruction had been complete in 1917. But on the theoretical level, the rejection of utopianism was swift. Just as utopianism is not subtle, it does not submit to detailed inventory. From the moment Gorbachev said he wanted to move to a market economy and democratic politics, no matter how much he procrastinated and claimed to be working for a "renovated" socialism, everyone understood Marxism was as dead and buried in the Soviet Union as it was everywhere else. Branko Lazitch has shown in an exhaustive article published in *Est-Ouest* in July 1991 how Gorbachev purged the key words of Soviet communism and thus was, in a sense, the "deconstructor" of its basic concepts. Words that had been essential to the value system of communism, such as "leading role of the Party" and "democratic centralism" and "proletarian internationalism" and "'scientific' socialism" founded on "historical materialism," these words were hidden away in the cellar, like the statues of the Polish "hero of socialist labor" in Andrzej Wajda's film, *Man of Marble*. "The truth is," Lazitch writes, "if there is ever a Nuremberg trial of socialism, it will not be difficult to establish the responsibility of Marx and Lenin: the doctrine is entirely Marx, the strategy entirely Lenin. All of communism's articles of faith were transplanted from Marx to Lenin. Their epigones merely parroted their untruths. No one ever revised any one of Marx's basic concepts no matter how erroneous it proved." The neo-liberal wave that had some effects in the West around 1978–80, reached communism in 1985. It was not yet possible to practice liberalism then, but it was the aim.

At about the same time, the shipwreck of the latest experiment in democratic socialism (not social democracy) gave another mortal blow to the utopia. The stunning repudiation of the French Left, which had been in power since 1981, following the European elections of June 1984, had repercussions that were felt throughout democratic Europe and beyond. I am not talking here of the agitation that filled that month in France, and how President Mitterrand played political games with the private school issue and then by naming a new prime minister, Laurent Fabius, with a "young" look. What I mean is that it was clear that in three years the Left had failed, and Mitterrand himself was drawing the consequences.

Of course there were some positive aspects to the government's policies between June 1981 and July 1984; but these were obtained by correcting socialist policies, not by applying them. This was the case, in particular, of the few successes, or let us say the damage limitations, that were achieved thanks to the austerity plan that was put in place after the second devaluation of the franc in June 1982, and, in particular, after the third devaluation and the Left's grave reverses in the municipal elections of March 1983. After all, these austerity plans went against the dogma enunciated in the Socialist bible, the Socialist Project of 1980 and the 110 Propositions of Mitterrand's election campaign. However one might evaluate these plans and their implementation, the fact is that they represented an abandonment, and a condemnation, of socialism. From this point of view, communist criticism was justified. Their own policies were madness, but the socialists had made the same promises. Of course, the latter claimed they were not making a U-turn, but no one else saw it that way.

Thus the new strategy of the French Socialist Party, the one that had been elaborated in 1971 in opposition to the old SFIO and Europe's social democratic parties, had by 1984 been a failure straight down the line. This eventually caught the attention of François Mitterrand.

It had been an economic failure, of which the broad lines are well known: the first drop in purchasing power since World War II, a rise in unemployment from 1.7 to 2.5 million, the "new poverty" and accompanying mendicity in the streets, depreciation of the currency, a rise in deficits notwithstanding a concomitant rise in payroll deductions, a foreign debt of $80 billion. This was the result of applying the socialist program during their first year in power. It was based on massive nationalizations and a consumer-based economic stimulus. You can approve or disapprove the subsequent policies, but at any rate they had nothing to do with socialism. The promised socialist miracle turned into a shambles.

It had been a failure in public opinion, as well. Laurent Fabius received favorable ratings when he took over as prime minister in 1984, but the Left in general continued to sink in the polls. In July 1984 the B.V.A.–*Paris Match* poll found 67 percent dissatisfaction with the way France was being governed, against 26 percent satisfied. Beginning with 1982, a year after he took office, the president had the lowest popularity in the history of the Fifth Republic. Opinion analysis showed that the Left had returned to its minority status in the country within a year of coming to power; this trend was deepened at the municipal elections of 1983, and it was badly beaten at the time of the European elections of 1984. Surveys and real elections had confirmed each other. Moreover, when these results are studied closely, it is clear that the reversal in public opinion was focused on the Left as such and on its key ideas, particularly its statist excesses.

And it had been a failure of the much-touted union of the Left. The Communists left the government in July 1984, underscoring a break that had been simmering for at least a year. It is important to remember that the founding principle of the new Socialist Party assembled at Epinay in 1971 had been: No enemies on the Left. This had led the following year to the party's endorsement of the "Common Program of Government," which owed more to the

Communist authors than the Socialist ones. The Socialists at Epinay made it clear there could be no left politics without the Communists, in opposition to the German Socialists' famous Bad Godesberg program of 1959, when they had rejected Marxism and any form of collaboration with communists. The French Socialists, on the contrary, were "re-Marxizing" themselves, rejecting any notion of governing from the center, calling for a "break with capitalism." Rarely has a political program been developed in such complete isolation from reality, but as Goethe said, sometimes the hardest thing in the world is to see what is before our eyes. The SP took a line different from every other socialist party in Europe excepting Greece's PASOK. With the end, in 1984, of the union of the Left (which had been interrupted in 1977 and renewed in 1981), both parties had reached the end of the ideological line, though they continued to pretend this was not so. In five years, the Communists had lost half their constituency, dropping to 11 percent of the votes. The SP, from 38 percent in 1981, had fallen to 21 percent in 1989 and 18 percent in 1992. Mitterrand had to govern with the support of just a fifth of the electorate.

And so finally it was an ideological and cultural failure. The government's education bill, which would have placed all private schools under state control and which had provoked the crisis of July 1984, was withdrawn behind weak face-saving gestures. But to understand this only in terms of religious schools would miss the point. In reality, most of the millions of French people who had been demonstrating against this legislation for over a year were primarily incensed at the ideological nature of the law. It was an old left-wing war horse: to bring all primary, secondary, and advanced education under state control and, in particular, under the control of the teachers' unions, which are under communist and socialist control. On this issue, as on others, the public was saying: "Keep the state out." And in pressing this legislation, the Socialist government was going profoundly against the temper of the times—and it committed the same folly in other cultural areas, for example in the way it made use of the state-controlled television network; its regulations of the press; in the creation of a new ministerial rank, "government spokesman," which everyone knew meant "minister of propaganda." The Left in power succeeded, remarkably, in alienating not only the people but the intellectuals in their majority—for the first time since 1789.

Indeed, on 26 July 1983 the "government spokesman," Max Gallo, published an article in *Le Monde* called "Intellectuals, Crisis, and Modernity," in which he expressed dismay over the blatant divorce between the Left and the intellectuals. This was new in France, and Gallo scolded the intellectuals for remaining silent, indeed for being hostile, toward the current socialist experiment. He noted the contrast with an earlier generation of intellectuals at the time of the Popular Front (1936) and the Liberation (1945). But what an avowal of failure! Needless to say the spokesman did not ask himself whether the intellectuals' desertion might be due to the Left's conceptual failure.

The importance of these events lies in the fact that they had repercussions that went well beyond France's borders. Until then, failures in other countries inspired by Marxist socialism (whether or not allied to the communists) could be blamed on external causes, on the heritage of the past, on a unfavorable context. You could blame persistent poverty, the legacy of a long dictatorship, underdevelopment, the activities (real, imagined, or exaggerated) of the CIA. The disasters of Third World socialism did not count; it was conveniently forgotten that Allende had ruined his country, and the Pinochet coup absolved him of any blame. The attempted "Prague coup" in Portugal in 1975 and the ruinous consequences of the early nationalizations were not held against socialism. These were special, even marginal cases.

But these kinds of excuses could not work in France. The socialists tried to blame their failures on their "heritage" from the Right, and even on a "plot," but this did not wash. In truth, all of public opinion throughout Europe realized that the French failure was socialism's. The French experiment, after all, occurred in a country which, despite a recession, was among the top five in the world in terms of per capita income. It was a country of republican tradition, in which democracy could lead to peaceful changes of government without any danger of a military coup. The Socialist Party was full of talented politicians, intellectuals, economists, social scientists. Brains were not the problem. At the National Assembly they commanded an absolute majority; they did not even need the Communist votes. No other party had benefited from such a luxury in recent French history. The recession weighed no more heavily on France than on other industrialized countries, on the contrary, and if it got worse, it was due to the Socialists' own policies in 1981 and 1982. These policies caused France to miss the recovery that began in the U.S. in 1983.

In other words, if socialist policies could work at all, there could be no conditions more favorable than those in France in 1981. And in less than three years the country was a shambles. Economic bankruptcy, political discredit, ghastly ratings in public opinion, overt hostility from two thirds of the population that is convinced the state is strangling their liberties in education and elsewhere. The worst blow was the cultural failure, the realization that the wreckage of French socialism stemmed from an intellectual failure, that the Left had misunderstood the modern world and had an ideology that worked no better in rich advanced societies than it had in poor backward ones.

This lesson carried a long way. The "French road to socialism" had no epigones. A large part of the work of Marxist intellectuals for the better part of the century had been devoted to proving that the consistent failure of socialists was not due to socialism. After 1984, this noble activity dried up. When you added the failure of democratic socialism to the increasingly well-perceived catastrophe of totalitarian socialism, either in its Soviet or Third World variety, you had to conclude that this time the evidence was all in and it was time to stop the waste. François Mitterrand was able to restore his own political popularity and win reelection in 1988; but this had nothing to do with socialism. The government of Michel Rocard, whom Mitterrand named prime minister after this election, adopted a program that had as little socialism as possible. True, the Socialist Party itself did better in the legislative elections of 1988 than it had in 1986, but it never recovered the majority that it began to lose in 1983's municipal elections, and even in the county elections of 1982.

An anecdote that illustrates the French Socialists' drastic and rapid loss of prestige occurred during this period. In 1982 Ricardo Utrilla, the editor, at the time, of the Spanish weekly *Cambio 16*, called me from Madrid and asked me to write an article showing how Spain's Socialists differed from France's. "The Right is saying, 'Look at what they did in France!' and Felipe Gonzalez [Spain's Socialist leader] is afraid voters will believe them."

The British Labour Party, too, understood after the bitter experience of three general election losses that it had to purge itself of its statist doctrines and its collectivist and high-tax programs. Neil Kinnock did his best to rid the party of these weights, but evidently not enough to convince the voters, and Labour went down in defeat a fourth time in 1992. Similarly, when Sweden's social democrats lost in the fall of 1991, this was widely seen as a rejection in the place where socialism was supposed to have worked.

Taken by surprise by the liberal (free-market) revival of the early eighties, represented by Reagan and Thatcher, the Western Left scoffed at the "flash in the pan" of liberal faddism. In practice, however, "liberal fads" were taking the place of socialist policies throughout the world. This does not mean successful liberal policies were being put in place everywhere, but it means that it was no longer shameful to aspire toward liberal democracy and market economics.

In their rearguard fight against the liberal revolution, the socialists, to be sure, were able to display their great talents for propaganda. This is the one activity they ever were really good at since, like socialism itself, it belongs to the realm of rhetoric. And yet the human race, including themselves, was marching in the other direction. Thus for example, President François Mitterrand could hold forth on economic policy in a way that would have embarrassed the turn-of-the-century German social democrat Edward Bernstein, while, in practice, he initiated the European Community's Single Act, which was bound to push France toward a liberalism more radical than it had ever known.

History will record that the president of the French Republic found himself astride the ruins of socialism even as he discoursed upon the failures of liberalism in a televised interview in 1990. To fully savor this spectacle, you have to be aware that this was a typical speech of ex-socialists (whether or not they acknowledged it). It went like this: "Okay, liberalism wins by default. All the more the reason to beware of its faults, in order to avert the dangers represented by fanatical liberalism!" It was granted that socialism was not superior to liberalism; but liberalism was still judged to be wanting. Utopias die slowly, and making wrong-headed equivalences is one of their last refuges.

But socialism and liberalism are not mirror images of each other. Socialism is a theoretical construct that precedes experience. It tells you there is a recipe, and if you apply it (the collective ownership of the means of production and trade), you will get a perfect, fair, and prosperous society. This is the very stuff of utopia. People who think this way assume that liberalism is a doctrine that is the opposite of theirs, that it makes the same promises and contains the same fanaticism.

But, in fact, liberalism is not a system of deliberate social construction. It is a mixture of political democracy and economic liberty that draws on experience and proceeds by trial and error. It does not guarantee justice and prosperity. But in a modern civilization, it is the necessary condition for trying to achieve justice and prosperity.

The disintegration of socialist utopianism in less than a decade is reflected also—and eloquently—in the evolution of the Roman Catholic Church from the 1988 encyclical "Sollicitudo rei socialis" to the "Centesimus annus" encyclical less than three years later. By their way of thinking, they would appear to have half a century between them. The former was the belated product of a period when a majority in the Church thought the Gospels could be given new life by being crossed with socialism. The latter appears to have been by a hand eager to refute the first, under the inspiration of ideas nurtured by recent intellectual changes. "Sollicitudo," while claiming to address economic and social issues, in the Third World especially, rehashed the debris of the conformist and unsophisticated progressivism that had been fashionable in religious circles during the previous two decades. Using the worn-out method of moral equivalence, it condemned communism and capitalism with, apparently, the same severity, calling both systems perverse and unimprovable. The two "ideological blocs" deserved each other and both produced "structures of sin," a nonsensically obscure formula that smacked of fashionable jargon. By contrast, "Centesimus" marks a bold break with three decades of backward progressivism and hypocritical equivalences. Which did not please everyone in the Church, judging from the vast and expert campaign of disinformation against this encyclical that was conducted within the Church itself.

A papal encyclical is a solemn letter from the pope to all the bishops in the world, and through them to the faithful. As such, it is always an opportunity to define important matters of doctrine and from there to reflect upon civilization. Thus encyclicals are documents with a profound influence on contemporary ideas and are, and should be, of interest to nonbelievers, or the faithful of other religions, no less than Catholics.

"Centisimus annus" was published on 2 May 1991, a Thursday. In the preceding weeks, when the text was known to only a small group of insiders, leaks insinuated that it was a violent attack against liberalism and market economics. The *Financial Times* (London) reported this on March 9 and the *Evenement du Jeudi* (Paris) followed suit on April 25. Throughout the world, this lie—for it was nothing less than that—was often repeated; and it is altogether likely that millions of people around the world got the impression the pope said the exact opposite of what he really said.

After May 2, it was not possible to blatantly distort the encyclical, since the actual document was available. Therefore, aware that a limited number of readers would go through all 144 pages of the text, a second wave of disinformation insinuated that the pope continued the "plague on both your houses" line of the previous encyclical, "Sollicitudo rei socialis," which, it is true, contained lines such as, "The Church's social doctrine is critical of liberal capitalism as well as of Marxist collectivism." But the historical fact is that the pope's thinking had evolved. He had had the same opportunity as the rest of us to study the anticommunist revolutions of Eastern Europe in 1989 and 1990. He had seen the material, and even more so perhaps the spiritual disasters that Marxist collectivism had produced, and he had taken this into account with profound intellectual honesty and changed his views. I feel I can take note of this objectively since I am not a Catholic. The fact is that the encyclical is clear. The pope avoids the escape of condemning all systems, which really amounts to condemning none and recommending none—in my opinion a serious avoidance of responsibility. The 1991 encyclical asks: "After the failure of communism, can we say capitalism has won?" And the answer: "The answer is surely yes if by capitalism is understood an economic system that recognizes the fundamental and positive role of enterprise, of the market, of private property, in short of free human creativity in the economic sphere, with the responsibilities this implies." However, adds the Holy Father, capitalism—for which he prefers the term "free economy"—is negative "if it is not exercised in a solid judicial framework which makes it serve overall human liberty," a definition of the very essence of liberalism.

The message of "Centesimus annus" is that a free economy must prevail, but that social life cannot be reduced to economics, which must be subordinated to moral and religious values with which Marxism, by contrast, is incompatible.

Since time immemorial, humankind has been practicing liberalism by any other name. It is no more perfect that the human race. Only utopians believe they have the power to achieve perfection. No liberal claims that a market economy is a formula for automatic success. The market will produce successes and failures, usually some of both. What is beyond dispute by now, however, is that a socialist economy will only produce failures. Of course in a capitalist economy there are poorly managed firms. Companies go bankrupt. Some countries fail to take off. But there are quite a few success stories too, which of course depend on other factors in addition to capitalism as such. But in socialist economies you can kiss success goodbye.

In the same way, political democracy allows us to choose our own leaders. It does not guarantee that all our leaders will be competent or honest. Voters can err or make mistakes. But to denigrate democracy because some democratic governments govern poorly is the equivalent of decapitating a patient to cure his migraine. Democracy does not do away with human defects—neither those of the voters nor those of the candidates. But at least it has the merit of not forbidding them from showing their qualities.

Freedom of culture does not guarantee that only masterpieces will be produced. But we do know for sure that cultural totalitarianism sterilizes talent. A free culture gives us great books and unreadable pap, ugly buildings, awful movies, disgraceful newspapers. Is this a reason to say freedom and slavery deserve each other?

Part of the cure for convalescing ex-socialists consists of getting beyond these equivalences. But the need to save face, joined to the survival of ideological nostrums long after they had lost all relevance, blocked the argument—as often happens in cultural history—while real life continued. At the beginning of the last decade of a century rich in paradoxes, it was no small irony to find a freer, unambiguous, categorical critique of socialism in the East than in the West of Europe. In liberal Europe, practice was ahead of theory. In postcommunist Europe, theory was ahead of practice.

CHAPTER NINE

HOW TO GET OUT OF THE CONSEQUENCES OF COMMUNISM

Communism was forced to annihilate itself. But before this it had annihilated all that makes a society, a state, an economy, a system of justice, a civilization. Thus there was no foundation on which to build anything over the wreckage. The only efficient institution in the communist system, the single party-state, had as its sole purpose its own perpetuation and the building of supporting networks on the outside. It ruled by coercion, corruption, repression, and terror. It could be reversed or overthrown only when there was nothing left to destroy. For the party-state to crumble, there had to be nothing left in society to kill. It became like a zombie. But this was without any positive value, because there were no longer any viable elements on the basis of which to start building a different society. The Party had annihilated even its own substitutes. This is why getting out of communism is one thing, and getting out of the consequences of communism is something else altogether.

When you die of an infection, the virus that subverted your organism dies with you. Epidemiologists therefore often argue that logically the virus ought not to kill its host. Yet it does so because it cannot escape its program. So it is hardly apropos for scientists to congratulate themselves on beating a virus when the patient goes down at the same time. Yet this was the sort of thinking that prevailed in 1985—90: Hooray, as soon as Gorbachev and other reformer-communists give them the go-ahead, these countries will bounce into democracy and market economics. There was a moment when it was widely thought in the West that getting out of communism presented no special problems; indeed, people began to talk about political democracy and free economies in the East as if these were already functioning. After all had not these nice reformers proclaimed these were worthwhile goals? Once again, this overlooked the sheer novelty of the communist phenomenon. The idea seemed to be that going from totalitarianism to democracy, from communism to capitalism, had been done many times, whereas this was a road that had never been charted. Prudence should have dictated at the least that we ought to prepare for areas where we and they would be driving blind. To get rid of communism was not to get rid of its consequences.

First of all there were the political and cultural consequences of having been deprived of democracy for too long. Helmut Kohl observed in June 1991 that denazification was easier in West Germany after 1945 than decommunization in East Germany after 1989, because Nazism had lasted twelve years to Communism's forty-five. Also, out of those twelve years, Nazism required three or four to fully acquire its control over German society. Despite its brutality, it was not able to extirpate entirely the previous culture. In East Germany by contrast, no one in 1990 had any memory of democracy. There had been no free election from November 1932 to March 1990. Moreover, openly neo-Nazi resurgences were far more virulent in East Germany than they ever had been in West Germany, a sure sign of the poverty of the political culture, youth's in particular. In the same way, communism annihilates all economic culture.

The major nonsense, with regard to economics, consisted of discussing Soviet economic reform on the model of reform or restructuring plans undertaken in Western or even Third World countries. These reforms were usually undertaken in a liberal direction—as was fashionable in the eighties—or in a social-democratic direction. Soviet or Polish leaders were described as "Reaganites" or "Thatcherites," or on the contrary they were encouraged to look like "New Dealers" or to favor the "Swedish Model." The problem with these fantasies is that for economic reform to take place, there must be an economy. But communism had annihilated the economy. As I have written many times, communism is not an economic system, it is a political system which, to rule, must destroy the economy. The crisis that overtook it in the beginning in 1985—or, more accurately, the crisis that it at last acknowledged in 1985—occurred because it had completed this achievement. There was nothing that a normal reform recipe could reform. This is why comparisons with all other societies, even primitive ones, were meaningless. A primitive or a poor economy is still an economy which at least has a chance of being improved. But to try to improve or reinvigorate a communist "economy" is merely to prolong or temporarily reinforce its destructive tendency. Brezhnev had understood this better than Gorbachev: the former chose "stagnation," which is to say decline at as slow a pace as possible; the latter chose "acceleration," a word associated with the early years of *perestroika*, and he got rapid disintegration. It is worth recalling that communism's final decline began as early as 1960 and worsened in 1970–75, the very years of "détente" when Western credits and transfers of technology were flooding the Soviet Union and Eastern Europe. They served only to worsen the disease instead of curing it. Czechoslovakia, which received less Western help after 1968 than its neighbors, on account of its brutal repression of the "Prague Spring," emerged in 1989 less ruined and less in debt than the others.* The paradox was that trying to help communism only aggravated the disease. When *perestroika* began, the West could not get a clear fix on the nature let alone the depth of the communist economic disaster. For long, "Marshall Plans" were proposed, as if the machine were fundamentally sound and merely in need of credits to get up to speed. On the contrary, the machine was fundamentally unsound. The problem was not insufficiencies, but itself. It needed not repair but wholesale junking. A common misconception was to refer to what was taking place as a "crisis," implying that some details were out of whack, whereas the system was acting in accordance with its nature.

In the history of Soviet reform, *perestroika* took on two successive meanings. At first it referred to "market socialism," a muddled notion which, in any event, excluded capitalism and private property. Then, in 1990, it began to refer to the transition to capitalism, to a real not a "planned" market, which implied a restoration sooner or later of private property. What the West never quite grasped, in either phase of *perestroika*, was that there was nothing to work with that was economically viable. They overestimated the salutary effects of "reforms." Economists referred to precedents whereby liberal pro-

---

*Czechoslovakia split, peacefully, into two distinct nations on January 1, 1993.
—TRANS.

grams, stimulated by foreign credits, would cure the ailing Soviet economy. They referred for example to Ludwig Erhard's 1948 reforms in Germany, or de Gaulle's monetary reform in 1959 (the Pinay–Reuff plan), or even the austerity program the French Socialists adopted in 1983 to repair the damage they themselves had caused with their earlier policies. And always there were references to the Marshall Plan. All these cases were cited, to take one noteworthy example, in articles by *Le Monde*'s economic columnist Paul Fabra in July 1990, "Why Help the Soviet Union" and "How to Help the Soviet Union." The misconception was always the same: getting a market economy damaged by bad policies or by war moving again is not comparable to trying to get back into the market an economy that has been stripped of all its basic mechanisms, its reservoirs of elementary know-how, including those it had acquired prior to the industrial period. From 1990 to 1992, 100 billion DM (deutsche marks) were invested in the eastern regions of the new Germany, with no result other than to expedite their decomposition. By contrast, from 1946 to 1952, 7 billion DM (in 1990 terms) had sufficed to finance the "German miracle" in the Federal Republic. At that time there were 55 million inhabitants, which means there was 800 DM in credit per person. In 1990 there were 17 million people in the DDR; the average credit per person—and over two years, not six—was, therefore, 6100 DM—only this time, there was no "miracle."

The *Treuhand*, the agency created in 1990 to dismantle and privatize East Germany's industry was, in 1992, still busy dismantling. Privatization turned out to be no panacea, for most of the enterprises left over from communism were of no interest to sensible buyers. They had not been upgraded since 1945 or 1950, and many since the days of Wilhelm II! They were good for the scrap heap and nothing else.

In Poland too, the firms that the Ministry for Transformation of Property wanted to privatize for the most part failed and had to be closed down. The most spectacular example was the famous Ursus tractor factory with its ninety thousand employees, which closed down in July 1991. Producing poor products at excessively high cost, there was no way this enterprise could enter the European economy. The Polish government wanted to privatize six thousand firms in three years. However, by July 1991 it had partially privatized seven. Four thousand were in liquidation. Unemployment in the uncompetitive East reached levels as high as 50 percent by the end of 1991. In addition to obsolete factories and untrainable workforces there was the scarcity, in Poland no less than in Hungary or East Germany, of lawyers capable of venturing in the briar patch of privatizations, particularly regarding land. The *Treuhand* gave up trying to decollectivize the land and turned the task over in 1991 to a consortium of private banks.

Without functioning telecommunications, lacking competent civil servants—despite their crushing bureaucracies—the former communist countries are lost without Western help, but they are not necessarily saved with it. Aid is wasted on them, since they do not know how to invest it productively. In January 1990, West Germany gave free electricity worth 50 million DM to freezing Romanians. No improvements were made, and the following winter the German government again provided 50 million DM worth of electricity. During the summer of 1991, the Romanian government inquired whether it might receive a larger allocation the following winter. It was surprised to hear the Germans reply that they could not provide aid indefinitely and that the Romanians ought to do something about fixing their system. If the West provided the ex-Soviet Union, between 1992 and 1997, with the same amount, proportionally, that Western Germany provides Eastern Germany, $30 trillion would be needed, according to the German federal chancellery. It is obviously impossible.

This also is why it makes little sense to refer to the New Economic Policy of 1921, as many commentators have done. The NEP worked—in particular, it "miraculously" brought food back to the markets—because in three years communism had not yet had time to destroy all the markets and all the farmers. After seven decades of collective farming and the destruction of Russia's millennial human capital on the land, it is not at all certain that "privatizing" agriculture will do any good. When, in 1987, the Soviet government offered long-term land leases there were very few takers, for the very good reason that there were very few real farmers left who knew what it meant to work their own land, let alone who knew how to.

How to rebuild agriculture without farmers, a banking sector without bankers, a distribution system without retailers—this is what they are up against. As Bronislaw Geremek said in 1990, "The weakness of democracy in postcommunist societies is not due to what happened before communism. The fundamental fact was the suppression of the market economy, a suppression which destroyed relations among individuals. Communism was founded on society being passive. Humanity sometimes goes down dead ends; well, communism was one of these."

The West did not understand postcommunism for the simple reason that it never really understood the unique nature of communism. Between 1985 and 1988 there was a considerable amount of enthusiasm based on economic take-offs and transitions to democracy, such as Italy in 1946 or Spain in 1976. As matters worsened even as reforms were supposed to be implemented, enthusiasm gave way to perplexity; market economics seemed to be rejected the same way a body rejects transplanted organs. "The consumer goods situation has deteriorated catastrophically," Gorbachev allowed with admirable candor before the Supreme Soviet on 19 October 1990. This was the paradox: you could not overcome the crisis without applying reforms, but the application of reforms aggravated the crisis.

The word "crisis," as I remarked earlier, does not properly apply here, since it is usually understood to refer to problems in a system that is still functioning and that, in fact, could come through the test stronger than before. In 1989 and 1990, Western observers began to perceive the paradoxical and contradictory nature of the exit from communism. Until then, and outside of a small number who had understood what was going on, the whole debate was based on two questions: Was Gorbachev sincere? Should we help him? The second question depended on the answer to the first, but in fact neither question was pertinent. Gorbachev, by the time he came to power, knew he had no choice: the old Stalinist system was finished and it was urgent to get out of it politically and economically. The Politburo and the Central Committee knew this too—that is why they made him General Secretary. The West considered the problem to be sincerity or lack thereof, which presupposed that "sincerity" would produce "good" reforms, which in turn were bound to lead to success. It never seems to have occurred to anyone to ask what the West was supposed to help Gorbachev for? To save communism? Or to scuttle it?

Mikhail Gorbachev himself stated with lucidity in his 19 October 1990 speech, as he presented a new economic program to the Supreme Soviet, "We could have kept the system going in its death throes, but we would have got to a historical dead end." But he added: "The Soviet Union is not forsaking socialism," a phrase that voids (and confirms) the preceding one. To not forsake socialism is, of course, to keep the system going in its death throes. Was this merely a rhetorical concession to the "conservatives"? By this date, Gorbachev had pushed the "conservatives" out of the way. Indeed he had crushed them, as he had at every decisive showdown in the previous five years, in the Party, in the Supreme Soviet, or in the Congress of People's Deputies. Prior to each of these confrontations, the Western media were filled with articles announcing ritualistically that Gorbachev was facing his gravest challenge ever. This time, he might fall to the conservatives! The latter always turned out to be in the minority and emerged from every confrontation weaker than before, until finally they were on the margins. In July 1991, just before the Plenum of the Central Committee, the *International Herald Tribune* headlined: "Gorbachev Faces Battle." *Le Monde* reported that he "would have to mediate between conservatives and reformers and avoid a split." The *Herald Tribune* observed: "But, as the Central Committee meeting is sure to demonstrate, many members of the Central Committee refuse to agree and want Mr. Gorbachev removed as party leader." The result of the vote was 243 for Gorbachev, 15 against. As early as the fall of 1990, it was Gorbachev who represented the conservatives against the "left-wing" opposition, that is to say the liberals and in particular the liberals in the Russian Republic, who demanded a much faster march toward capitalism. The "conservative" resistance to Gorbachev was not located in the assemblies, but in the old power centers, as the coup on 19 August 1991 would show. These centers would have been weakened and overwhelmed if Gorbachev had followed a bolder policy, as Yeltsin kept telling him to. Really applying the liberal reforms and autonomy for the republics would have neutralized them, as would have Yeltsin's suggestion to interdict Communist Party cells in the workplace. Gorbachev refused to do this, and he resisted putting the new Union treaty, which redefined (albeit in a confused and half-hearted way) the relations among the Soviet Union's constituent republics, into practice. Since 1989, the general impression was that Gorbachev slowed down rather than accelerated the march toward democracy. He never announced a policy without immediately afterwards decreeing its opposite; thus, in his famous speech of 19 October 1990, announcing a race toward a market economy, he concluded by warning that the first step must be to reinforce the central authority! The chaos was such, he said, that the Soviet Union required "administrative methods" to avoid a collapse in production during the winter which would definitely finish off the economy. Thus, after six months of negotiations during which all concerned agreed to jettison the command economy and the control over the republics by the Soviet central power, the president's first ukases strengthened both. Formed in the image of the impossible problems he lived with, Gorbachev's ideas became the faithful reflection of an incoherent reality. Blithely announcing incompatible policies in the name of reform, he did not realize that applying them simultaneously guaranteed they would all fail.

The repetition of this vicious circle, added to the growing awareness of the extent of the damage in the ex-communist countries, led finally to a new perception and interpretation of post-totalitarian evolution. Beginning in 1990, four new themes, less optimistic than earlier, began to appear. Simplified, they were as follows:

First, the extent of the disaster, and of the West's underestimation of it, was better understood. The full extent of communism's ravages had not been measured adequately, nor had anyone understood the depth of the destruction to the economy, society, culture, human resources, environment, morality, political life, even public health. In the West it finally began to be understood that fixing this, without usable materials, would be more dubious and a longer undertaking than was thought.

Second, it suddenly became permissible to say out loud that *perestroika* had failed. It had been evident since the spring of 1988, but it was considered tactless to say so. The only permissible question was, "Is Gorbachev sincere?" This was simply a continuation of the only "détentist" thinking of the seventies, founded on the hypothesis that communist economies could function properly if helped along. Finally acknowledging that *perestroika* could not work, it followed that Western aid was useless. Which led directly to the third new theme in Western perceptions of the Soviet Union, namely a re-evaluation of the question of whether or not to help Gorbachev and how.

Turning over these three themes under every conceivable angle led to the last: getting out of the consequences of communism—it was at last understood—was an unprecedented project. The media reflected this new concern about Soviet chaos and collapse. The CIA was accused, first by the Soviets and then by its own reappraisals, of having been too optimistic about the Soviet economy. Then newspapers began reporting shortages of bread, of cigarets, of just about everything, and that massive famine was imminent. It was almost impossible to pick up a newspaper during the summer of 1990 and not find a story about the suffering Russians. Before long, it became a cliche to say that *perestroika* not only was ineffective, but that it was pernicious. The *Economist* (4/28/90) published an article titled "Perestroika: and now for the Hard Part," which concluded that the concept was intrinsically contradictory. The crucial frontier between state and market had not been crossed.

Thus in 1990 it became permissible, in the Western media, to explain why *perestroika* was not viable and that socialism was not reformable. I had published an article three years earlier making this point, which simply had the effect of getting me the reputation of "not liking" Gorbachev. I referred to the Yugoslav experiment, which Branko Lazitch recently had summed up in an article in *Est et Ouest*, proving that everything Gorbachev had proposed the Yugoslavs had tried since 1950 and, despite enormous quantities of Western aid—their per capita foreign debt was equivalent to Brazil's—their economy, like the Soviet one, was on the brink of complete disintegration. In 1989, the American secretary of defense, Dick Cheney, had been rebuked by President Bush for saying that *perestroika*, inasmuch as it was a refusal to choose between two systems, could not work. In the *Washington Post* on 30 April 1990, the same Dick Cheney made the same prediction ("again," the newspaper pointed out), and this time he was not reprimanded. The stampede then began, with newspaper headlines like "The Illusion of *Perestroika*" (Michael Ignatieff, the *Observer*, May 7), "Gorbachev's Last Assets" and "Perestroika's Failures" (*Le Monde*, May 23 and June 6), "Why Gorbachev Is Failing" (*Newsweek*'s cover story, June 4). Valéry Giscard d'Estaing, the soul of moderation, allowed that "the crisis in the Soviet Union would worsen" (*Le Figaro*, July 30). This was putting it mildly since the press was reporting bread shortages; Pierre Briancon, the Moscow correspondent for *Le Point* and *Liberation*, reported that the Soviet economy had for at least a year gone from stagnation to catastrophe. Already in November 1989, 1400 Soviet economists, meeting in Moscow at the invitation of Leonid Abalkine, at the time Gorbachev's principal economic adviser (he kept changing them), declared that "The changes introduced since 1985 [i.e., *perestroika*] have merely improvised upon the system of centralized planning which has run the Soviet economy since 1920." But what else could be done without opening the gates of universal chaos against which Gorbachev was always warning?

Gorbachev, for his part, scarcely sought to hide his difficulties and he regularly called Western capitals for help. But in the West serious doubts were developing on the usefulness of this help. The question was no longer, "Should we help Gorbachev?" the answer to which was automatically "Yes" if he was judged to be "sincere." The question now was: Can we help Gorbachev? Is Gorbachev capable of purging the vice that renders the Soviet economy unreformable and therefore Western aid useless and even unuseable? Why was he forever putting off the application of the reforms he announced, especially the most important and needed ones, that would make it possible to definitively get out of the Stalinist system? The West was beginning to get an inkling of the cost of economic totalitarianism, the persistence of its damage, its hold on the social fabric. To justify his requests for aid, Gorbachev no longer claimed he would put a modern economy in place in a few years. The goal now was only to preclude devastating chaos that could have, he never failed to insinuate, destabilizing consequences in Western Europe.

Communism, as we should now only too well realize, not only destroyed material wealth and the means of producing it, it destroyed men and their capacity for entrepreneurship. They do not even know what this is. In 1988, the Deutsche Bank gave the Soviet Union 3 billion DM ($1.7 billion) in credits to modernize its industrial plant. The Federal Republic indicated that it was pleased to contribute in this way to the future success of *perestroika*. Since 1985, Western leaders were in the grip of a circular argument about the necessity to support Gorbachev. They favored the granting of credits to the Soviet Union in order to get its economy in shape. But despite the credits, the economy kept crumbling. In the West another argument then came to the fore: aid must continue in order to support Gorbachev and prevent him from falling. Why? Because only he can successfully carry through *perestroika*. But is not *perestroika* a failure? No doubt; but this failure accentuates the danger Gorbachev is facing; therefore, it is necessary to support him since the West is in favor of *perestroika*. The arguments in favor of subsidizing *perestroika* were based on the same circular logic that was used to justify communism in the name of hypothetical future results that it would have been sacrilegious to sacrifice because of short-term problems. But the issue was not to sacrifice or not sacrifice, it was to realize these goals were impossible to achieve, for reasons that were intrinsic to communism just as they were intrinsic to *perestroika*, which is its intellectual child. These intrinsic qualities are where the analysis should have been focused, in order to form a policy that corresponded to the real events that were taking place, not on some imaginary scenario which no amount of financing could bring to life. To be sure, the motivation for helping Gorbachev became increasingly diplomatic rather than economic.

The West feared the downfall of the man who had allowed central Europe to regain its independence, Germany to be reunited while staying in the Atlantic Alliance, and who had put the Soviet Union for the first time on the side of a broad alliance of Americans, Europeans, and Arabs, during the Persian Gulf conflict that began in August 1990 with the Iraqi aggression against Kuwait. These arguments were important. Gorbachev was aware of this, since he soon became a master at trading political concessions for credits that he found ever harder to obtain on the basis of normal economic considerations. His meeting with George Bush at Helsinki, at the beginning of the Gulf crisis, furnished a classic example of this kind of bargaining. There were, then, solid foreign policy reasons for wanting Gorbachev to stay in power. And at the same time, the Western governments were terrified at the prospect of political, ethnic, and social chaos in the Soviet Union—chaos which Gorbachev was unwittingly provoking through his indecision, his incoherence, his procrastinations, his timidity in the face of the no-doubt heroic efforts that were required to truly get out of communism. Say what you will about the policies of Peter the Great, he put them in practice—which is what Gorbachev failed to do despite the comparisons that were made between him and his predecessor at the helm of the Russian empire. When decisiveness was required, Gorbachev let his country's economy flounder in its swamp of laziness, incompetence, and racketeering.

Which is what the Deutsche Bank discovered at the end of 1989 when it asked how its money had been used in the preceding eighteen months. In the first place, the Germans learned that the Soviets had no clear idea of the machines they needed to buy to modernize their obsolete industry. They were not even capable of drawing up a reliable inventory. After a year, most of the three billion marks remained unused. The president of the Deutsche Bank, Alfred Herrhausen (whom the Red Army Faction would murder at the end of the year, just before it was discovered in the records of the East German secret police that Western terrorists had always been financed, armed, trained, housed by the secret police of the communist countries) went to Moscow in June to explain to officials at the highest levels that they were not proceeding rationally in requesting money which they did not use. This, he pointed out, risked discouraging German bankers from advancing other funds. Yet at the beginning of December, with the credit line about to expire, a billion DM were still available. The other two billion had served no purpose. The new machines that had been purchased in the West were abandoned in warehouses or broken down into their component parts and sold on the black market instead of being installed in factories. This would seem to have proved that a communist economy simply could not acquire Western technology and therefore could not be aided by conventional forms of economic aid. This was increasingly well understood in the West, but policy-makers continued to pretend it was not. In June 1990, West German banks accorded a fresh credit, worth five billion DM, to the Soviets, guaranteed by the Federal government. True, Germany was, at this point, involved in the last and most delicate phase of its reunification, and preparing to sign a peace treaty that would put a definitive official end to World War II. Essentially political, the underlying motives of this loan, and others that would follow, had little to do with "saving *perestroika*," which no longer meant anything. Few observers failed to see this. On 23 June 1990, *Le Monde* noted that the "political loan was extraordinary in its amount and in being publicly guaranteed, and was designed to help Gorbachev overcome his economic problems." The last part of the sentence was pure formula. The journalists watching the Soviet Union knew very well that Gorbachev would not "surmount" anything, and their newspapers were filled with stories about the "final fall" of the Soviet economy.

Up till this point, the end process of communism had been misunderstood because the nature of communism had been misunderstood. Gorbachev sustained this misconception as long as possible in order to make the West pay for getting out of communism, just as his predecessors had sustained other misconceptions to make the West pay to keep communism going. The only difference was, not that *perestroika* was more viable than communism, but that—and of course this was significant—*perestroika*, as communism's funeral march, consisted of receiving subsidies in exchange for forsaking the military aggressiveness of communism. Lenin had described imperialism as the "supreme stage of capitalism," but it turned out that *perestroika* was the "supreme stage" of communism. It could no longer compensate for internal weakness with external power. The fact remains that communism is an irreversible political phenomenon, in the sense that it can disappear only when it has finished destroying the society it has seized, without leaving any foundations for a society that might take its place. No Communist regime has ever willingly evolved into anything other than itself. To suggest communism is reversible the way other regimes are, simply because it is not eternal, amounts to saying a fire is reversible because it went out after burning down the entire building. Unlike other great political changes of the past, there was nothing to take its place when communism ended, neither the seeds of a renaissance, nor a "cunning of history," nor "creative destruction." Rarely did history give rise to such a purely negative phenomenon. It was inevitable that the exit of communism should lead to a period of anarchy, a passage through the void proportional to the length and seriousness of the earlier disease.

Mikhail Gorbachev's "health problem" on 19 August 1991 was supposed to be a euphemism for a "conservative" counterattack on *perestroika*. But was it really? The events of August 1991 and Gorbachev's brief house arrest might be interpreted this way if his reform policies had succeeded or had been in the process of succeeding. But it bears remembering that his policies were considered to be failing for some time and even by some of his closest and most supportive advisers, such as the economist Stanislav Shatalin, who asked him to resign in a spectacular open letter at the end of 1990. Gorbachev was criticized as much from the reform side, who reproached him for his contradictions and procrastinations in moving toward democracy and a market economy, as from the conservative side, which feared this evolution. For three years, economic production and the standard of living had been dropping, and they continued to drop. Anarchy was spreading through a system that was no longer communist without having become liberal, that was no longer totalitarian without having become democratic. Gorbachev was floundering interminably in projects for a new Union, without finding any clear solution for the major issue of how the republics should relate to the center. There is no doubt that conservative ultra-communists harbored ill-intentions toward Gorbachev, but it is unlikely they would have dared move if his policies had been working. The Communist Party was much weaker in 1991 than in 1985. Had Gorbachev put in place a new political economic system that worked in an acceptable way, the conservatives would have had no pretext for trying to overthrow him. They could not have challenged a popular leader. The point is that Gorbachev was anything but. Returning to Russia in 1991 after fourteen years in exile, Vladimir Bukovsky was struck by the degree to which Gorbachev was "hated." Stalin, Bukovsky observed, was admired and feared; Khrushchev was an object of scorn; Brezhnev was despised. But Gorbachev was the first Soviet leader whom the population simply hated.

No doubt, he did not deserve it, when you consider what he was trying to do and what he in fact was able to do in the areas of freedom and international affairs. But on the most vital issue, reforming the structures of Soviet society, Gorbachevism was a graveyard of *outworn ideas*, upsetting to reformers as well as to conservatives though for opposed reasons. Soviet society had become ungovernable. It was sinking in a vacant lot, between the wreckage of collectivism and an aborted liberalism. The blocking of the conservative plot underscored the end of neo-Brezhnevism as well as Gorbachevism and the timid reformism of *perestroika*. The road to democracy could not be the return of Gorbachev to power. Thus while the attempt to restore communism in August 1991 demonstrated that the democratic renewal in the world was vulnerable, it nonetheless also demonstrated how deeply the democratic current runs. The vehement reaction to the putsch showed that Gorbachev's unpopularity was not due to a rejection of democracy, but on the contrary to a desire for reforms more extensive than those attempted during *perestroika*. The failure of the putschists, and the concomitant rise of Boris Yeltsin, the enemy of the center and the Communist Party, clearly showed which way majority opinion was heading in Russia. Indeed, the putschists did not even represent a majority in the Soviet communist party. But then, neither did Gorbachev represent a majority of the reformers. After going through the motions of returning to power on the 22nd of August, Gorbachev dragged himself through a few more months of being the president of a disintegrating Union. Abroad red carpets were still laid out for him, but at home his presidential chair shrank by the day. On November 14, a confused weak compromise, signed unenthusiastically by seven republics and refused by five others, including Ukraine, transformed the defunct Union of Soviet Socialist Republics into an undefinable "Union of Independent States," which brought with it the end of the job of president which had been created by and for Gorbachev in June 1988.

Gorbachevism was neither a maneuver designed to save the totalitarian system, as certain Western experts believed, nor was it a clearly thought through and firmly managed policy for a transition to democracy and market economics, as the West's "Gorbygroupies" thought. It was a refusal—or an inability—to choose between the two. The tragedy of Gorbachev is that he represented neither the past nor the future, and he found himself crushed by both at the same time.

Thus from 1989 to 1992 what we have witnessed is not a revolution, which suggests the idea of creation, of discovery, of something new, but rather a return to square one, or more exactly an attempt to return to square one, that is to say to the position before communism. Communist societies at first try to regain the usage of the precommunist characteristics, and they fall back on the time before they entered the totalitarian tunnel. When they emerge from it, they find, intact and even in more volatile form, the realities and problems that totalitarianism was supposed to have annihilated, but which in fact it had merely placed in deep freeze. Nationalism, family, religion, capitalism, private property, parliamentary democracy, the rights of businesses, free trade unions, freedom of the press, of commerce, of retailing—all the questions that had been raised in the nineteenth century found themselves raised, unchanged, in the communist countries at the end of the twentieth.

But the difference is that they were less well equipped to deal with them than they had been in the previous century. With annihilated economies, populations lacking all experience of entrepreneurship and competition, no financial markets, an incompetent administration, obsolete technology, a political class starting at zero and needing to learn the democratic a–b–c, the governments are without a clue on how to save the store and can do little more than pile on inappropriate or contradictory decisions. When the totalitarian state stops controlling everything, it no longer controls anything.

So would it be best to begin by letting a society coming out of communism return to the state of nature? The failure of the reforms of 1990 suggested as much, in particular for those countries that were most annihilated by communism, the Soviet Union and Romania. In the East it appeared that no one knew how to return to a market economy. Without changes disaster was inevitable. But changes also were bound to bring disaster. In the West, governments, businessmen, journalists began to question Gorbachev's chances of success and took note of his inability to make key decisions. It has been remarked that between 1985 and 1989 the Soviet Union received ample credits, but no modernization of industry was undertaken, let alone realized. "Where did the money go?" lamented a Soviet economist quoted in *Le Monde* of 10 July 1990. The money evaporated before the reforms that were passed in 1987 could be set in motion. Gorbachev's empty boasts of doubling the GNP by the year 2000 rang hollow already: the truth is that the GNP fell by half between 1985 and 1990. This fiasco did not stop him from making the reckless promise that he could put a market economy in place in less than two years. While he was making these laughable statements, it became clearer by the day that Western money and technology could not save the Soviet economy. As the economies of Eastern Europe became sponges for Western investors, Soviet borrowers increasingly came back empty-handed from their fund-raising trips. The perennial headache returned: Should we help Gorbachev? Richard Nixon, *Le Monde*, *Le Figaro*, *Time*, *Newsweek*, among others, raised the previously heretical question in the summer of 1990. "Can capitalism take root in the Soviet Union?" *Newsweek* asked dubiously. Gorbachev, for his part, made the same appeal for help to the G-7 summit in Houston that summer as he had made a year earlier when the leading industrialized countries had met in Paris. At that time, the consensus had been that Gorbachev should not be pressured to relax the Soviet hold on central Europe. It was thought to be in bad taste to use the crisis of communism to separate the Soviet Union from its satellites! The latter did without any help from the West, as usual. But a year later, the G-7 were not sure about the value of irrigating the Soviet economy with their capital. Bush, while encouraging business circles to give Gorbachev a hand, nonetheless was more skeptical than the persistently generous Mitterrand and Kohl, the latter in particular whose political motives were obvious. Frightened by the bill, though, Kohl exclaimed: "We Germans cannot help the Soviet Union alone!"

In point of fact, they were not alone. Mikhail Gorbachev could not travel abroad without getting a little something from just about everybody. In the fall of 1990 he obtained a billion and a half dollars in Spain, a billion in France. Italy gave him several billion in November. But this charity looked increasingly like emergency food relief, rather than a thoughtful vote of confidence in *perestroika*. The West was mainly interested in saving Gorbachev, who played shrewdly on Western fears of chaos that would envelop them as well. "My program of change is entering a critical stage [again!]," he wrote to the G-7 in July 1990, "and I appeal for Western economic support for it will benefit all humanity."

The implication was that if the West failed to do its job, it might wake up one morning to find a Soviet general had taken Gorbachev's place. He told the Spaniards that if he did not obtain the help he needed, there was a risk of returning to the dictatorial command economy. What he neglected to mention was that the West had never been stingy in helping him, and at any rate the Soviet Union was still a command economy. As far as help was concerned, he had just bartered German reunification for 50 billion DM ($1=DM 1.5), and still was no more able to get reforms going than he had been in 1987, 1988, or 1989. And yet the blackmail still worked. Felipe Gonzalez himself fell for it: "It is in the interest of the Spanish government to invest in *perestroika*."

The interest of the Spanish government, like that of all of Europe and the United States, would have been to invest, not in a lost cause but in a serious operation. For the help to serve a useful purpose, the first necessity was to rid the Soviet Union of the ruins of socialism. A free economy could not be built on them. It was becoming increasingly clear that Gorbachev's stubborn claim to be able to "direct" the transition to a market economy with the methods of a command economy—on top of the absence of any kind of "market culture"—was one of the main obstacles to the resurgence of normal economic behavior.

Thus, after five years of *perestroika* the reality began to come into focus, though a straightforward structural analysis at the start would have sufficed. The West saw that direct economic and financial help served no purpose—as, indeed, Andrey Sakharov had warned them till the end of his life. Next, it had to be admitted that, after half a decade, announced reforms remained just that; either they were never applied or they were reduced to nothing when they were applied. Moreover, Gorbachev and his economic advisers piled on the incoherences, never seemed to know what they wanted, nor to believe what they said. They changed their minds from one day to the next, giving the impression they did not believe in the possibility of reform and were resigned to chaos. Gorbachev's "subjectivism" was comparable to Khrushchev's, thirty years earlier (it was to bring him down that the Party leadership coined that sin). It became apparent that

129

Gorbachev's political authority was melting as the Union came apart. Decisions that might have been useful depended less and less on him. It was turning out that the political exit, as well as the economic exit, from communism was turning out to be far more laborious than in most of the former satellite nations.

Henceforth, criticism of Gorbachev in the West came from others than those skeptical observers who had doubted from the start the viability of *perestroika* and who, in consequence, had been accused of relying on "anti-Soviet reflexes" instead of thinking. Now the détentist conservatives, the reformist communists, and the non-communist left, which from the start had been most committed to the success of Gorbachev's "third way," joined the doubters. This was the case, for example, of the French Socialist eminence Claude Estier, who had been a fellow traveler and then became a confidant of President Mitterrand. He prepared an economic report on the Soviet Union for the Senate, of which he was a member, in which he took note of a "generalized recession" and a "worsening of shortages," and "unfinished projects." Even as Mitterrand and the government were encouraging French businessmen to invest in the Soviet Union, the Estier report was full of data that should have discouraged them. On top of the enormous budget deficit there was now a trade deficit—new for the Soviet Union—and nonpayments to foreign suppliers. If anyone was counting on reforms to help, Estier warned that the reforms already passed "did not have the desired results." The cooperative sector, created by legislation in 1987 and meant to employ a third of the active population only employed 1 or 2 percent. Farm property was still not redefined, and in consequence agricultural production continued to fall.

In spite of these striking facts, which journalists and experts were describing often, the EC's executive authority, meeting in Dublin on June 25 and 26, ordered the Commission "to inquire of the Soviet Union regarding its needs, in order to provide short term credits and support for long-term structural reforms." The Council still had not grasped that the Soviet Union was a patient dead by the time the cure started.

An in-depth understanding of the system, rather than a superficial view of the immediate situation and Gorbachev's speeches, were needed to see the sheer uselessness of wasting credits on the Soviet Union's economy. It could not absorb these credits any more than the human body could transform solar energy without chlorophyll needed for photosynthesis. This was demonstrated strikingly by two events that occurred during that summer of 1990 when Gorbachev, Yeltsin, and their advisers were interminably discussing yet another economic reform plan.

The first was a fantastic harvest—three times more abundant, for grains alone, than the previous year's. Such favorable climatic conditions had not been seen for decades. However, the Soviets proved incapable of reaping this harvest. It rotted under foot, or was wasted in bins and trucks, or even, when it managed to get to its destination, was lost for lack of adequate storage facilities. In a normal mediocre year, between a fourth and a third of Soviet agricultural production was wasted this way. The very abundance of the 1990 harvest provoked shortages because it overwhelmed the bureaucracy and disorganized a system that already was scarcely capable of harvesting, transporting, storing, and distributing. Potatoes and wheat were rotting on the ground or in railroad stations, and rationing was being reintroduced. It hardly took a genius to realize that credits were not what this system needed.

The second event had to do with the price of oil, which shot up from $18 to $35–40 a barrel in a matter of weeks due to Iraq's invasion of Kuwait. Though it was the number-one producer in the world, the Soviet Union could not take advantage of this, due to the obsolescence of its equipment and the inadequacies of its extraction technology, which prevented it from increasing production. Much of this, such as natural gas, was normally wasted during extraction anyway. On the contrary, oil production actually decreased compared to 1989, provoking the vice-prime minister Leonid Abalkine to say that the Soviet economy was in its worst shape since World War II. Financial credits would have helped neither oil nor gas production. The Soviet leaders themselves were aware of it, since they went so far as to consider granting concessions to American firms to get the oil out. In the midst of such a shambles, it is difficult to judge which was more responsible, the old socialist system or *perestroika*.

Throughout the summer of 1990, Moscow was abuzz with the lyrical-sounding "500 Days Plan." They got it in their heads to develop a market economy in five hundred days. Why five hundred? It took the West five hundred years to achieve something approximating a market economy. And the West started without the disadvantage of having just been through the communist grinder. And how to proceed in these five hundred days? From June to September, the debate continued between "radicals" and "conservatives." The latter pushed for a brutal destruction of centralized planning, the former lurched about in the swamp of a "planned market." On top of this conflict a second one was juxtaposed, between the Soviet Union and the Russian Republic and, in a more general sense, between the Soviet Union hanging on to its role as the "center" and all the other republics, seeking autonomy or even outright independence. There were two obvious issues: Does Gorbachev know what he wants in terms of economic policy? And if he does, can he impose it on the republics? Gorbachev furnished contradictory answers to the first question. "We are talking about a mixed economy," he said in a speech on September 18. "Private property will have an essential role in a very limited sphere, and an extremely restricted role in most of society." He was, therefore, not talking about a market economy as the West understands the term. In a sentence reflecting the confusion in his country, Gorbachev said in the same speech, "The market democratizes economic relations, and socialism is unthinkable without democracy [sic]; so by reforming property relations, we are going to lay the foundations for a truly healthy base for authentic collectivism: therein lie the roots of our economy's real socialism." What this meant was anyone's guess; it was, in fact, mindless. Meanwhile, however, the Western press was celebrating the "500 Days Revolution" as the *New York Times* headlined an editorial on October 6, and saw this misconceived program—which no one had even bothered to read—a "decisive turn" that would take the Soviet Union irreversibly down the "road to capitalism." By October 16 they were in for a disappointment: the program was published and it was clear that Gorbachev had backed off from all the decisions that would have constituted real breaks with the command economy.

As to the question of his political power in relation to the republics, his answer was to obtain for himself the power to rule by decree. But whatever for did he need such powers in putting in place such insignificant reforms? The less authority he had in the country, the more power he had on paper. Did he believe he could thus stop the republics from deserting? In reality, his program was born dead. It was a "plan for a country that no longer existed," as French historian Hélène Carrère d'Encausse said. His innumerable theoretical powers could not compensate for the timidity of his actual program, nor for his growing inability to impose the center's authority on the republics.

In point of fact, what was left of the Soviet Union at the end of October 1990?

The Supreme Soviet had just granted to Mikhail Gorbachev the right to govern for 500 days by ukase (decree), the very term formerly used under the Tsarist autocracy. The Western press reported that the "parliament" thus had granted the "president" absolute power.

Yet this terminology is misleading. For the Supreme Soviet is no more a parliament, in the Western sense, than Gorbachev is a president elected by universal suffrage. The Supreme Soviet comes out of the Congress of People's Deputies, whose 2250 members had been elected in March 1989 following a procedure that was surely an immense improvement over the earlier totalitarian methods, but that remained only semidemocratic. A third of the deputies were selected by various organizations: the Communist Party, the trade unions, the women's union, the young communists, the scientific academy, the committee for peace, the philatelist union, etc. The other two thirds were elected either by the nationalities or by the Union, by universal suffrage but without time for real multi-party elections to be organized. This did not prevent the voters from expressing their disapproval of communist candidates and of dismissing them. A year later, Gorbachev was elected to the presidency by this same congress, indirectly and not by universal suffrage. His was the only candidacy and it had been proposed by the Party.

At this point freedom had been spreading in the Soviet Union, but it remained a country that had not achieved political democracy. In the former satellites, elections had taken place under universal suffrage, albeit, as in Romania, with manipulations. The first truly significant politician elected by direct universal suffrage in the USSR was Boris Yeltsin in June 1991, to head the Russian Republic.

Gorbachev justified the use of ukases by referring to the urgency of the need for economic reform. It is true the country was not on the brink of the precipice; it was at the bottom of the precipice. But then why the months of procrastination? Elected to the presidency in March, crushing his conservative opposition in July at the Congress of the Communist Party, did he need special powers to choose between the radical plan of Stanislav Shatalin and the more timid one of his prime minister, Nikolai Ryskov?

Throughout the summer he appeared to favor audacity. But in the end he chose compromise. Yet this so-called synthesis, which proposed at once free enterprise and a reinforcement of bureaucratic control, a market economy without capitalism, looked like nothing so much as Georg Christoph Lichtenberg's famous "knife without a blade lacking a handle."

In fact, this program did not go much farther than the legislation of June and July 1987, which was intended to privatize industry without abandoning socialism, give land to the peasants without restoring property, create joint ventures without foreign stockholders, liberate prices, and turn the ruble into a competitive currency. These laws were supposed to have gone into effect on 1 January 1988, but they broke down right away. Giving the president accrued powers was not the issue, since his decisions were not obeyed. It did not seem possible they ever would be, so great was the inertia.

It became clear that the transition to a market economy could not take place in the empty shell that the Union had become. The center was the source of the evil; how could it also be the solution? Gorbachev's first ukase was to order that hard currency earned by the republics should be turned over to the Union. He was maintaining, in other words, the old system. The Western press, finally noticing that Gorbachev's reform was not for real, began to editorialize that "his plan did not merit Western financial support," as the *Times* of London put it in October 1990. Even the Germans, tired of throwing good money after bad and with the reunification of their country accomplished, began to find it of less crucial importance to help Gorbachev, particularly with estimates of the cost of rebuilding the former East Germany rising all the time.

The "500 Days Plan" was supposed to go into effect on October 1. It was put off to November 1, and then to an indeterminate date. As reform broke down once again, Gorbachev, as usual, obtained additional powers for himself and proposed a new reorganization of the central power. But his real problems were not institutional; Gorbachev could acquire all the power he wanted; he was in any event caught between the accelerating economic collapse and the disintegration of the Union. The Gorbachev period was finished, at least as an attempt to strengthen and democratize Soviet society while saving the Union with a mixture of market and socialism nurtured by a magic potion called *perestroika*. Gorbachev was still president, but he no longer controlled the country. Commentators now agreed the experiment had failed; Hélène Carrère d'Encausse and Martin Malia referred to the Union in the past tense. The idea took hold that

Gorbachev was a ghost presiding over a phantom country. Toward the republics as with regard to the economy, Gorbachev kept taking contradictory measures. He claimed to accept autonomy even as he reaffirmed the center's preeminence; he proposed to move toward the market while keeping locks on that made it impossible.

At a press conference on 23 November 1990, Gorbachev suddenly insisted that he wanted to maintain a strong central power, which would keep control not only of defense and foreign policy, but also economics and finance, real property and the means of production. It felt like a twenty-year leap into the past. He did it again on November 29, reaffirming the leading role of the Party, that Leninist pestilence which was supposed to have been set aside in March. He banished the eventual possibility of private property in land. This was one the key aspects of the reforms under discussion for three years. Four days later, the parliament of the Russian Republic voted to reestablish private property in land, but tied in such restrictions that, once again, the reform was meaningless. These suffocating regulations reflected Gorbachev's will, and they undercut a far more ambitious proposal of Boris Yeltsin. According to the final draft, Russian peasants could own land, but they could only sell it to the state—and only after ten years! In short, the essential element in private property, the freedom to reinvest one's capital wherever one wants, disappeared with this law. This was typical of the whole *perestroika* imbroglio. First he proclaimed that such and such a measure would never be accepted, then Gorbachev decreed it, and finally fixed it in such a way as to render it useless. Thus the retail "cooperatives" were asphyxiated with taxes of 70 to 90 percent on profits, and long-term land leases were proposed in conditions so restrictive and onerous that they discouraged all but a few. Incessant legal changes were not an incentive to risk a venture into the market economy.

In public relations, by contrast, at least abroad, Gorbachev's tactics won him a reputation as an indefatigable reformer, who could not let a week go by without decreeing some new change. Since few people remember what they read in the newspaper six months ago, or even what they wrote there, they are unlikely to discern the new guise under which an old and never-applied reform is being introduced. In July 1991, Gorbachev, having managed to get himself invited for the first time to the G-7 Summit (the annual meeting of the world's leading industrial states) in London, set in motion a "new" program of economic reforms, this time with the help of Harvard economists. As

Paul Fabra, *Le Monde*'s economic columnist, put it in a lucid and profound analysis of this grab bag, the preposterous program was good at expressing ideals but short on means of action. Shrewdly, Gorbachev announced before going to London that he would present "concepts" rather than a detailed program. He was presenting himself as a theoretician rather than a leader. Yet, even though his powers had accrued again in December 1990, it was as a lecturer rather than as a man of action that he impressed the G-7—if action means choosing, deciding, doing. He was not having any of that. It was the same with the Union treaty; it was never possible to know who was in favor of what. One day Yeltsin was supposedly supporting Gorbachev; the next day, the Russian Republic recognized the independence of Lithuania. Another day, Gorbachev exulted that Armenia was signing; the following day, the Armenian president denied it. It was disconcerting. You could have quoted Dante, in reference to Gorbachev: "Te, che fai tanto sottili / provedimenti, ch'a mezzo novembre / non giugne quel che tu d'ottobre fili."* It was an unending game of political legerdemain. Of course, he denied having dictatorial powers, even though he was governing by ukase. Even in the defense sector, the center could no longer play its normal role: the army was demoralized, disorganized, subverted by the recalcitrance of young draftees unwilling to serve outside their own republics. By mid-November, a number of renowned intellectuals headed by the historian Yuri Afanassiev, struck by Gorbachev's incoherences, asked him in an open letter to either fight the crisis or resign.

Which, to be sure, did not mean anything. There was no constitutional way to resign, and to "fight the crisis" was merely a euphemism for going along with it. By now the Soviet Union was a basket case in need of emergency humanitarian aid. In fact, on November 29, Germany put in place an airlift to bring supplies to the major Soviet cities. It was like Ethiopia—but an Ethiopia with a record harvest and not wracked by war. And how to be sure the care packages would make it to the people in need, and would not be stolen by apparatchiks? The 1991 Soviet budget predicted a 50 percent drop in revenue from oil exports (the principal source of hard currency), entirely because of corruption, obsolete equipment, incompetence.

---

* "You disperse yourself in so many little things that by November you don't even remember what you undertook in October."—TRANS.

Communism was only too successful in extirpating from society all foundations for returning to civilization. That was the goal of Lenin and Stalin. *Perestroika* was too timid to have a chance. It seemed bold to trusting Westerners because it tried to transport certain market characteristics into a framework that remained basically collectivist. But this was not possible; reform and collectivism are not compatible. And market economies depend on a collection of factors each of which is necessary for all the others. It cannot be programmed. The conditions have to be present, and then left alone. Foreign credits are insufficient to transform a communist economy into a capitalist one.

Thus it was that from the July 1991 G-7 summit, with the unprecedented attendance of the Soviet president, the West finally understood they had misunderstood *perestroika*. What has been less remarked is that it was also from that time that the West understood the reconstruction of the East could not be fueled, primarily, by Western capital—a view that had informed Western policy throughout the *perestroika* period and that, indeed, went back to the détente period of the early 1970s. Henceforth, Western governments recognized, and stated, that credits would be useful only after the market was in place not during the "transition."

Not that the West was unanimous in its degree of severity regarding the new hard line. The Americans and Japanese were more severe than the French, the Italians, or the Germans. But even a fervent advocate of helping Gorbachev like Helmut Kohl could say in London: "Those who felt that we should open a huge bag of goodies have been wrong from the start." There could not be a more eloquent image of the Western reversal on the way to set Soviet reform in motion. Since politics are partly a matter of symbols, the praise Gorbachev received in London was surely significant, but the belle of the ball would surely have preferred to receive the hoped-for 100 billion dollars than the platonic title of full member of the international economic community. Gorbachev was in the position of someone who had finally got himself admitted to the most exclusive club, but who did not have permission to go near the buffet.

At the previous summits (at Paris in 1989 and at Houston in 1990), he had got into the habit of calling attention to himself by sending a letter to his capitalist friends. This allowed him to steal the show, and he never failed to include the bill. When he stayed away, he got money. Now that he was present, all he got was advice. The point was that the G-7, now as generous with their praise as they were stingy with their cash, applauded Gorbachev's brilliant presentation of his plans, but could not help but notice that his new "concepts" were little different from the reforms that supposedly had been put in practice on 1 January 1988 and were not as far-reaching as the "500 Days Plan," which had not got off the ground in 1990. After six years, in short, the West's leaders had finally got it: investments that can stimulate a capitalist economy have no effect on an economy petrified by bureaucratic centralism.

It is worth recalling that after the failure of the Moscow putsch of 22 August 1991, Edward Shevardnadze made an extremely grave statement, accusing Gorbachev of having to a certain degree created the conditions for the coup by going off to rest in Crimea instead of staying in Moscow during the critical time. The ex-Minister of Foreign Affairs in effect accused his former boss of abandoning his post and thereby letting the coup take place, adding these terrible words: "assuming he did not instigate it." Many are those in the former Soviet Union who lean toward Shevardnadze's hypothesis of an at-least passive complicity of Gorbachev with these strange putchists, all of whom were his own close advisers, put in their positions by him. In this perspective, the putsch's origin is to be found at the London G-7 summit in July, when Gorbachev, though invited for the first time to attend, did not receive the credits he sought. Apart from the uselessness of giving him credits the Soviet Union could not absorb, the U.S. had two political conditions: the end of all military and financial aid to Fidel Castro and a massive reduction of Soviet military spending. To which the Japanese added a condition of their own: the return of the Kurile islands, annexed by the Soviets in 1945. Gorbachev said he could not accede to these conditions without being challenged by the Army, the KGB, the Party, and the military-industrial complex. He used his habitual argument: "If you do not continue to help me, I will be overthrown, and it will be curtains for democracy in the Soviet Union and for *perestroika.*" The idea is that Gorbachev set up the putsch in order to make the West feel guilty. At any event, whether or not Gorbachev had a role in the putsch, the guilt reaction occurred; there was no shortage of leaders and commentators who exclaimed, "If we had given Gorbachev the money he asked for in July, there would not have been a coup in August!" Interestingly, however, the coup's failure did not restore Gorbachev's standing, on the contrary it undercut what remained of his authority. Moreover, Boris Yeltsin hurriedly announced, in the days following the coup attempt, that Russian troops would be leaving Cuba and the subsidies would cease, adding that the Kuriles too were negotiable. Since then, the liberal reforms accelerated rather than slowed down, and the Communist Party was banned, the KGB dissolved. It would seem, therefore, that the West's firmness in London turned out to be more effective than more concessions would have been. Far from wrecking the chances for *perestroika*, Western firmness finally got it going. As to substantial reductions in defense spending, this was for Gorbachev the hardest decision. Thus he was caught at his own game of announcing grand plans when George Bush on September 27 announced U.S. plans for massive and unilateral nuclear disarmament. Gorbachev was in a typical contradiction: reducing military spending was necessary economically, but daunting politically.

Economic development is not merely a transfer of loot, but the creation of new wealth. Only true growth over the centuries allowed the human race to improve its numbers and longevity. Moreover, development is not the same thing as wealth. Certain countries became rich thanks to oil or looting, but did not develop; that is to say, their economies did not become modern, diverse, innovative, efficient. Development leads to wealth, but wealth alone does not produce development.

Western economies grew because of the way they were structured and they way their structures were modified. Several factors combined to produce four basic technological revolutions over five centuries. First there was intellectual and scientific freedom (the suppression of which crippled Islam). Second there was freedom of commerce. Letting seller and buyer argue over the price of a product without interference was an advance that is not as self-evident as it seems. It depended on the gradual ripening of the market and the habits accompanying it, in other words on the commercial texture of society. When communist economies were suddenly released from the straightjacket of fixed prices, they did not make progress—they exploded.

In the sixteenth century, the changes that freed economic activity from political and religious authority provoked the most important changes in Europe. It became possible not only to create enterprises, but to sell, to advertise, to make gains and losses. Backed up by property rights grounded in law, enterprises did not only promote self-interest and imagination, they became laboratories of experimentation and innovation. N. Rosenberg and L. E. Birdzell put their fingers on the principal factor of development when they write: "The West, practically without thinking about it, gave to private enterprises a power of decision that proved essential in sustaining economic innovation: they, henceforth, would decide which projects would be banked on, which would be dropped." (*How the West Grew Rich*, 1986)

Freedom to invest is, in effect, the freedom to choose among possible innovations. It also implies the willingness to pay for failure—which the state never does. Capitalism, Peter Drucker points out, is not only profit, it is profit and losses. It is above all a "culture," the establishment of a society in which the law institutionalizes competition in the race to innovation. Communist societies demodernized; their technology always seemed obsolete, they took part in virtually none of the inventions of the century (except through industrial espionage and the theft of technology): this seems to certify that there is a profound incompatibility between communism and innovation. This is what Boris Yeltsin understood when he launched, in November 1991, a program of overthrowing all of Russia's economic institutions. The program may well fail, but the patient certainly will die anyway, if it is not tried. Even in Czechoslovakia, a communist society "once removed" by comparison with the Soviet Union, Vaclav Havel lamented a year after the "velvet revolution" that "the main task remained to be done." For demodernization seems to bring with it a killing of the body. The reforms did not eradicate the core of the totalitarian system, or were able only to merely scratch it. An in-depth study of Czech agriculture concluded that the collectivization of the land destroyed the very knowledge of farming. Nothing like this had happened since the neolithic era. It is astonishing: nature ruined by collectivist pollution, human ingenuity demolished by habits of slavery. You could say of communism what was said of Attila: "Nothing grows where he has been."

Everything eventually will grow back. Mankind never tires of anything, and particularly of its own mistakes, which it leaves for posterity to deal with. But everything will grow back on soil cleansed of the sterile dust of totalitarianism. It was naive to believe in the viability of a reformed communism. For five years, the more *perestroika* sank, the more Western governments said it must succeed at all costs, in order to avoid what Gorbachev called the "Lebanonization" of the

Soviet Union and universal chaos. So when the chaos began, the West had no policy ready for dealing with it. A better understanding of communism and of the peculiar problem of getting out of it would have led them, on the contrary, to think: chaos is inevitable, so let us prepare for it. They would not have been caught unawares. "Worsening Soviet Crisis Leaves U.S. at Loss," headlined the *Herald Tribune* (29 November 1990). This is what happens when you base your policies on what you would like rather than what is likely. The analysis should have ruled out the hypothesis of a "pragmatic" communism tempered by "realism." Communism cannot come back to reality because it is not born of reality. It bears no relation to reality. To return to reality, communism must annihilate itself, just as it annihilated reality in order to find itself.

This is the only way to explain the incomparable desolation of the post-totalitarian landscape. The paroxysm of poverty, anarchy, confusion, in the postcommunist countries, especially in the Soviet Union, is without historical precedent, either in its origins or in its consequences. Contrary to the collective catastrophes of the past, communist destruction is not due to war, nor a barbarian invasion, nor a natural cataclysm, nor an epidemic. It is due entirely to an idea.

Communism is the first case in history of a system for the suicide of humanity that is not partly but wholly born of the human mind. Madness and cruelty, to be sure, had in the past concocted other utopias, but none have ever been so completely applied, at any rate for such a length of time and on such a scale. Having finally got past the fantasies of "historical materialism," we must understand that there were no "practical problems" in the early years of the twentieth century that created "objective conditions" rendering Bolshevism "necessary." Conversely, of course, Bolshevism did not find solutions to any of the real problems that humanity faced in those years. On the contrary, wherever Bolshevism established itself it rendered these problems insoluble—even long after its own disappearance. Certainly, the questions raised by socialists in the nineteenth century had a basis. But to the extent that answers were found to them, they were found by capitalism, never by socialism. Communism was not a product of real facts; there is therefore no way it can find its way back to them. Indeed, facts chase it out. Communism is not so much a product of history as much as it is a hiatus in history, an evolutionary syncope, an eruption of systematic delirium in the great chain of human events. As an accident, it is far more serious than a social experiment that failed; rather, it is a comet that surged outside of all social experimentation, even bad ones. Had communism been merely an execrable political system, it could have been improved; *perestroika* would have been viable. But it was far more than that, and far worse. It was a pure creation of the mind, not produced by any sort of historical determinism. It is an invention that has its source in ourselves—in each of ourselves—otherwise there could be no explanation for the fact that, "helped by an immense force of illusions and terror, and pushed by the army of crime" (as Michelet said of Spain under Philip II) it could have had such a stunning ideological success, despite its practical failure and the martyrdom of its innumerable victims.

The former American ambassador to Prague from 1983–86, William H. Luers, in a column in *Newsweek* (26 June 1989), suggested that our descendants would think of "communism" much the way we think of "alchemy," a vague, confused, pretentious phantasmagoria. He is probably right. However, alchemy never killed anyone, nor did it enslave billions, nor did it ever kill and deport tens of millions. As an intellectual extravagance, it was an innocent pastime. During the campaign preceding the German general elections of 2 December 1990 (the first for the reunified country), a poster was displayed in a city of the former East Germany that showed Karl Marx making an appeal: "Proletarians of all countries, forgive me!" Alas, those who should have asked for forgiveness were the proletarians themselves. The poster artist surely had a funny idea, but Marx was not the guilty party. After all, any one has a right to concoct some intellectual fantasy if it diverts him to do so. The really guilty ones are those who take him seriously. Communism originated in the minds of men. It had nothing to do with "degrees of development of productive forces," "contradictions between the infrastructure and the superstructure," and other "dialectical" silliness. There is no Marxist explanation for Marxism.

The real origin of Marxism resides in the human capacity to dismiss reality. This capacity will always be latent. Sooner or later it always returns to the surface; hence the totalitarian danger will never go away. It will take other guises, to be sure, behind which we will not recognize it; it will use different appeals. But we must learn from our experience so that we may instruct our posterity to be on guard against new and unpredictable reincarnations of this threat. And after all, why else write about politics if not to sharpen our ability to see these things. Though we can oppose ourselves to the totalitarian threat, the totalitarian temptation will never die, for it is inherent in mankind. We can learn from political philosophy not to escape the temptation, but to avoid it. Otherwise, how can one explain the hallucinations of so many eminent men, many of whom were by no means communists, and who saw "song-filled tomorrows" in notes that were from the start nothing other than a funeral dirge.

From the start: this was so as a political and social theory, and also as an empire. From the 1970s, authors referred increasingly to the Soviet Union as an "empire." And they were right to do so, for Moscow's expansionism had never been so menacing as during the years following World War II, while within its own borders the Soviet Union was, in effect, the last colonial empire, imposing its Russian and Leninist hegemony on recalcitrant subject peoples. However, comparisons with great empires of the past were valid only up to a point. Leave aside Napoleon's, which was a carnival empire staged by a adventurous military genius incapable of creating anything durable. An empire that depends on one individual is scarcely an empire. Napoleon was brushed aside after barely twelve years, though as the heir of the Age of Enlightenment and the French Revolution he left behind him innovations in institutions, culture, architecture, gastronomy, witticisms, furniture, and paintings, which is more than can be said for communism. Empires worthy of the name are grand multinational entities which a diversity of peoples and cultures cohabit for a substantial period.

From this point of view, it is not possible to compare the disintegration of the Soviet Union with the end of previous empires. The "decline and fall" of empires is an historical enigma, when we look at the empires of Rome or Byzantium or the Ottomans or Spain or Austro-Hungary, or China, or the Mayas, because before coming apart these conglomerations produced great civilizations. Their disappearance is intriguing because at their apogee they were fascinating, and indeed have left parts of themselves to the common inheritance of mankind. It would be an insult to them to compare them to the seventy-five sterile years of the Soviet Union, which produced nothing that is worth retaining in the history of civilization apart from some poor jokes like "socialist realism" and scientific frauds like Lysenko. The only good books of the period were those written against communism, clandestinely. Montesquieu's question, since 1776 better known as Gibbon's—what was the cause of the Roman Empire's decline and fall?—is not a useful reference for understanding the Soviet Union. The comparison is false at every level. First of all the Soviet pseudo-empire was ridiculously short. Second, its failure is no enigma, since it was never a success. The mystery is not in the fall but in how it lasted. It did not even decline, for to decline you first have to have risen. For decades it hid its incurable failures and then it collapsed all at once.

By contrast, the decline and fall of real empires sometimes took centuries. Indeed, even during their decline they were often at their brilliant best. They created, even as they were decadent, new standards of living, heights in the arts and in letters, science, advances in law, medicine, poetry, philosophy. Did the Soviet period produce any of these? The end of what Michael Rostovtzeff called the "Roman world state" was not only the fall of the Roman Empire as such, but of ancient civilization more generally—Greek, Hellenistic, and Roman. When it fell it had existed for twelve or thirteen centuries, and anyway, it fell without dying, for its legacies are still very much alive among us in our culture, institutions, philosophy, morals, laws, aesthetics. This simply bears no comparison with the seven sinister and sterile decades from Lenin to Chernenko.

As it disappears, communism leaves not even the hint of a contribution to civilization. On the contrary, it almost put an end to our own. In doing that it taught us an extraordinary lesson, an expensive one no doubt but which—for that every reason—we should be loath to forget. There is a great temptation to say now that, all things considered, communism was a mistake to be sure, but it came and went and really we made too much of it. Such an irresponsible view would set us up to fall in to the next trap, which will be new, unexpected, and against which we would be unprepared. I hope and I believe this will not happen. Let us not drown the nightmare in a pleasing amnesia! The one thing to thank communism for is that it grimly demonstrated how far murderous foolishness can go in humiliating all of mankind. Let us admit the degree to which we nearly fell for it. As in the case of nazism, communism will be remembered for its grotesqueness and its hatefulness. I hope the wound to our human pride will keep the memory of this phenomenon present in our minds. For to guard against a relapse, I confess I am counting more on our hurt vanity than on the scruples of conscience, less on the clearsightedness of intelligence than on the setbacks caused by our wilful blindness.

PART THREE

DEMOCRACY IN THE THIRD WORLD

CHAPTER TEN

FROM DEMOCRACY TO THE MARKET

OR FROM THE MARKET TO DEMOCRACY?

When in the 1980s the failure of communism revealed that the socialist camp was in many regards even more underdeveloped than the so-called underdeveloped countries, the Third World began to suspect that there exists a link between political democracy and economic development. On the matter of getting beyond the consequences of communism, as on the issue of getting out of poverty, the question of the relation between the market and democracy began to occupy the center of the debate on what makes a good society. This debate reached the developed, democratic world as a matter of fact, and a neoliberal school of thought got the ascendancy over those who believed the state should intervene in economics and culture. Increasingly, the idea that there was a strong causal relationship between economic and political freedom gained strength, and it was seen that in political liberty there must be implied freedom of information, of opinion, of thought, of research, without which there can be no development. Thus, the decade of the eighties witnessed not only the fall of communism but, as well, an intellectual attack on "Third Worldism." Development, it turned out, is not just enrichment; it is a form of civilization of which the different elements, not all of which are physical, are complementary. Among other things, the waste of the help given to the ex-communist countries confirmed a thesis which, until then, was heresy among the "Third Worldists": namely, that foreign aid can worsen underdevelopment instead of alleviating it, so long as the institutional mechanisms and the human skills necessary to take advantage of the help are not there, as well as the instruments of democratic control that can oversee that it is put to its intended use.

This argument was heard more and more toward the end of 1990, when the Soviet Union and Central Europe, far from moving forward after their revolutions, seemed to be standing still or, worse, moving backward. The main reason for this halt seemed to lie in their inability to make the transition to the market, or a reluctance to take the hard measures necessary to make the transition, even when the transition to democracy undeniably had got under way, by means of changed institutions and elections. Developing countries found themselves with comparable difficulties, for most of them had adopted, somewhat like the communist regimes, combinations of economic statism and political despotism. Agricultural collectivism and bureaucratized cooperatives succeeded in turning the most fertile lands into importers of food products. Many had rejected the market, imposed currency and price controls. Their monetary policies were unrealistic, removed from the international context. They had made colossal investments in wasteful and megalomaniacal and unproductive industrial complexes. They had ruined themselves with arms expenditures. Their nationalized banking systems were sterile, preventing credit from functioning according to economic criteria. Protectionism blocked competition from the outside, leading to the deterioration in the quality of homemade products. A labor-intensive work force rendered any return to the market impossible without large-scale unemployment at least in the short term. Overall, the population tended to get poorer, even as the political and bureaucratic class got wealthy through corruption.

Obviously, not all Third World countries were, or still are, afflicted by these problems to the same degree, but it is impossible not to notice the similarity between them and the ills that destroyed communist societies. The analogies, imperfect as they are, gave currency to an ancient but long-forgotten idea: the suppression of the market, which is justified in the name of protecting the interests of the poor, in reality answers the aspirations of a despotic minority in the political and bureaucratic classes, allowing it to corner both the power and the wealth. Not content with subjugating and impoverishing the rest of the population, they deceive it. Lying, in the face of the evidence of reality, is a precaution taken by the ruling classes in the Third World almost as much as in the communist world. To do this, however, requires that information be controlled by the state, with the resulting asphyxiation of culture. Statism, with its creation of high, middle, and low strata in a new nomenklatura with countless little associated profiteers, is the instrument of the new class system, in which material well-being depends on belonging to the official sphere. It is legitimate to conclude that the reason it is necessary to suppress the market in order to suppress democracy is that there is a connection between democracy and market which is not accidental. As the analysis of the failures of communist and Third World regimes both led to this conclusion, new weight was given to the notion, indeed the conviction, that the two sides of liberalism, political and economic, cannot be separated. But how did Third Worldism lend itself to this critique as much as communism?

"Third Worldism" claims poverty in the Third World is caused by the supposedly pernicious interventions of foreign capitalism. The original sin in this way of thinking is colonialism. Following the end of the colonial era, the external cause of their poverty is reconstituted as the Third World nations were subjugated to the needs of the rich nations. Simple as it sounds, this is the basic Third Worldist idea, amplified by its theory of "dependence," "unequal exchange," and "domination effect." In effect, it is a form of xenophobia, which confers on the ruling classes of the underdeveloped countries three key advantages: It turns people's attention away from their own incompetence and dishonesty; it saves them the trouble of examining the internal causes of poverty and reforming the devastating system behind them; and, finally, it allows not only all the blame, but the entire solution as well, to be situated conveniently far away. Fundamentally, it allows them to argue that the only solution to their problems consists of foreign economic aid.

The intellectual foundations of this fraud are to be found in the old doctrine that economic and social problems can be solved through redistribution. Whatever the teachings of their own history and the lessons to be drawn from the debacle of command economies, socialists and Third Worldists persist in an old prejudice: inequalities in wealth must mean that one side (either within a national or international context) is getting more than its fair share. So, the "thieving minority," meaning the rich, viewed as rich individuals within a nation or more broadly the richer nations, must give back its excessive take. Of course this requires making the hallucinatory assump-

149

tion that a given quantity of wealth is self-generating, and the task is to distribute it fairly. Thanks to this simple strategy, everything would improve—power, culture, knowledge, responsibility, initiative, happiness, culture, health, work. All you then have to do is distribute parts of the whole bag of goods to everyone, making sure no one gets more than his neighbor.

But authoritarian distribution does not produce progress, unfortunately. On the contrary, it often destroys it. Progress comes from many factors. They are too complex to be planned; but they are sufficiently fragile to be permanently queered, and even paralyzed.

Communist and ex-communist countries cannot, in all credibility and decency, blame their shipwreck on the imperialism of the democratic nations; yet they often imitate Third World countries in expecting that the solution to their problems will come in the form of Western handouts. Their favorite sophism consists of saying that their own conversion to economic efficiency presupposes capitalist generosity and cannot succeed without it. But the experience of *perestroika* proves just the opposite: it was, in part, due to premature foreign aid that it failed.

The joining together of democracy and the market is therefore the only way out of communism as well as underdevelopment. The important point is not only that this proposition is true, but that it is increasingly acknowledged in these last years of the twentieth century. We owe some thanks to communism for having demonstrated by its own failure how true it is. But many countries of the Third World did not wait for *glasnost* to show, from 1985, the full extent of the communist catastrophe, to oppose Third Worldism and to criticize statism. From the late seventies, liberal thinking emerged in Africa and Latin America and influenced a generation of statesmen. To be sure, turning this thinking into practice required overcoming barriers, particularly in Africa. It is harder to rebuild a free market than to destroy it. In 1990, researchers at the World Bank reviewed all the attempts that have been made since 1945 by a number of developing countries to liberalize their economies in the area of foreign trade. Of thirty-six attempts, only fifteen succeeded. Nonetheless, the "liberal restoration" led to a series of courageous economic experiments, which were preceded or accompanied by restoration of political democracy in Latin America in the late 1980s. As to Asia, more precisely the Far East, the successes along the Pacific Rim have given it a claim to being the precursor, or the inventor, of the liberal way out of underdevelopment. At the end of the 1960s, a group of United Nations experts issued a document called the Pearson Report (which took its name from the former Canadian prime minister) that foresaw no chance whatsoever for an economic take-off in South Korea. In 1990, another group of economists decided to rank Korea not among the "developing" countries, but in the "first" world itself. Not only had its growth rate been remarkable for twenty years, but it had moved into political democracy. No doubt, its democracy was imperfect, but the only thing that is perfect in politics is imaginary socialism.

Until about 1980, when you voted in Europe you made a conscious choice between two kinds of society: capitalistic or socialist. Ten years later, socialism is not an option. There is only one choice, democratic capitalism. Disagreements concern the best way to manage it. There are still differences between left and right, but they are within liberalism. This is a decisive change. For what really prevented the left from existing is socialism. So long as the left defines itself with reference to socialism, there will be no left. The difference between left and right now concerns the best way to reconcile solidarity with efficiency, and no longer efficiency with liberty. In 1956 Gunnar Myrdal, who was to receive the Nobel Prize in economics, said as if it were a given, "Socialism is the only way for underdeveloped countries to grow." It sounds like something from another age, yet it remained conventional wisdom for at least another quarter century.

In the Third World, the new way of thinking has two distinct starting points, one economic and one political. But they join together. From the economic point of view, this becomes evident: development only takes place through the market, and not through central planning as has long been thought. From the political point of view, it becomes clear that far from being "formal," democracy is creative, playing an active role in the material and cultural takeoff. At the summit of La Baule in June 1990, African countries with special ties to France were told by President Mitterrand that democracy is the condition for development, not the reverse. This was a complete turnaround from the conventional TWist theme, which until then the Socialists—and the speaker himself—had supported.

But must the equation of market and democracy be taken literally? No: it does not always happen this way. The take-off in Europe preceded its democratization by two centuries or more, and it was almost lost to totalitarianism twice in this century. The industrial strength of Hitlerian Germany, the energy of Japan prior to 1940, of

Franco's Spain in the 1960s, or of Pinochet's Chile in the last years of the dictatorship prove that there can be economic success without democracy. This is also the evidence of the oft-cited "four dragons" of East Asia, which went from underdevelopment to overdevelopment in the space of one or two decades, astonishing the world by the rapidity with which they entered the "rich" club, even as their governments remained authoritarian and even to a certain degree statist. For that matter, many knowledgeable observers of Japan would not call it a real democracy and would question whether its economy can be called liberal.

These elementary facts remind us that life is too complex for ideologies and their prefabricated categories. Marxism is false; but the rigid and literal opposite of Marxism is false as well. It is interesting to note that in the period when communism and TWism were being called into question, during hundreds of conferences and in innumerable speeches and papers, those who had lived under communism insisted the market had to come first, while those coming from the TW thought democracy must come first. For the former, the restoration of a market economy conditioned the restoration of democracy, political pluralism, and cultural freedom. The latter, who did not need persuading that there is a link between prosperity and the market, nonetheless saw in the establishment of democratic control the precondition and the key to any economic revival. The reason for the different emphases is that people who had lived under communism were all too acutely aware of the annihilation caused by socialist planning and the need to live as beggars off the West; whereas people who lived in the caricatural regimes of the Third World believed the first order was to get rid of the venal and predatory despots who stood in the way of any sort of development.

Both were right. Both spoke of what they knew only too well. No one was suggesting that the victims of communism did not suffer under political tyranny, or that the victims of TW dictatorships did not suffer under the ill-effects of their administered economies; it was a matter of placing the emphasis on the egg—or on the chicken.

It is pertinent to demand political democracy right away, first of all because it is a value in itself, and then because it makes it possible to fix economic mistakes, or at least prevent them from continuing beyond a tolerable time—which is precisely what totalitarianism allows. To understand this was to rid oneself of the Marxo-TWist prejudice that held liberty to be an illusion so long as there were inequalities. Even those Soviet citizens who were the most sarcastic about Gorbachev's economic fiasco in 1989 or 1990 objected to excessively critical Western observers. They pointed out that it was like being born again, however grim the economic scene, when you could speak out against the government without fear of being arrested or dismissed from a job; or find newspapers that at least resembled an opposition press and said in the full light of day what previously could only be said in samizdat; or be able to go to a concert and hear Rostropovich, until then forbidden to enter the country; or see a debate on television between Sakharov and Gorbachev at the Congress of People's Deputies; or for that matter to have been able to elect those deputies, even if in elections that Westerners would have considered less than fully democratic. After all, democracy in the West began with limited suffrage. You can complain about liberty being incomplete, but bear in mind that it always is, even in advanced democratic societies. Liberty has progressed in Europe little by little since the Middle Ages. It is a historical fact that you can have certain liberties and rights in a regime that is not strictly speaking democratic; conversely, a state with all the outward trappings of democracy, notably universal suffrage, may well treat its citizens like a tyranny. This is what Latin American regimes are notorious for, but it is true of France too, where the chief of state, though he is elected, has powers worthy of a monarchy, and where the legislative and judicial branches cannot be considered fully independent. There is no democracy without elections, but elections alone, even in a multi-party system, do not democracy make, particularly if they grant disproportional and uncontrolled power to the elected leader.

There are countries where development occurred despite the inexistence, or the limited application, of democracy. South Africa is such a country. But in cases such as this, the state did not confiscate the economy (even if, as in the South African case, it interfered heavily in it). Free enterprise and free markets survived. By contrast, where the absence of economic freedom is added to political dictatorship, there is persistent poverty—underdevelopment is sustained by authoritarianism. This is what the vast majority of Africans are subjected to.

Black South Africans represent less than one twentieth of the 600 million people who live on the continent of Africa. It is quite right to feel passionately about their rights, and to rejoice at the democratization of their country, which has been underway since 1989. But there are many more Africans, and somehow Americans and Europeans do not seem to care about them, at least not from the angle of democracy and human rights. However, whereas the dismantling of the apartheid system in South Africa has progressed steadily (particularly since February 1991), the rest of Africa has not stopped sinking deeper into misery, dictatorship, civil war, and tribal genocides. The West repeats in this Third Worldist context the same error they made with regard to "postcommunism," and which consists of showering credits and aid on countries where the structures cannot make use of them and where the despots are likely to steal them.

African profiteers indignantly reject as "neocolonial" any suggestion that economic aid be linked to reform, since reforms would reduce the portion of this aid which they could keep for themselves. For example, in Mali the better part of the aid that was received to alleviate the damage caused by the drought of 1984 went into the building of summer homes for the rulers. As a matter of fact, the Malians called these places, which everyone knew about, "drought villas." Cases like these, which could be multiplied *ad nauseam*, underscore the organic link between political and economic dictatorship and therefore, by contrast, between democracy and the market. Absent the market, help and debt forgiveness simply reinforce the dictatorship. A few tens of millions of francs given by France in 1990 to the worn-out Vietnamese Communist regime had the direct effect of bringing down the worst wave of repression and arrests in ten years. The same year, President Ratsiraka of Madagascar was able to continue to tyrannize and repress his population thanks to President Mitterrand's ill-advised decision to wipe out his debt with regard to France, which presumably brought to French taxpayers the satisfaction that they were financing one more dictatorship. Able to stay in power thanks to Mitterrand's generosity, Ratsiraka was in position, in August 1991, to order fire opened upon a large and peaceful demonstration that was demanding his departure. These are some of the paradoxes of Third Worldism.

It is interesting to note, by way of contrast, what happens when real investors, who could set in motion real development, investigate the opportunities available to them. According to *Le Monde*, a delegation of the *Confederation nationale du patronat francais** visited Madagascar in November 1986. "Beyond the speeches, everyone was

---

*This is similar to the National Association of Manufacturers, but it has substantially more influence since it is consulted on social legislation.

able to assess the damage done the economy of this country by ten years of constraining statist administrative straightjackets. The French CEOs were given a report when they arrived by an independent consulting organization, which had the effect of a cold shower. Mr. René Lapautre, chairman of the delegation, tried to encourage his colleagues by saying: 'If you are asking me why we do not go home right away, it is because, first of all, there is no flight tonight. However, the time may be ripe for some positive evolution here, and maybe we are in a position to get it going'."

Of course, they got nothing going. Mr. Lapautre was probably thinking of vague commitments to liberalize the economy. Leaders of command economies always make such promises when they are on the run and they need a few billion more from the international community. The tune is familiar: The catastrophic situation to which "Malagasy socialism" in Madagascar (read: predatory dictatorship) has led since the "cultural revolution" (the bloody purge) of 1972 influenced the president to adopt a "more open" policy (openness to Swiss bank accounts where he will place the money he gets). But the said president wants anything but normal investments, which would lead to the loosening of his grip on the economy, and therefore lessen his political power and his control over the whole country.

Like the communist pathology, the Third Worldist one is simultaneously and inextricably both economic and political. It is therefore striking evidence of the link between democracy and free market. The market alone is not always able to provoke development, but development never takes place where there is no market. At any rate, economic statism suffices to block it, surely and without exception, just as it strangles democracy.

It is argued, however, that while there can be no democracy without the market, there are market economies without the free market. This is a sensible argument; but when you look at the examples upon which it is based, one always notices that the connection between democracy and market prevails in the end, whereas the antagonism between democracy and command economies is never overcome. The industrial revolution, which was made possible by freedom of enterprise and exchange, developed in countries that were far from fully formed democracies. But their history shows the close link that grew between the building of democracy and economic development, if for no other reason than that the latter requires progress in education and freedom of information.

This is illustrated, too, by those countries which, since World War II, were economically successful thanks to the spirit of enterprise and competition, even though they had authoritarian governments. Their economic liberty led to political liberty. The market served as the lever of democracy. More—and this is what people who have experienced totally planned economies strive to explain—the market is itself a first step toward democracy. The very fact that it creates and protects a coherent category of behavior, of relationships, and of power free from the central control of the state limits the latter's power and prevents it from overstepping its sphere. This is so even in an authoritarian regime. South Korea, before democratization began in 1985, had a dictatorial regime, but the market provided civil society a substantial slice of autonomy. Life for the ordinary citizen was far more free than in North Korea, where the state's ownership of everything and control of all exchanges annihilated social, individual, and intellectual freedom. This is why in authoritarian systems that have a market putting increasingly irresistible pressure on the political authority the transition to democracy is prepared, as it were, rendered possible to the point of being ineluctable. In systems of collective ownership of the means of production and exchange, on the contrary, "transition" becomes a vicious circle in which the market is needed to stabilize democracy, and democracy is needed to rebuild the market. Countries which, thanks to capitalism and private property and the market, were able to develop without democracy are therefore quite different. While it is true that democracy and development do not always go together, it is also true that a society with a market economy is never completely antidemocratic, and economic freedom sooner or later leads to political liberty. Economic freedom implies that there exist together private property, capitalist investment, and the market.

While the fantasies of a "socialist market economy" can make us laugh as the last tricks that socialist magicians are trying to pull off to miraculously marry collectivism and the market and give birth to a market without private property, there is another fantasy, far more real, that needs to be rejected. This is private property with a market; that is to say, private capitalism that is dependent on the state (not to be confused with state capitalism). In this case, private capitalism cleans up because of privileged relations with the political power, which protects it from foreign and domestic competition. Here, the capacity to enrich oneself comes not through economic smarts, but through smart connections with politicians. The capacity increases not by means of the capitalist's productive talent, but by his proximity to power. This noxious mix poisoned Latin America, among other places. Thickheaded as they are, Marxists (whether or not they are theologians) claim this is the continent of the "capitalist jungle," when in fact capitalists here are in the zoo, risk-aversive and protected from a real market. This coupon capitalism goes against trade unions that are no less cowed, a closed shop unionism that rejects the labor market just as the bosses refuse the product market. In this type of society extreme wealth and extreme poverty are side by side far more than in a real market economy, whose tendency is to drive the large majority into the middle class.

Getting out of such a system is not as difficult as getting out of communism, but it is painful nonetheless. There are privileges and sinecures, valuable superfluous jobs in the state bureaucracies and nationalized firms that are financed by inflation. Heroic courage was required, in Brazil, Argentina, Venezuela, Peru, Bolivia, to try to rationalize and reverse the situation. It is exceedingly difficult to break the sterilizing cronyism that holds together an obese public sector, racketeering unionism, and private statism. Moreover it tends to be all the more difficult as private statism becomes less and less so, for every crisis that it periodically plunges into brings with it a new wave of nationalizations. This is what happened in Mexico in 1982 and in 1988 in Peru, when Lopez Portillo and Alan Garcia, respectively, believed they could overcome the cataclysms they had brought about by nationalizing the banks. Latin America is still referred to as one of the poorest continents. The Western media perpetuate this cliche. The implicated governments encourage it, as much to cover up their own mistakes as to obtain the best possible conditions when they renegotiate their foreign debts.

In reality, for decades Latin America has belonged to what the World Bank calls "intermediate income countries," better off than the "low income" countries of Africa and Asia. Since 1940, Latin America as a whole has sustained a growth rate of 5 percent per year. No European country has sustained such a high average rate. But it is saw-shaped growth, with wide gaps from year to year and extremely uneven from one country to the next, as well as among regions and social classes within countries.

Nonetheless, the growth is real. From 1950 to 1985, real income per capita doubled, in constant dollars—from about one thousand to two thousand annually in 1975 dollars, meaning it had reached the level of Western Europe in 1950, three times the level of the poorer regions of Asia and Africa. At $2420, Mexico's real annual per capita income in 1985 was higher than Italy's in 1960 ($2313), and considerably higher than Spain's ($1737) in that year. (Spain's per capita income in 1985 was $4390.)

These numbers show that it is false to speak of "worsening poverty." The disparities of wealth in Latin America, the misery of part of its population, the stunning bankruptcy of public finances, the inflation that destabilizes daily life and sterilizes investment do not come from fundamental underdevelopment. These ills stem from waste, the origins of which are political.

Demography cannot explain Latin America's difficulties. The population explosion did not stop real economic growth from occurring in Brazil and Mexico. In Colombia, which is an intermediary country by Latin American standards, per capita income more than doubled from 1945 to 1980, while in the same period population grew from 10.2 million to 27 million. What is more, population growth in Latin America was not among the highest. The continent entered what demographers call a "demographic transition": a drop in the birth rate and in fertility. This accompanies industrialization, urbanization, and the growth of the service sector.

Economic thinking became realistic in the Spain of the 1960s. The change came two decades later in Latin America, where an irresponsible approach to economic facts is still widespread, and with it the full panoply of lies, myths, and incoherent ideas.

Was it not obtuse to refuse, throughout the eighties, all oversight by the IMF, even as these countries were preparing to suspend debt repayment and contract new ones? Latin American governments became masters at putting the arm on lending institutions in the name of sacred aid to the Third World, even as they rejected any sort of oversight. Indeed! "We cannot pay our debts with our people's hunger," declared President Sarney on Brazilian television (20 February 1986), stating that Brazil would no longer meet its obligations. Brave words—one would like to be sure the money that was not paid back really went to the people.

Following the bankruptcy of Mexico in 1982, the *Financial Times* commented: "Eminent Mexican public figures took the lead in taking dollars out of the country to put them in Swiss bank accounts and

Connecticut and Californian real estate." If there is a forbidden question in Argentina, Brazil, or Mexico, it is: "Just how did you use the money you borrowed in the seventies and eighties?" It is sort of paradoxical to cry poverty when you are—as is Brazil—the world's eighth greatest economic power, the third in the Western Hemisphere (behind the U.S. and Canada, and sometimes ahead of Canada), when exports in 1986 were worth $23 billion (two thirds of which were industrial products), for a foreign trade surplus of $10 billion. This surplus had to be used entirely to service interest on the debt, and that was unfortunate, even intolerable. But then, what was the cause of this absurdity? It was precisely because they did not want the answer to this question to be known—that the Latin American countries rejected all IMF oversight and that they invented the theory of "dependence."

The Latin American countries' dependence on the more industrialized countries was a theory that the famous Argentine economist Raul Prebisch had elevated to the level of a metaphysical dogma. It is better to blame foreigners when you need guilty parties. Of course, the real guilty party was the system of political-business cronyism, corporate-unionism, and bureaucratic statism. As I noted earlier, Latin American trade unions do not defend the interests of workers. Rather, they monopolize jobs for their own members, who pay off their officials for the privilege. The workers who cannot afford to do this have a choice between unemployment and emigration, which is why there is an exodus to the U.S. This system functions at the expense of the working masses as well of foreign investors, and the latter, for this reason, are getting rarer. Ever fewer of the hated multinationals are present in Latin America. If there is an area where, to use the phrase of Bertrand de Jouvenel, "political facts are economic causes," it is surely Latin America. The ruling class is made up of administrators far more than capitalists: it holds capitalism hostage, but it does not practice it. A public sector as immense as it is in debt provides this class with wages far above the average. Octavio Paz calls the system "patrimonial," meaning thereby that the politico-bureaucratic class, including its servants and its clients, runs the country as if it owned it. The beneficiaries of the patrimonial system, the intellectuals in particular, pay their dues by promoting leftist ideas. The rhetorical camouflage deflects against "imperialism" discontent that should by rights be directed at the governments. Robust eloquence is required to turn a Vera Cruz watermelon vendor against the GATT or the Bank for International Settlements, but with some perseverance and patriotism, it can be done.

Archaic garrulousness and reality denial persisted in Latin America longest with regard to economic problems. Nonetheless, the popular protests that accompanied the Mexican presidential election of July 1988—actually less fraudulent than usual—confirmed the general trend of the period: people in developing countries want democracy no less than anywhere else. The Mexican example is all the more telling because this country has, since the 1920s, occupied a position that was somewhere between real democracy and pure dictatorship. This is not uncommon in the Third World. The challenge to this masked dictatorship in a country as well-known as Mexico had ramifications in many other countries.

It is one of the mysteries of the way information is used today, but the odd thing is that until then, the Mexican system had a generally good press, either through a deliberate misperception or a strange conspiracy. It was never on the black list of tyrannical regimes. But when enough Mexicans got together to provide visible and influential opposition movements, and decried the reigning fraud, the media in the U.S. and Europe finally got around to explaining clearly how the system functions. By means of a strange and shrewd construct, an oligarchy, the well-known PRI (Revolutionary and Institutional Party), since 1929 has monopolized power for itself.

Electoral fraud was, for many years, relatively insignificant in the omnipotence of the enormous bureaucracy based on patronage, from the powerful "godfathers" in the president's intimate circle all the way down to the most humble rural functionaries on the *ejidos* (collective farms), passing by the state governors. Many people voted for the PRI because it was their way of earning a living, and many others did not vote. Union leaders were part of the oligarchy. For example, the PRI's candidate for the presidency is "nominated" by the farm-workers' union, even though in reality he has been chosen already among the party barons. Though he is assured of victory, the candidate conscientiously campaigns for several months. It is the populist, paternalist side of this form of domination: the future boss of bosses must visit the people, go to remote villages, offer homage to the system's profiteers, console the victims. He pretends to seek their votes: in reality he is renewing their contract. This democratic pantomine often fools foreigners, all the more so since Mexico always has had "opposition" parties, carefully formed and subsidized by the ruling party. What was new in 1988 was that the two opposition parties this time turned into real adversaries to PRI hegemony.

The system's logic is that the political hijack produces an economic hijack as well. In Mexico, the real masters are not the entrepreneurs or the capitalists or the multinationals: they are the politicos, who hold the keys to economic activity. It is much more than conventional corruption, though much less than totalitarian collectivism. It is generalized cronyism. Every economy agent must cut the political class (including the bureaucrats and the union leaders) in, in order to launch an enterprise, make it work, and be alive when the profits are distributed. The system is not new. It can be seen in other civilizations, for example in the Later Empire, as it is described by Michael Rostovtzeff in his *Economic and Social History of the Roman Empire.* "By institutionalizing the state's policy of looting," he writes, "the reforms of Diocletian and Constantine rendered all productive economic activity impossible. But this did not prevent great fortunes from being made; on the contrary, but it changed their character. The new fortunes were not made by the creative energy of certain individuals, nor by the discovery and application of new sources of wealth, nor by improvements in industrial or agricultural or commercial enterprises; on the whole, wealth was made by taking advantage of a privileged position in the state in order to embezzle and exploit both the state and the people." Similarly, Ibn Khaldoun, the only genius produced by Arab political philosophy, wrote in the fourteenth century: "A ruler who engages in commercial activity works against the interests of his subjects, interferes with fiscal revenues, and prevents competition; he dictates the prices of materials and products, which can cause many bankruptcies. When the sovereign acts like a hunter and when this behavior spreads, it touches everything and causes a slowing down of business which, too, spreads." In 1990 and 1991, Mexico's President Salinas began to put an end to the statist strangulation of the Mexican economy by creating "free trade zones" for foreign investors and starting to take apart the *ejidos.*

This model goes a long way in explaining the debt problem, and how the money borrowed abroad did very little for productive investments within—when it did not purely and simply disappear. It also explains why those who hold power this way mask their looting under a leftist and "revolutionary" rhetoric, accompanied by violent xenophobic diatribes, aimed at blaming foreigners for economic difficulties. Most intellectuals, who are themselves beneficiaries of the system, sharpen this rhetoric. The press is not entirely run by the single party, but is under sufficient control to be about as free as are elections. Superfically, there is no censorship. But if ever it attacks the core of the system, the latter strikes back, as, in an instructive case, President Luis Echeverria did to *Excelsior*, Mexico's leading daily, in 1976.

Excelsior had gone beyond the line that, traditionally, the honorable opposition and the tame press were not supposed to cross. Criticism must go far enough to appear free, but not so far as to bother the administration. Concerned with maintaining the democratic facade, Echeverria did not go directly against *Excelsior*. Instead—and this should be appreciated by specialists of indirect despotism—a few hundred peasants were brought by bus one morning to demonstrate before the newspaper's building. Their ostensible aim was restitution of the lot on which the building was built, and which had been stolen from their ancestors a century ago. The crowd grew. They settled on the square where the building was located. Blocking traffic, they became the capital's major attraction. Raising the stakes, the peasants demanded not only restitution, but interest to compensate them and their ancestors for what they might have earned. Touched by their plight, government ministers studied the case and determined that they were surely within their rights. A petition of support was circulated by intellectuals. Legal experts claimed they had a case, lawyers offered to defend it, without fee. High-ranking prosecutors let it be known that *Excelsior* was bound to lose their suit. Economists and bankers studied the case and without charge calculated the estimated fine. The fine was so high that to pay it, the paper's owners would have had to close the business. They got the message. They fired the editor in chief and the handful of reporters who had the guts to go against the system's unwritten rules. Within an hour of this, the peasants had calmed down. They forgot the wrongs done their forebears and returned to the bosom of their villages and of the PRI.

Luis Echeverria, in the *Excelsior* affair, gave a nice lesson in indirect despotism—made possible by the existence of a political party which, while not totalitarian, was hegemonic. He represented the very type whom Octavio Paz calls, "constitutional dictators called presidents." He found no contradiction, not long afterward, in attending an international conference on information in Acapulco and referring to the North American press as being "enslaved by money." He retired a few months later, with one of the biggest personal fortunes in the Western Hemisphere. However, it was not as great as the fortune accumulated by his successor, Jose Lopez Portillo. The latter, too, was a "progressive." He nationalized all of Mexico's banks.

There was a time when increasing the economic role of the state implied a true concern for social justice. Then, with little experience to go by, it was not well understood what happened when this was done. Today we know this is pure hypocrisy. This state, supposedly protector of the poor, is, as Octavio Paz, who is a genius at pithy phrases, puts it, a "philanthropic ogre." This kind of statist intervention must be distinguished from another kind, which is referred to as a refutation of liberalism: this is where the state puts itself in the service of productivity and the market. Actually, there are a number of great economic success stories in the latter years of the twentieth century that are far from being models of liberalism and democracy. There were for example the last years of the Pinochet dictatorship in Chile. There were the examples, each with its own singularities, of the four "Asian dragons" of Hong Kong, Taiwan, South Korea, and Singapore, where the state certainly played an important role in directing a market-oriented economic take-off without ideological preconceptions.

The state indeed interfered, but on the basis of economic not ideological criteria. Its policies remained empirical, subject to change according to whether or not they worked, and never hiding political ambitions behind a phony economic program. This pragmatic approach whereby the state sees its role as a facilitator of enterprise must not be confused, either, with the "entrepreneurial state" of—for example—the French Fifth Republic. Notorious and endless are the list of mistaken ventures undertaken by French policy-makers after 1958: in aeronautics and space, in steel, in information science, in low-cost housing, in subsidized agriculture, they persisted in taking no account of the market; in choosing industries and exports to subsidize they persisted in backing losers and finding customer-countries that would not pay their bills. In an outstanding illustration of this sort of administrative ineptitude, certain prices that had been frozen in 1945 were not freed (by decree) until 1979. Interestingly, it is only from this point that French inflation began to come under control.

By contrast, there is such a thing as "liberal statism," in which the state serves the market instead of trying to outperform it. Much of what has been written about the Japanese government's role in the economy does not resist analysis—if I may permit myself a pun, the notorious MITI is largely mythic. One of the driving forces of Japan's foreign trade is, not planning or coordination, but intense domestic competition. Thus, in information science, key to dynamism in so many other industries, Japan is the only country with fourteen competing firms, all of them private. As far as competition goes, MITI had recommended in the early eighties that several automobile firms merge. Fortunately the manufacturers found the idea stupid and nothing came of it, which if nothing else proves that MITI powers of coercion are limited! MITI or no MITI, the Japanese economy is light years away from an administered, let alone a command, economy. When it appears that the government is intervening, it is in reality pushing in a direction already staked out by private investors, themselves following technological progress and a competitive market. It is also worth noting here that in Asia's "four dragons," this sort of statist liberalism proved to be the best ally of social justice. Absent authoritarian redistribution, income distribution in these places is in reality more equal than Sweden's!

The dividing line here is less between statism and market economy as between a true and erroneous conception of the role of the state. It could be said that by extending it everywhere, collectivist societies are, paradoxically, societies without a state, in the sense that the state gets involved in all the areas where it does not belong and loses its effectiveness in those very areas where it is needed. There always seems to be a great void where the state should be when administered or command economies fall apart. In its World Development Report for 1991, the World Bank confirmed its earlier reports by observing that competitive markets and improved productivity are the only real factors that matter for development, but it adds that the state must provide the judicial framework and the guarantees of law and order without which these factors cannot have the desired effect. If the states of the "miraculous" Pacific rim have intervened effectively in the economy, it is because their interventions were in the direction of the market. Still, the essential point is elsewhere. The essential point is that the state must—for it alone can—create conditions of security without which there can be no economic life, in particular no viable enterprises, because there is no confidence in long-term stability.

According to the Bank, domestic stability, on the average, augments a country's growth twice as much as does foreign aid. This estimate, which of course is very approximate, gains significance when you consider that "developing countries" have averaged, since 1948, about one coup attempt every five years. What foreign or local entrepreneur can work in such uncertain conditions? It is easy to gloss over the "selfishness" of finicky entrepreneurs who are ever ready to put their capital to "flight." If states were less inept, less corrupt, and less interfering, capital would stay home. Wars—I will return to this—and military spending also wipe out all efforts at economic take-off. A 1991 study of the International Monetary Fund criticized excesses in this area, showing that foreign aid always has had the effect of increasing military spending.

Also—and this should be germane in view of the current preoccupation with democracy—the less a state is democratic, the more of the national treasure it wastes on arms. This brake on economic development depends on the form of government: absolute monarchies lead in waste, followed by military dictatorships and by socialist dictatorships (a minor distinction in practice). Multiparty democracies spend the least, in percentage of GNP, on arms. Economic regressions by wars in the Third World are not due only to the fortunes spent on the arms with which to fight them. The regressions are prolonged by the losses caused by these wars. A ridiculous episode like the "soccer war" between El Salvador and Honduras, which was provoked by a game that turned sour in 1969, lasted exactly 100 hours. Two thousand people died. One hundred Salvadorans working in Honduras had to return home in a hurry to unemployment. Half of Salvador's oil refineries were destroyed. The "Central American Common Market" scheme was held up for years.

Developing countries and countries coming out of communism do not require a state that will administer the economy, but a good administration, competent and honest. In order to privatize and return to the free market, a state is needed to develop and pass legislation that can define property rights, legalize private property, and create incentives for the "logistics of privatization," which is to say the re-creation of the network of professions that are indispensable in a liberal economy: lawyers, accountants, investment bankers, financial advisers, and financiers. The real alternative is not between more state or less state. It is between a good state and a bad state. There can be no good state without a free market, and a market cannot function without a good state, which means a democratic state. There is no such thing as a pure market and no such thing as a pure state either. But their complementarity can emerge and become creative only within a framework of democratic capitalism.

It cannot be stated without qualifications that democracy is the necessary condition for economic take-off; but most of the evidence we have shows that where democracy is totally suppressed, there is no possible take-off. There must be some sphere of autonomy—hence, the beginning of a free economic space which is the market—which allows "civil society" to gain some independence vis à vis the state. It is this independence that allows both the economy and democratic institutions to grow. They help one another as are developed not only material wealth but voting rights, press freedom, the separation of powers, access to education, and human rights. From all this there follows a natural reduction of inequalities. As with all creation, economic creativity requires freedom to flourish. Also, by separating civil society from the state, the market forms the foundation of democracy. The market, by its nature, is a threat to totalitarian power and weakens all authoritarian power by diffusing decision making throughout society. Also, it is forced to forge links with the outside world, thereby putting an end to the isolation of the population on which absolute power depends. Democracy goes well beyond the market, of course, achieving dignity, morality, happiness. Democracy inverts the ancient relation between citizen and state: no longer does the state appropriate the citizens for itself; rather, the citizens create and control the state. These are banalities, but they were novel in the Third World and the countries coming out of communism in the 1980s. To live decently in a well-ordered society and to enjoy human rights in a free society were seen, at last, to represent two sides of the same aspirations.

It was, therefore, real progress in the Third World when the importance of democracy to development was understood. It is sometimes said, in explaining why it took so long for this to be seen, that Third World countries should not be judged by the same standards as Western societies, whose cultures ought not to be "imposed" on others. What does this mean? That the peoples of the Third World do not want to be prosperous? Despite much work in the past twenty, and especially the past ten, years on questions of development and political systems, not to mention simple common sense, the mutual interests of exploiters and imposters, of local tyrants and their Western accomplices, have resisted the demolishing of the Third Worldist mythology. The mix of guilt and ignorance suits too many people for it to go away easily. Those who went against the fashionable view of the Third World and the causes of its poverty had to take a great deal of insult and injury. Nonetheless, they got an idea across that is summarized thus by the French journalist Guy Sorman: "The poverty of nations is not a fatality; rather it is the consequence of bad policies founded on bad ideas." These were, simply put: underdeveloped countries were better served by centralized planning than by the market; dictatorships or fake democracies (so long as they were socialist) are better suited than are democracies to put such centralized planning into practice. And of course there was also the fantasy that the poverty of the Third World was due to looting of its resources by the rich nations, a fantasy that shifted the blame from corrupt and inept rulers to foreigners.

To see things clearly and finally get beyond the status quo, it is important to spell out the details of Third World despotism. Beyond abstract characterizations, however useful they may be conceptually, such as "patrimonial system," it is essential to understand that Lopez Portillo, president of Mexico from 1976 to 1982, had named his son Minister of the Budget, his mistress Minister of Tourism, his sister director of state television, his cousin director of the Cultural Development Fund.

Africa has suffered the most from Third Worldist fraud and the absence of democracy. Significantly, in the sixties the experts were predicting doom and disaster for Asia and saw in Africa a rather rosy future. As late as 1969, the World Bank-sponsored Pearson Commission observed that South Korea was condemned to permanent dependence on foreign aid. A few years later South Korea was reaching average annual growth rates of 5–10 percent. By 1990, India was exporting wheat to the Soviet Union and Romania; Thailand was selling rice to China; Indonesia had huge food surpluses. In twenty years, the Asian population grew by 50 percent and food production per capita grew by 20 percent. In black Africa, food production per capita dropped by 20 percent between 1975 and 1990. These contrasting results are both distressing and encouraging. For they show that despite a supposedly desperate situation, Asia did well; is there not reason to hope Africa can do the same?

What are the causes of Africa's slump, and how might they be addressed? There is no doubt that the drought has got much worse since 1980. Yet, although dryness can explain fluctuations in food production, it cannot explain its constant decrease since 1965! More harmful have been the armed conflicts, repressive regimes, violence that has exterminated populations or forced them into emigration. And while the resistance of African peasants to technological innovation has slowed progress, far more pernicious have been mistaken policies. African leaders, favoring industry over agriculture, which they taxed even as they fixed prices, in effect destroyed food production and condemned their countries to dependence on imports. Contrary to a widespread myth, it is not true that African agriculture was sacrificed to production for export, for that has been failing also. In 1965, 73 percent of the world's production of palm oil was African. In 1980, Africa produced only 27 percent, while Asia represented 68 percent of the world's production. Nigeria, the world's leading exporter of palm oil in 1960, is now an importer of palm oil. Eleven percent of the world's banana market was held by African countries in 1960; it was less than 4 percent at the beginning of the 1980s. The market is now dominated by Latin America and the Philippines. Similar regression can be noted in the production of cocoa, coffee, cotton.

The outstanding example of African socialism was Tanzania under the presidency of Julius Nyerere, who retired in 1985 after thirty years in power. Universally acclaimed as the "conscience of the Third World" and so forth, what he actually did was to provoke a 27 percent collapse in his country's agricultural production in the space of a generation. State farms for the employment of members of the president's party (the only one permitted), state monopolies for the distribution and sale of products, and incompetent and corrupt state grain brokerages discouraged farmers, who saw themselves forced to sell their grain at prices three or four times below what they could have got on the world market.

Indeed, a meeting of African economics ministers at Addis Ababa in May 1985 admitted that "African liberalism" might have been more appropriate than "African socialism."

Nevertheless, the democratic wave was slow to gather strength in Africa in the eighties. At the end of the decade, you can count six countries that have started on the democratic road, while in more than forty others the single party and the strongman are still the norm. Paradoxically, Namibia, a former German colony mandated to South Africa by the League of Nations in 1920, saw the first really free elections, under U.N. supervision, in 1989. Zambia had free elections in 1991, which resulted in the (peaceful) replacement of President Kaunda. South Africa has been moving toward democracy faster, or less slowly, than most other African countries. Ironically, the African National Congress, if it comes to power through democratic procedures may undermine democracy in that country because of its continuing adherence to statist control of the economy.

In Latin America there were only four dictatorships left by the mid-80s: two of the right (Chile and Paraguay) and two of the left (Nicaragua and Cuba). Five years later, only Cuba remained. The return to democracy in Nicaragua was the first time a communist regime had accepted the verdict of the ballot. The fall of Marcos in the Philippines in 1986, of Duvalier in Haiti the same year, elections in Pakistan and South Korea in 1988, all these trends reinforced the sense that democracy, after so many setbacks in the twentieth century, was once again the inspirational force of the modern world.

The interdependence of democracy and the market was understood in the Third World before it was grasped in the communist world. Another factor for development is, of course, education, not only in the sense of universal literacy, but in the appreciation of rigorous standards of logic, of respect for the truth, of the importance of accurate information. At the twenty-second summit of the Organization of African Unity in 1986, Edem Kodjo, former general secretary of this organization, put it this way: "We have avoided the issue of political reform. We must replace monolithic and oppressive autocracies with systems of liberty. There is no development without freedom of enterprise, without freedom of thought, without basic human rights." And, four years later, the Chilean economist Jose Pinera exclaimed: "There is no reason for misery on our continent. We are not a poor continent, we are a continent impoverished by our political leaders, trade unionists, businessmen, intellectuals, who have refused to accept that economic freedom is the necessary complement to political freedom as we strive for prosperity and peace."

From Africa to Latin America, the Third World was rejecting Third Worldism.

CHAPTER ELEVEN

IN PRAISE OF ELECTIONS

OR WHY IT IS BETTER TO BE RICH AND FREE THAN POOR AND OPPRESSED

Getting out of Third Worldism, like getting out of communism, means first of all liberating oneself of an ideology. Which already is a great deal, since man's most stubborn trait is his refusal to see the pernicious consequences of a favored idea. Man's unlimited capacity for suffering and failure caused by persistence in error argues in favor of his detachment from the world's material goods. Man is only too happy to sacrifice his own best interests to his prejudices. The fanatic does not die for his ideas, but of them. So to give up an ideology represents a supreme sacrifice, though, unfortunately, it is insufficient to furnish a substitute. To see an error and to correct it simultaneously happens only in the abstract, not in real life and even less in the life of societies, where errors and customs flowing out of them remain part of the landscape. It is therefore legitimate to ask whether certain societies realistically can make the transition to democracy, or whether they are stuck in the habits and mentalities of their own past. Similarly, how many societies can make the transition to economic rationality? As was seen throughout the eighties, it is one thing to adopt a liberal rhetoric, another to turn in into practice.

These questions lead to a well-known problem: Are there civilizations, religions, mentalities, that are incompatible with democracy or with economic modernization, or both? It would be foolish to say that a given human group is, in the abstract, predisposed against democracy and economic growth. The question is meaningful only if it is placed in the context of a specific historical moment, when the group in question can be appreciated for the institutional, cultural, technological environment in which it is. Also, depending on one's criteria, certain societies may be viewed as democratic from one point of view but not from another. Thus, it would seem that European society as a whole was closer to democracy in the eighteenth century than in the twelfth. As a general proposition, this seems evident. And yet, if you examine towns, it becomes evident that they were far more independent from the central authority in the twelfth century than in the eighteenth, and even in the nineteenth. Medieval cities often functioned as real democracies, and not necessarily for the benefit only of the rich. They enjoyed substantial autonomy, which they would lose in later centuries to the monarchical, imperial, pontifical, or even republican powers. They ran their affairs through debates among "citizens," or "bourgeois," and the accords among the social classes were often more respectful of their various needs and interests than would be the unilateral and distant decisions taken by monarchical administrations or republican bureaucracies. Political democracy is not necessarily impossible in societies where beliefs and hierarchies appear to a westerner to be founded on the worst kinds of intellectual and moral perversions, such as the caste system in India.

There is no doubt that in every Indian village, the dominant caste controls the vote, which is nominally by universal suffrage. But viewed whole, the Indian political system finds its balance, precisely, in the suffrage of 500 million voters, men and women, who, despite low levels of literacy, can judge which are the democratic parties.

Studies in electoral sociology in India have invalidated the notion that Western-style electoral institutions are merely "grafted," parodies without substance. They are that, certainly, where tyrannies violate the rules of democratic pluralism, where candidacies and choices are not free—which is to say almost everywhere. But the rape of democracy is not evidence that true democracy cannot work. "All of Indian history since 1947," writes Jean-Alphonse Bernard, "proves that political democracy has been the driving force of development." Unfortunately, the biggest export of the West to India (and the Third World generally) has not been parliamentary democracy but authoritarian state centralism. What Tocqueville already had attacked, administrative centralization, accompanied by a parasitical bureaucracy, rules in India as it does in most of the Third World. The growth of the public sector allows a new privileged class to drape itself in the pretext of social justice, at the expense of other sectors of the population that are less adept at defending themselves politically. In India there is a network of controls that multiply the opportunities for corruption and slow the implementation of decisions. According to Bernard, India's political problem is less a conflict between tradition and modernity than it is an excessive concentration of power at the center and the summit.

While this optimistic judgment is fair on the whole, I think it overlooks some of the inconveniences of tradition. On the day in 1957 when Nehru inaugurated India's first nuclear reactor—and it is worth noting that its technology was entirely imported, not invented—a child was kidnapped on a main road near Delhi and sacrificed to a local goddess.

Nonetheless, experience shows that elections always are valuable, if they are conducted honestly. And if they are followed by other elections. The people can fool themselves or be fooled; therefore, they must have the opportunity to effect corrections. The requirement of democratic consultations at regular intervals is one of the constitutive bases of democracy. Misanthropes have a point when they say Hitler came to power democratically in 1933. But they forget that after this victory, Hitler never gave the people another chance to express themselves. Democracy means always having a choice, it does not mean always making the right choice. There cannot be democracy if freedom of choice is not forever. "One man, one vote, once," as the ironic African saying goes, is not democracy, it is plebiscitary Caesarism, which, as historian Jerome Carcopino put it, consists of getting support from those whom you annihilate politically.

Despite doubts about the discernment of peoples with little political sophistication, one is often surprised by the sensible way in which they vote, when they are able to. Despite controls on information flows and the betrayal of their own elites, their judgments remain sound. As the late Venezuelan journalist Carlos Rangel used to say, whenever Latin Americans vote freely, they choose moderate parties of the center left or the center right. This suggests that Latin America's supposed extremism is imposed on them by elites, not freely chosen. It is worth recalling even today, because the example is so instructive, that despite the myths propagated by the European and North American lefts, the Chilean people in 1970 did not vote for the revolution proposed by Allende. In a three-way race, over 60 percent of the votes went to conservative candidates. Allende would have been well advised to respect this instead of trying to ram through unpopular radical changes that brought on the catastrophe of a military coup that cost him his life.

There are two kinds of elitism. There is the antidemocratic elitism of self-chosen elites, and there is meritocracy, founded on examination and competition. I am of course referring to the former here; it assumes the people do not know what they want and that in consequence they do not have to be consulted.

But people often enough see their own interests pretty clearly and know how to give voice to them. When the elites condescend to listen to them, they may well make choices that go against the desires and calculations of antidemocratic elites, throwing these pretentious mentors into a comical disarray. An outstanding example occurred in Nicaragua's elections in February 1990, when the Sandinistas were defeated. This defeat was so unexpected for some sensitive souls that some foreign correspondents were seen crying when the results were announced. Not a few of these had been in the country for months and even for years, which suggests that their ability to observe their own surroundings was somewhat atrophied. For whatever one might have thought of the dictator Anastasio Somoza, overthrown by the Sandinistas in 1979, and however pernicious his regime may have been, the fact was that ten years of rule by the "nine comandantes," referred to derisively as the "nine somozas," had left ordinary Nicaraguans far worse off. Nicaragua's economy was the worst in the hemisphere, with a standard of living below that of Haiti. Consumption had dropped by 70 percent. Salaries—in terms of purchasing power—had fallen by 92 percent! Inflation was out of control: a dollar got you a thousand *cordobas* in January 1989, thirty thousand in June. Nicaragua, a small country that had never had a military draft, had seen its army grow from fifteen thousand to eighty thousand men and the Sandinistas claimed they wanted six hundred thousand men under arms, which would have meant virtually every able-bodied male. Four hundred thousand, in a population of two and a half million, had chosen exile. Against all this misery, the opulence of the communist nomenklatura and its friends from abroad, called the *internationalistas*, was blatant and shameless, with the Sandinistas occupying the homes of Somoza and his cronies.

While the anticommunists and Nicaragua's neighbors, notably the presidents of Costa Rica and the U.S., demanded free elections to test the Sandinistas' legitimacy, the international Left neglected to press the issue. Even the Socialist International, which after all was not committed, as far as anyone knew, to single-party dictatorships, supported the nonelected junta in Nicaragua. But given its accomplishments, the surprise is that the results of the elections surprised anyone.

Yet even before the polls closed, French television was saying the Sandinistas had won. On Monday morning, as the ballots were being counted, the BBC World Service predicted a Sandinista victory by 52 percent. Weeks earlier, the *Economist* had given 51 percent to the Sandinista leader, Daniel Ortega, against 24 percent for his opponent, Violeta Chamorro. The real results: 55.2 percent for Chamorro, 40.8 percent for Ortega. Even the ultra-serious *Frankfurter Allgemeine Zeitung* had foreseen a 60–30 victory for Ortega! As early as January, the Gallup organization and a reliable Venezuelan opinion survey institute had discerned a strong anti-Sandinista trend, but most foreign observers (governments as well as journalists) had fallen for the surveys commissioned by the Sandinistas themselves. Obviously, their error was rooted in a profound misunderstanding of the situation in Nicaragua.

First error: the U.S. had opposed the Sandinistas from the start (just why this should absolve them from their despotic rule is another issue). False: the U.S. supported the Sandinistas and gave them economic aid in 1979–80; it opposed the consolidation of a pro-Soviet dictatorship.

Second error: the contras were creatures of the CIA and were former Somozistas. False again: the CIA helped the contras, but they sprang up on their own, peasants in rebellion against the Sandinista confiscations of their produce and the military draft. Nine contras out of ten, particularly from 1985 on, were children when Somoza fell.

Third error: the failure of socialism in Nicaragua was due to the civil war and the American-imposed embargo. False: the war was bankrolled entirely by the Soviet Union. The embargo could have hurt exports, but it could not explain the internal misery in a country that traditionally had a rich agricultural sector. Indeed, Nicaragua had an agricultural surplus worth $106 million in 1987, though no one, except the nine "comandantes" knows where the money went.

The list could go on, but let us hear one more: Violeta Chamorro's victory was due to American money. It is correct that the U.S. Congress very openly and officially provided for $3.3 million in aid to her campaign. However, while the media hammered away at this, they neglected to mention that the Sandinistas blocked currency movements, which meant the Chamorro campaign only received two hundred thousand dollars in time to make any use of it! Meanwhile, the Sandinistas had been receiving between $3 and $4 billion annually from the Soviets. Throughout the campaign, the opposition was virtually clandestine, whereas the regime was everywhere.

Neither side was perfect, to be sure. But why were the free world's media so determined to prove the anti-Sandinista opposition could not possibly be democratic or represent the aspirations of the people? Why did the media, the Socialist International, Amnesty International close their eyes and ears for ten years whenever there was evidence that human rights were being violated by the Sandinistas, or even that they were committing crimes against humanity? Already in October 1983, two ex-Sandinistas, Leon Nunez and Zacarias Hernandez, had been invited by a Paris-based organization, *Résistance Internationale*, to discuss some of these issues. The French government, at the time run by a Socialist-Communist coalition, would not grant them visas. In June 1991, Sandinista killing fields were discovered. Public opinion had been told for ten years that the Sandinistas respected human rights. That this was a lie is a further argument that elections are indispensable.

All the more so as the Nicaraguan people drew conclusions from the Sandinistas' failure that were not only sensible, but moderate. With over 40 percent of the votes, Ortega's party was out of power, but remained an important factor in the country's political life. The voters did not want a purge or a violent reaction or a new dictatorship: they wanted multiparty democracy. Their democratic sense was superior to that of most of the traditional elites, which have a tendency to use their victories at the polls to try to eliminate their adversaries and consign them to the political margins.

No matter the factors that can skew an electoral verdict (leaving aside out-and-out fraud), including for example one-sided propaganda, misleading slogans, a poorly informed and credulous population, it is the rare election that does not bring out fresh teachings that even the sharpest analyses would not have perceived. Good analysis can point toward possible directions—in France, for example, from 1983 the rise of the extreme right; but only elections can provide a real map of what is going on. Opinion polls are done with great precision, but real elections often shake them up in unexpected ways. Even when elections confirm opinion polls, they give the latter an irrefutable validity, and they also bring additional information the polls did not pick up. For example, the "illegal" referendum (read: not wanted by Gorbachev) that was held in Lithuania on 9 February 1991 with a participation of 84.4 percent, and 90.5 percent of the ballots cast favoring independence, showed two things. First, there was even more pro-independence feeling than many believed, including the local communists or ex-communists. Next, and this was more surprising, the numbers showed that the non-Lithuanian minorities (Russians, Ukrainians, Belorussians, Poles) also had voted for independence. Which indicated that these groups did not fear, as Gorbachev claimed, being oppressed in an independent Lithuania. The reason for this resided probably in their desire to get out of the sinking raft that was the Soviet Union and gravitate, with an independent Lithuania, toward the Western economic world. Only elections could show this perfectly realistic consideration.

This lesson was reinforced in the "illegal" referenda which followed, in Estonia and Latvia, in March. For here the indigenous population was far smaller, due to deportations and murders by the Soviets over the years, and a policy of forcibly sending Russian settlers: only 52 percent of the population of Latvia is Latvian; 60 percent of Estonia is Estonian. Nonetheless, over 73 percent voted for independence in Lativa, nearly 78 percent in Estonia (with participation levels of 88 percent and 83 percent). Even (or especially) in the West, the expectation had been that the Russians would vote against independence.

It would be easy to harp on Gorbachev's success in his own referendum on 17 March 1991. Three out of four voters said yes to his question on whether they wanted to stay in the Union. Yet the result is surprising when put next to the fact that in the preceding year, the fifteen republics belonging to the Soviet Union had declared their desire for independence from the central power. But the contradiction clears up when the text of Gorbachev's referendum question is read: "Do you believe it is necessary to conserve the USSR as a renovated federation of equal and sovereign states, in which human rights and the liberties of all the nationalities will be fully guaranteed?" The question was thus framed in such a way that it had to receive an affirmative response from conservatives wishing to preserve the Union, as well as from reformers who wanted the opposite, that is to say the sovereignty of the republics and the self-determination of the nationalities. But as soon as the result was in, the Kremlin concluded that the Soviet voters had simply approved "maintaining the Union." Suddenly, there was no longer any talk of sovereignty, equality among the republics, liberty for the nationalities. Indeed, the Kremlin announced that the referendum would be constraining for all the republics, including the six that had not taken part in the vote. These were the ones that had always considered themselves foreign to the Soviet Union, victims of forced annexations. As to the others, did they want to "maintain the Union" or did they want a federation of equals that rejected the authority of the central authority, the heritage of Stalinism? The ambiguity was inevitable, given the way the question had been put.

These loaded questions are not a new ruse in plebiscites. In 1870, Napoleon III asked the French public to ratify the following proposition: "The people approve the liberal reforms instituted in the Constitution by the Emperor since 1860." Everyone had to vote yes: republicans who were for the reforms but against the emperor; and the Bonapartist party, which was pro-emperor but antireform. There was no alternative.

Elections can go in any direction, including against democracy. Even here, they provide invaluable instruction. Thus, it was with some astonishment that Albania was seen, in March and April of 1991, to vote by a majority of two to three for the Communists. In the preceding months, the pathetic sight of Albanian boat people abandoning everything as they tried to reach Italy, suggested that in a free election there would be a clear rejection of the ruling Communists. This indeed occurred in the cities, but not in the countryside. Sixty percent of Albania's people are still on the land—twice as many as in France or Italy in 1945. Surrounded by communists and knowing no others, since no other party had the time to organize outside the cities, the peasantry voted conservatively. Also, the rural and urban votes in this country corresponded to specific ethnic allegiances. Add the votes of the army, the police, and the party members, and the Albanian result is understandable. During the preceding year, the Albanian communists had changed their name, following the current East European fashion, and had taken care to give to each peasant family a plot of land and a cow. During the campaign, they claimed that the opposition social democrats were the party of the prewar landlords who would confiscate the plots of land and the cattle from the peasants. The ill-informed and inexperienced electorate fell for this shabby electoral ruse, but the following summer the

Albanian boat people were at it again, trying to reach Italy because there was no food at home: voting with their feet.

The practice of democracy requires a minimum of information, and people dulled by long years of censorship require political education. In order to make a choice, you need to have some comparative references. An instructive example of what this means took place during the first general elections of reunified Germany, 2 December 1990. At first sight, the principal electoral debate was between the Christian Democrats under Helmut Kohl and the Social Democrats under Oskar Lafontaine and their respective conceptions of German reunification. The environmentalists, or Greens, had no reason to fear they would lose ground, since protection of the environment had become a sacred cause in the West, practically on a par with human rights. But after the fall of the Berlin Wall in 1989, a striking fact had made a powerful impression on Western minds: pollution in communist countries was unbelievable, incomparably worse than anything seen in the West; and of these, the former DDR, or East Germany, won the championship as destroyer of nature.

This apocalypse—for it was nothing less, literally as well as metaphorically—made voters realize that the Greens had been lying. For their virulent campaigns had pointed the finger only at the capitalist countries, and their main interest was Western unilateral disarmament. Their real aim was to put ecology in the service of pacifism—but a pacifism that would only apply to the democracies. The ecologist fraud reached an apogee of sorts during the catastrophe at Chernobyl in 1986. For though the most serious nuclear accident ever occurred in the Soviet Union, it was against the Western nuclear installations that our pacifists and ecologists protested. The Greenpeace organization did not utter a word about Chernobyl. The German Greens, assembled at Hanover, denounced NATO as the "main cause of the arms race and of the dangers to world peace." They demanded the abolition of the German army, the police, and the counter-intelligence services (not a word about the East German or Soviet ones). In Holland, the Socialist leader Joop Den Uyl campaigned under the slogan: "No missiles or reactors." In Great Britain and the U.S., nuclear programs under way were indefinitely put on hold. The Western press announced uncritically that the accident could have occurred anywhere, which was false. All the experts agreed: the Soviet installation was built without protective confinement and in criminally insecure conditions. In fact, it was learned in 1991 that a no less shoddily built reactor was operating in Bulgaria and threatened the planet with a radioactive explosion. The Bulgarians then had the nerve to say that they would shut it down only if the West built them a new one for free! Liberated Eastern Europe still had a highly developed habit—learned under communism—of parasitism and irresponsibility. (When the Chernobyl reactor melted down, it took the Soviet authorities several days to mention the risks posed by the radioactive cloud.)

Thanks to *glasnost*, it was the Soviets themselves, three years later, who gave us the appalling truth about the environmental and human devastation caused by the Chernobyl accident. Thus the Soviets unmasked our heretofore silent ecologists. At this point the Western press took up the theme. For example, in April 1990 the popular monthly *Geo* gave its millions of French and German readers a crushing report, "Disaster in the Soviet Union," on Chernobyl and other eco-disasters in the East. The powerful, widely read, and influential German weekly *Der Spiegel* called its 8 January 1990 cover story on East German pollution, "The Poisoned Kitchen."

A few comparisons with the "capitalist" countries give an idea of the state of the environment in the ex-DDR. It major river, the Elbe, carries eight times more mercury and one hundred times more dangerous pesticides than the Rhine. The earth too is affected: in certain regions the ground is so contaminated that even earthworms are becoming extinct. The yield of the overfertilized lands of East Germany is half of those in West Germany, in spite of the latter's strict limitations on the use of chemical fertilizers. Another eloquent comparison is the electro-power center at Boxberg, with its coal furnaces: it puts more dioxide in the atmosphere than all the electrical power centers of Denmark and Norway combined. The chemical factory at Buna (near Halle) dumps more mercury into the river Saale every day than that West German industrial giant, Bast, dumps in the Rhine every year. These facts were shown on countless television programs. Viewers had never seen such filthy water, fetid smog, dense smoke, toxic ashes swirling in the air, waste dumped in empty lots and on beaches as far as anyone could see. In April 1990, the European Community's environment ministers—by then to no one's surprise—called East Germany the "most polluted country in the world," and Bitterfeld (a city of thirty thousand, 175 kilometers south of Berlin) the "most polluted city in the world."

Reading such reports, how could the German voter still have any faith at all in the Greens? Their most bitter enemy scarcely needed any public relations help to demolish their credibility. Nature itself, if I may say so, took care of that.

Even a vast country like China, which has relatively little industry and 61 percent of whose population (in 1986) was still on the land, is one of the worst cases of pollution and destruction of nature. Lack of data—and of curiosity—caused the Western media to come late to an environmental catastrophe that, as *Time* put it in a cover story in 1991, had brought the country to the edge of no-return. It is apparently one of the mysteries of socialism that it manages to pollute as much as it does even as it produces so little.

Often, it is harder for universal suffrage to make itself heard than to express itself. Since 1982, the people of El Salvador were sending a constant and unequivocal message to the governments and foreign observers kind enough to pay attention: namely, that they are, by majorities that regularly attain 80 percent, opposed to the guerrillas of the Farabundo Marti Front. Each time the latter has called on people to boycott an election, they have turned out in record numbers to vote either for the Christian Democrats or the right-wing Arena. A call to boycott, for the great democrats of the Front, has meant an order to gun down people waiting in line at polling places. It would therefore seem that the least that can be said for these voters is that they take their civic duty seriously, since they risk their lives to perform it. Yet the international Left, including the Socialist International, for ten years persisted in seeing in the Front the representative of the "people." Somehow, the parties that over and over got overwhelming majorities of the votes did not qualify. One way to keep this skewed perspective was to insist the elections were fraudulent. But from 1982 this tiny country never voted without an army of foreign observers on hand, and these never noticed more than marginal fraud. Finally in the legislative and municipal elections of 1991, the Front had the magnanimity to let people vote without being shot at. The Salvadorans proceeded to give over 44 percent of their votes to the ruling Arena (National Republican Alliance), 28 percent to the Christian Democrats, and 9 percent to the conservative National Conciliation party—over 81 percent for the parties that somehow did not express the "people," while 12 percent went to the party supported by the Front. This seems to be a clear vote; yet the BBC and *Le*

Monde, to take two examples, described the elections as "victories" or "strong showings" for the Left!

At any rate, despite what its supporters in the foreign press said, the Front did not consider the elections to have been a success since it denounced them as fraudulent. Yet, the Organization of American States had sent one hundred observers to monitor every aspect of the election. The "Democratic Convergence" supported by the Front did indeed progress a little, but it was perfectly obvious that the single great message of the vote was that the people were fed up with the guerrillas. Within a few months, following the cessation of Soviet aid to Cuba and therefore of Cuban aid to the Salvadoran guerrillas, the Farabundo Marti Front negotiated a cease-fire with the government, and one of its main clauses was to fold the guerrillas into the national police.

In these cases, universal suffrage expressed itself straightforwardly because the information needed to make a clear choice was right there. But matters are not always so simple. Democracy is founded on information, but information is often founded on deceit, confusion, or at least an ambiguity that misleads voters.

Suffrage can be abused by demagogues—often with the help of voters' apathy. This weakness is inherent to democracy. It was spotted by the best minds of fifth and fourth century B. C. Athens. Without as much practical experience of democracy as they had, Jean-Jacques Rousseau asked in *The Social Contract* whether "the General Will can err." Two centuries of democratic experimentation provide the answer: Of course it can err—but not for abstract reasons. Democracy errs and is abused for concrete reasons, which have to do with the impossibility of always making all the information available to voters that is necessary for sound decisions. Add to this the propensity of political rhetoricians, today called "charismatic leaders" or "media favorites," to take advantage of their audiences. When you consider how easily this happens in advanced democracies, with high levels of education and abundant and varied media, it is easy to imagine how readily more backward populations, who do not benefit from a vigorous free press, can fall for these inconveniences. I must insist here, incidentally, that illiteracy as such will not prevent people from making sound judgments when the choices are clear. Indeed, they often show much better judgment than intellectuals in advanced countries. They are perfectly able to draw the lessons of their experience; in particular they know how to tell a failed regime or party to quit. But it is more difficult for them to make a choice for the future. Thus, in the Peruvian presidential election of 1990, the people clearly saw it was time to get rid of the ruling party, Alan Garcia's APRA, a nominally social democratic party that had lurched into collectivism with catastrophic economic consequences. Thus, so long as the contest was between the APRA's designated candidate and the free-market party organized around the novelist Mario Vargas Llosa, there was little doubt about the outcome. But then there appeared a third-party candidate: Alberto Fujimori, a Peruvian whose parents were Japanese. He appeared to come from nowhere, though in reality he was secretly aided by APRA, which was determined to block Vargas Llosa.

Fujimori proposed an economic recovery without pain, that is to say without the austerity measures that Vargas Llosa said were rendered inevitable by the disastrous policies of the past few years. Economically unsophisticated, a majority of Peruvians naturally preferred this; it was only too easy to let them think, also, as Fujimori did, that if he were elected Japanese credits would rain down on the country. The Peruvians, who surely deserved better, fell for it and elected Fujimori.

Nonetheless, there was one factor that remained constant throughout these misfortunes, and this is the rejection by the voters of the party of the sitting president, with its cronyism, its statism, and its socialism. Vargas Llosa's eventual failure did not translate into any sort of comeback for Alan Garcia, who was knocked out in the first round of voting. Both second-round candidates favored a return to the free market; the difference was that one said it would include some pain while the other claimed it could be painless. In short, the voters were perfectly able to assess for themselves the meaning of the APRA years. On the other hand, they were susceptible to demagogic messages regarding the country's future and the policies that would have to be adopted to save the country. As soon as it is a matter of making judgments about the future, people become gullible.

The gullibility of Peru's voters quickly turned to bitterness after Fujimori's election. The crisis was so deep that the new president found himself forced to apply Vargas Llosa's program, with the aid of several of the latter's advisers and with a brutality that turned out to be all the more brutal for being unexpected. Indeed, as soon as he was elected, Fujimori asked for help from Hernando de Soto, the economist who had revived classical liberal thinking in Peru and, in fact, throughout Latin America. De Soto's classic, *The Other Path* (1986), had been prefaced by Vargas Llosa; and his Institute for Liberty and Democracy, which he had founded in 1979, was the center of Latin American classical liberalism. Fujimori even offered de Soto the job of prime minister in July 1990, but he turned it down while remaining an unofficial adviser. By February 1991, several policies advocated by de Soto, favoring liberalization and deregulation of the economy, were before the legislature in the form of bills: they were chiefly concerned with making it easier for peasants to own land, and for entrepreneurs to start businesses, as well as tariff reductions. At the same time, the director of the Institute for Liberty and Democracy, Carlos Bolona, became finance minister. Thus, Vargas Llosa's "liberal solution" was being applied, willy-nilly, by his rival.

The same sort of confusion affects voting in countries trying to get out of communism and its consequences. So long as it is a matter of signifying clearly their rejection of the totalitarian system, the voters express themselves with lucidity because they know what they are talking about and they know what they have experienced. No amount of demagoguery can deceive them on this score. In Hungary, in Poland, in Czechoslovakia, in the DDR, the former communist parties, even with new "socialist" labels, received deep humiliations. Even in the Soviet Union this was clear in the elections of March 1989—even though these were not based on universal suffrage—and those for the presidency of the Russian Republic in June 1991. But it was another matter when it came to choosing among diverse programs for political and economic reconstruction. Here, the lack of well-organized opposition parties and the poor preparation of the voters, after decades of vegetation in the totalitarian night, hampered voters' understanding of their own problems.

In any event, the tendency to fall for illusions, the desire to reconcile opposites, is not a characteristic only of so-called underdeveloped ex-communist countries. It is also quite common in established democracies, whose intellectual founders were well aware of the problem. In the late eighteenth century, for example, Jeremy Bentham in opposition to Rousseau affirmed that it was perfectly possible for majorities to err grievously. Nevertheless, he argued that over the long term majority opinion, so long as it is given the opportunity to correct past errors, is the surest indicator of the public interest.

This utilitarian optimism should overcome the objections of skeptics who maintain that voters in poor countries are too "ignorant" to make good use of the ballot. History is full of examples of "enlightened" despots whose mistakes were far more catastrophic than the occasional errors brought on through universal suffrage.

There is, on the other hand, a more serious problem in democracy than the supposed incompetence of the masses (and for that matter the elites) to govern wisely. This is the unwillingness of the majority to respect the rights of the minorities and, perchance, trade places with them. The reluctance to compromise, and to permit peaceful transitions of power, is probably democracy's gravest problem.

Friends and defenders of democracy generally start from the principle that the threats against it or the barriers to its development always come from above: states, military establishments, religious leaders, "money," parties with monolithic ambitions. This is a belief deeply anchored in our democratic culture and in the romantic vision of the fight for liberty. Unfortunately, it must be recognized that people—ordinary people, in their legions—are intolerant and opposed to pluralism, human rights (others'), freedom of expression, and even universal suffrage! This is a fact and it should not be avoided.

After all, the Nazi and fascist phenomena, including Argentinian Perónism, grew out of powerful popular movements. The book-burning riots directed at Salman Rushdie's *The Satanic Verses* were the work of British citizens, who had not yet heard the Ayatollah Khomeini's order, since it had not yet been issued, to kill the author. The 1989 elections in Sri Lanka resulted in hundreds of deaths—not because they were fraudulent, but because they were fair and the losing minority refused to accept the verdict of the polls.

In this regard, the democratic education of the West was not so very different. The street riots that shake places like South Korea and the Philippines and Pakistan are scarcely worse than the historically sacred "revolutionary days" that regularly bloodied the streets of Paris from 1789 to the Commune of 1871. Even granting that this violence grows out of oppression, the question is whether the rioters really aimed for a pluralistic democracy or for their own dictatorship. Even thinkers close to the humble masses have had their doubts; it was Simone Weil, who uttered this blasphemy: "The oppressed in revolt never were able to found a society that was not oppressive."

In the years following the establishment of universal suffrage in France and Great Britain, the vote was not used heavily by the masses.

The "people"—followed in this by the "revolutionaries" of 1968—saw in elections a trick designed to prevent them from seizing power and establishing their own dictatorship. They viewed the vote as a way to channel violence away from the final battle. Much maturity is required, much time, much trial and error, and much learning of good manners, before a society learns to accept the prosaic but redeeming value of the suffrage. Moreover, it takes time even in an established democracy to accept that power not only can only be acquired by the ballot (and not the bullet), but that it must be shared with the side that lost the last time. A self-confident democracy will even, sometimes, associate the opposition in the work of the government, if only to avoid sordid settlings-of-scores during transitions. This can be seen in the U.S., in Great Britain, in Sweden, and even in Italy. In less pluralistic democracies such as France or Spain, the legal conquest of power is followed by the hounding of the opposition out of all the positions of power where it had a foothold, including positions in the media that are directly or indirectly controlled by the state. This is a moderate substitute for execution, jailing, or banishment of opponents.

Universal suffrage can be pitiless, sparing the losers' lives but destroying their careers. This led certain classical theorists, in a spirit of toleration, to suggest that regimes of limited suffrage were more effective at establishing a fair balance of power among the various groups that compose society. Walter Bagehot, author of *The English Constitution* (1867), observed the coming of universal suffrage with the following comment: "Until now England has been a free country; it is going to be a democratic one." This was scarcely an exaggeration, for even in mature democracies it is often forgotten that winning elections confers the right to exercise power, not keep it all for oneself. Yet the latter, unfortunately, is what all too often happens. In a classic expression of what might be called the "primitive mentality" in democratic evolution, the Socialist deputy Andre Laignel—though a professor of constitutional law at the University of Paris—addressed the opposition, during a parliamentary session, with the following words: "You are legally wrong because you are politically in the minority!" In this view of things, the majority party forgets that it is one part of society. It is tempted to consider itself all of society, if only temporarily, and then to make the temporary permanent. In a description of Felipe Gonzalez's hold of power in Spain that could define the French Socialists as well, it was said that "he is a politician who has put the state in the service of his party."

Here again, the ancient Greeks had seen the problem and analyzed it. In the anonymous "Constitution of Athens," which has been attributed to Xenophon and which dates from about 425 B.C., democracy is said to lead to the hegemony of one group—the demos, or "popular classes"—over all the others. Pseudo-Xenophon argues that democracy is no less intolerant than oligarchy. It wants to destroy its opponents, and indeed in the following century Demosthenes, reputed a "moderate," demanded that even those citizens who were inclined toward oligarchy be deprived of their rights and excluded from the Assembly. This brings to mind the so-called law of the suspects, which the Jacobins passed in September 1793 and which provided for the elimination of people merely suspected of having sympathy for tyranny. And Plato and Aristotle too grappled, each in his own way, with this real, but not insurmountable, democratic contradiction.

True democracy is not the tyranny of the majority. It is power sharing—primarily by the limitation of executive power by the legislative and judiciary branches of government. Power is shared, also, because of the existence of opposition parties, whose opinions on public affairs must be accorded respect. Finally, a printed press and other media, independent of government and parties, provide still another check on power. When these different elements come together instead of staying apart from one another, they result in dictatorship, either overtly or, more frequently, under the cover of a sham democracy. Separation of powers, party pluralism, and freedom of information are the conditions of democracy—and of development. This is the only system that, under the rule of law, provides at one and the same time for an efficient executive and the possibility of dismissing it. It is the only system that can prevent those who control the state from taking the national wealth for their own use. It is the only system that guarantees the autonomy of the civil society, which is the source of all economic creativity. The experience of history tells us over and over: as a way of running society, democracy is better than dictatorship not only from a moral point of view, but from a practical one as well.

Now the idea of sharing power is precisely what is rejected in the Third World, both by the elites and by the masses. For example, in Africa, in the Maghreb no less than south of the Sahara, the fight for democracy is not between authoritarian regimes and people devoted to liberty. The people do not appear to be taken with liberty any more than their dictators—they seem no more able to imagine and accept diversity: and liberty is, above all, diversity. This is the cause of their persistent poverty, for wealth cannot be created without a diversity of economic initiative. There may be something in Islam, on the one side, and in tribalism, on the other, which favors political intolerance; at any rate, "power is not shared in the African mind," as *Le Monde*'s Jacques de Barrin put it.* The same could be said of wealth, and it was with complete candor that the commission charged with writing a new constitution for Nigeria in 1976 defined the aim of politics as the opportunity to acquire wealth.

In Cameroon, it is said of someone who got a government position that he "is getting grub," and of someone who loses such a job, that he is "losing his grub." It is scarcely surprising that poverty is on the increase in this environment, and it is somewhat abstract to debate whether or not Africa is "ready" for political pluralism so long as the economic consequences of a single-party system are not appreciated. Sub-Saharan Africa, South Africa excepted, has a GNP equivalent to Belgium's. The real danger to Africa is not the mythological "neo-colonialism" upon which its despots from Algeria to Zaire continue to blame their own incompetence, but the very real possibility that it will find itself completely outside the increasingly unified global economy, in which it will have fewer and fewer products to sell and less and less means to buy. There is no mystery here. Africa has been destroyed by civil wars, the consequence of the African notion of power in which sharing it is inconceivable. Permanent intertribal warfare has been Africa's lot since independence. Angola and Mozambique, as soon as they acquired theirs from Portugal in 1975, began the massacres and the destruction of anything like a stable agriculture. The civil war in Nigeria cost two million lives between 1967 and 1970. Countries, tribes, religions, dictators—there seems no end of the ways Africans find to ravage their lands and decimate one another.

Masters at blaming others for their troubles, the Africans claim the ex-colonial powers left them with artificial states in which rival ethnic groups are forced to coexist against their will. And, they add, the same powers either prop up regimes that serve their interests, or finance and support guerrilla groups that attempt to bring down the

---

* Jacques de Barrin in *Le Monde*, 19 October 1991.

governments in place. Both accusations are valid (and can be applied to the Soviet Union, the U.S., and South Africa, as well as to France and Great Britain). But what sort of frontiers could the ex-colonial powers leave? Should they have created as many states as there are tribes? This would not have stopped the intertribal wars, particularly since tribes that regularly have tried to exterminate each other, such as the Hutus and the Tutsis of Burundi, live on the same territory. It is usually the governments that are threatened by rebels that appeal for foreign intervention. The intertribal massacres in Liberia in 1990 were not due to any sort of foreign intervention, but only to the ambitions of local gangsters. Ideological dictatorships, in such places as Maputo or Addis Ababa, were always caused by the reluctance of the local Marxists to share power or hold internationally supervised elections.

At the end of the twentieth century, Africa is the area which, next to Afghanistan, can make the dubious boast of having the most refugees. In 1991, nearly one out of every two refugees in the world was Afghan, but there were nearly as many African refugees. Liberia, Somalia, and Togo added starving hordes to these numbers in 1990 and 1991. They are the tragic symptoms of failures which are almost invariably political in nature.

In the African political culture, endless warfare and the statist smothering of the economy are part of the same conception of power. Without grasping this, one cannot understand the ruin to which Africa has come. The prodigious intellectual efforts that are deployed to mask this fact would be comic if they were not pernicious. They attempt to blame Africa's problems on everything except human action, as if history were made by anything but men. The U.S.-based Worldwatch Institute publishes well-documented monographs on global environmental and demographic trends. But its concern to blame all catastrophes on environmental degradation and overpopulation leads it to a reading of history in which no room is left for human action. In one paper, "Reversing Africa's Decline," Lester R. Brown and Edward C. Wolf blame said decline on the deterioration of the natural environment, soil erosion, deforestation, desertification, and changes in the climate—due, according to the authors, to excessive population growth. It is as if a historian explained Europe's disastrous situation in 1945 by reference to a succession of hard winters since 1939, or summer heat waves, or mysterious population movements due to demographic surges, and without mentioning any form of causality more tragically and directly rooted in human initiatives, decisions, and actions—including military operations, bombings, deportations, exterminations. The natural causes of misery that Worldwatch so ably catalogues are real, but the effects that the institute connects to them are in fact due to African politics. Uganda's excellent coffee, which at one time was highly prized, has purely and simply disappeared from the world market—not because of soil erosion but because of Idi Amin. Between 1967 and 1979, the dictator exterminated the peasants who knew how to grow it and drove out the merchants who knew how to export it. The rest is words.

Of course poverty caused or worsened by despotism is not unique to Africa. According to a United Nations study issued in August 1991, the cost to Iran of its war with Iraq in the 1980s was on the order of a trillion dollars. Add to this the consequences of the repressive stupidity of the mullahs, it is understandable that in twelve years of Islamic government, between 1979 and 1991, the Iranian standard of living was reduced by a half, and a quarter of the active population found itself without work. Loss of life must have reached—no one is sure—several hundred thousands. As to Iraq, which started the war, its natural riches should have made it one of the world's most prosperous nations, but it too found itself at the end of the conflict impoverished with no clear result. Then it ruined itself thoroughly by starting the Gulf War by its invasion and rape of Kuwait. Among the victims of this criminal expedition are the four hundred thousand Palestinians who were living in Kuwait; they lost all they had and went off to Jordan to starve. The entire Persian Gulf region, which could be one of the most flourishing on the planet, instead has been turned into a field of ruins—not because of vast, complex, and mysterious historical or economic processes, nor because of Western imperialism, but because of dreadful decisions taken in Iran and Iraq by a handful of tyrants lacking the slightest legitimacy.

In Southeast Asia, Bangladesh—consistently succored by international and nongovernmental organizations—had little chance of taking off so long as its political culture subsisted. Since its birth in 1971, when it seceded from Pakistan, this country's political life has been dominated by coups d'état. Whoever was president killed off his political adversaries until he too was assassinated. Finally there was progress in 1991 and more or less honest elections took place, though the losing side announced it would not recognize the results. While it is surely true that Bangladesh finds itself in an exceptionally violent climatic zone, it would be doing its dictators a service to explain the country's problems only by referring to the cyclones that have often devastated it. Another pathetic and absurd case can be seen in Sri Lanka, whose economic growth from 1977 to 1984 was broken by the revolt of the Tamils and their interminable and murderous struggles against the Singhalese.

The ideological biases of modern social science, with its predilection for abstract and impersonal models, have tended to eliminate human causality from historical and sociological analyses—and to eliminate, in particular, the notion of power. Despite the evidence provided in our century by such giant experiments as the Nazi cataclysm in Germany, Fascist Italy, Islamic fundamentalism in Iran, not to mention the Soviet Union and Communist China, we still find it difficult to face the idea that countries and, indeed, entire continents, might be devastated, their populations starved and decimated, and civilizations annihilated, as a result of the kind of power that is held there. And yet, that is the main reason for most of our misfortunes.

There are two kinds of underdevelopment: inherited and induced. The former is not, strictly speaking, underdevelopment; rather, it is nondevelopment, or predevelopment. It is the level of preindustrial economies. Their productivity is low, but they have an agricultural base, arts and crafts, trades, commerce, all of which function in a coherent if fragile way, vulnerable to climatic upheavals or epidemics. These economies do not need to be repaired but helped to grow, or to evolve by helping them connect with the factors that lead to growth. These factors are political and cultural as much as they are economic and technological. The West's own story over the past two centuries, with the spread of literacy, democratization of life, innovation, investments, demonstrates that this road to development is slow. However, in spite of crises and regressions, it works.

By contrast, induced underdevelopment is the consequence of the authoritarian application of a false economic doctrine, which is to say wilful error compounded by a rejection of democracy, which makes it impossible to correct the error. This pernicious combination can send advanced countries back into underdevelopment, as happened in Argentina, Czechoslovakia, East Germany. Applied to the traditionalist societies of the Third World, it breaks their strengths and confuses them without providing the factors needed for the take-off that leads to a growth economy. Most of the countries that we call underdeveloped destroyed the traditional forms of economic organization without introducing the modern ones and thus find themselves in a dead end. The destruction of traditional agriculture in favor of collectivization has proven to be the most grotesque of calamities, worsened in many cases by megalomaniacal projects of heavy industrial development, due to idiotic imitation of Stalinist perversity. How many "underdeveloped" countries have thus been banished simultaneously from both past and present by a handful of sectarian leaders! They can at best vegetate in one of history's empty lots, where tradition has been uprooted and where the future cannot grow.

These countries can be classified in several categories, according to the degree to which they are marked by the disease that sapped their resources. Very few remain whose governments, usually antidemocratic, left them a chance to recover the elements that could put in place the conditions for growth, following the stages of development followed by the West. One of the nostrums of Third Worldism consists of saying that these civilizations should never have imitated the Western capitalistic model, and that to recommend they do so is Eurocentric arrogance. Perhaps. But in that case, why follow another model, no less Western—the communist model, or at best the authoritarian socialist model (or simply a bureaucratic command economy)? If you are not going to imitate the West, then why ape its worst inventions?

In a first category of underdeveloped countries are a large number of straight-out communist regimes: Vietnam, Cuba, North Korea, Laos, Cambodia, mainland China. Even among the former satellites of the Soviet Union, and in the Soviet Union itself, several countries or regions that are not usually classified in the Third World could be labeled "developmental disasters." They have material and natural resources that should allow development, but if you look at their standard of living, their quality of life, and their life expectancy, they are underdeveloped. And they certainly cannot be described as "victims of capitalism," though they wish they were. To be a victim of capitalism you have to have something to sell to countries with solid currencies and an economy sufficiently interesting to attract investments.

In a second category are Third World countries which, without having belonged formally to the communist bloc, adopted Marxism-Leninism and formed close relations with the Soviet Union and its satellites, often in the military and police areas. Here you find such countries as Benin, Burkina Faso, Congo, Guinea, Equatorial

Guinea, Madagascar, Vanuatu, Zimbabwe, Tanzania. Officials of the latter's ruling party, created by Julius Nyerere, all went for advanced training in East Germany's Communist Party School until 1989. Then there are those, belonging to what might be called an even more catastrophic subcategory, that managed to combine the devastations of Marxist-Leninist political organization with civil war or foreign war or both; the best known cases are Afghanistan, Angola, Ethiopia, Mozambique, Nicaragua, and the former South Yemen—where it is worth recalling that in 1986 alone a minor spat between rival factions of the local communist party caused at least ten thousand deaths, in a country whose population is about two and a half million.

In a third category are countries not formally in the Soviet camp and whose political-economic systems are not explicitly Marxist-Leninist but that, nonetheless, practice a kind of socialism which cannot be called anything other than totalitarian. Algeria represents almost the classic example of this sort of regime. "The FLN-state was, without doubt, a totalitarian regime," writes Nicolas Baverez in one of the best studies of this country.* The founders of Algerian totalitarianism, Ahmed Ben Bella and Houari Boumedienne, identified the market with colonialism. In consequence, they undertook to insure their country's economic independence through agrarian collectivism and industrial statism. The result was that agricultural production fell by a third in twenty years even as, due to rapid population growth, food imports reached 60 percent of consumption. The myth of independence had turned into food and financial dependency. In 1990 Algeria's foreign debt was $25 billion, half of the GNP; debt service was $8 billion, two thirds of export earnings. But the remainder of the earnings from exports, due to hydrocarbons (gas and oil), subsidized basic services and products. As Baverez puts it, Algeria's "planned growth" turned into a *subsidized economic sector*, worsened by industrial stagnation. In 1990, the five hundred firms owned by the state were operating at one-third capacity and employed 30 percent more manpower than necessary. Inevitably, the system was corrupt from top to bottom of the state machinery, which required payoffs for everything it did. According to a former prime minister, Abdelhamid Brahimi, from 1980 to 1990 $26 billion in public funds were stolen this way—about the amount of the foreign debt. The

---

* "Algeria: Chronicle of a Foretold Failure," *Commentaire*, Winter 1990–91.

"Algerian model" became a scarecrow for foreign investors. It was hardly "multinational capitalism" that threatened the country, since it would have been crazy to invest there. To escape complete bankruptcy, the Algerian government was obliged in July 1991 to accept the "disgrace" of selling to foreign firms part of its nationalized oil resources.

This grim novel (unfortunately only too true) raises the question of whether these countries have any knowledge of history, and if they have, why they refuse to draw any lessons from it. I have devoted some attention here to Algeria's case, because it represents a paradigm of almost pure idiocy. But in the race to failure, it has competition; Burma, for example, destroyed by the despotic socialism of Ne Win from 1962 to 1988; or the "revolutionary" military officers of Peru, fans of Albania's great Enver Hoxha, who managed to reduce their country's GNP by two thirds between 1969 and 1980. In a striking example of historical ledgerdemain, among the thousands of commentaries written on Peru's grim situation in the 1980s, there is almost never any reference to the insanities of the previous decade, even though they are the key to the subsequent catastrophe. The fact is that the Third World has been victimized far more by the idea of "systems" than by the idea of money, and it has been weakened far more by its refusal to accept the market economy than by the presumed ravages of capitalism. Development failed not because of democratic capitalism but because of a stubborn refusal to adopt it.

This is the reason too for the countries of the fourth category. Even as they conserve the fundamental characteristics of the market and stay within the community of liberal economies, they are burdened by a noxious degree of statism, although they do not go all the way to authoritarian or totalitarian socialism. I have referred already to the Latin American system, but many other countries, in Africa and Asia, work less well than they might because of the brake on their development represented by statism. These include some major nations, notably India. It is not often recalled that in 1927 Jawaharlal Nehru, then thirty-eight years old and therefore no longer exempt from responsibility due to youthful idealism, visited the Soviet Union. He liked what he saw there. He returned from his trip sold on the virtues of centralized economic planning and twenty years later, having become prime minister of independent India, he made it his duty to supply his country with a class of bureaucrats reflecting the ideas and methods of those who ran the Soviet Gosplan, the Soviet economic planning commission.

Fortunately, British parliamentary democracy, which had taken root in the former colony, prevented Nehru from sliding down the totalitarian slope, although Indira Gandhi came perilously close to it during the so-called state of emergency in the seventies. Political democracy was subsequently restored, but the ruling elite and the press continued to be actively pro-Soviet and, what was worse, they continued to favor the heavy bureaucratic machinery of Soviet-style centralized planning. Despite the creative energy of business men, despite Rajiv Gandhi's courageous attack on the command economy in 1986, and despite the clearly liberal orientation of the government that followed his after he was murdered in 1991, it can be said that India lost precious time due to Nehru's Soviet sympathies and the centralizing and statist policies that he adopted. Similarly, even those African countries that are reputed to be oriented toward the free market, notably Ivory Coast, Gabon, Kenya, suffer from two ills that turn off creditors and discourage local entrepreneurship: paralyzing governmental bureaucracies and political authorities that remain the final arbiters of how wealth shall be used and distributed.

In sum, there are very few nations that are underdeveloped due to large international economic forces—on the contrary, these most often were prevented from operating. In most cases, underdevelopment was prolonged or worsened due to the application of pernicious economic doctrines by ruling cliques interested in power and enrichment, or—often simultaneously—due to the destruction of lives and property in the course of repression and civil wars. It is fair to conclude that underdevelopment is caused by the absence of democracy, that is by the lack of economic and political liberties. The most damaged countries are those that were called "progressive" but that ought to be called "regressive." But with a handful of exceptions, the Third World languishes in persistent weakness that is caused by political and economic despotism.

The Third World itself, as we know, became aware of this during the last two decades of our century. Like the ex-communist countries, it has begun to favor political democracy and market economics. But there are structural and cultural obstacles to getting beyond intentions.

One way to understand why liberal reforms fail in centralized systems is to consider the difference in chemistry between a mixture and a compound. When, as the bureaucrats say, you "inject some market forces" into a collective or command economy, you get a mixture, which does not create a new dynamic. By contrast, in a real market economy, the diverse substances that make it up create a new combination, which cannot revert to its former constituent parts. The new combination possesses the solidity of an original and homogeneous substance. Partial liberalizations fail often, because recent "converts" to the market forget this fact, or do not understand it, and think they can "improve" centralized economies with a small dose of the market. Partial reforms provoke brutal tremors—although the partial successes in Mexico under Carlos Salinas or in Argentina under Carlos Menem are worthy of note—because they only reform, or perhaps only can reform, certain aspects of the system, but others are needed as well. They must do away with subsidized capitalism and featherbedding unionism, not to mention the legions of government bureaucrats that inevitably come with these privileged conditions, and this is not something that the interested parties can easily accept. This became clear in East Germany, whose conversion to a normal economy, following unification with the West in 1991, proved to be far more painful than the optimists had thought. It turns out, unfortunately, that you really have to start all over in order to rebuild. This is why Third World countries that have maintained traditional economic structures (even preindustrial ones) find it easier to adapt to modern market economies than those that adopted the socialist model, with all the privileges and protections this implies. At the death of Sekou Touré, Guinea was a ruined country, inhabited by people with atrophied mental habits who for over twenty-five years had become used to expect everything from the state. It was an enervated herd, lacking willpower and any sense of solidarity, with no concept of what it means to take an initiative. In these conditions, foreign aid is sterile. Quite apart from money that is stolen, it does not spur growth: on the contrary, it encourages immobility. Straightforward aid—a humanitarian duty— should not be confused with real aid for development, which requires political and cultural changes.

Now it is true that South Africa, which has the only modern economy on the African continent, suggests that interdependence of democracy and development is not an absolute rule. However, South Africa, prior to the abolition of apartheid, was a democracy—for whites only. Therefore, the problem was not to bring democracy to South Africa, but to extend it to all. By fighting for their rights, South African blacks got an education in democracy. This is not to suggest apartheid was good for them, obviously, but it does contrast with the experiences of the masses elsewhere in Africa, who knew of no other changes than alternating dictatorships and civil wars. As in Western Europe in the nineteenth century or the Venetian Republic in the Middle Ages, South Africa had an embryonic democracy, against the background of a market economy, where full citizenship was limited to a small minority. And, as happened in Europe, it was inevitable that the rights of citizenship would spread to all. Once reforms were put in place leading to universal suffrage without racial discrimination, it appeared that the process of democratization was imperiled more by violent clashes between different black ethnic groups than by the aftereffects of apartheid.

This practice, however limited, of democracy, and the education it implies, is missing entirely in the rest of Africa and in the Arab world. Nevertheless, there has been some progress, first in that there has developed some awareness of the evil effects of the old despotic system, and second in tentative efforts to practice democracy. In 1990, Gabon and Ivory Coast for the first time held parliamentary elections in which two or more parties competed. Benin, following Burkina Faso, foreswore Marxism-Leninism and chose a new constitution by referendum.

Latin America counted eleven dictatorships in 1980; in 1991 there was left only one: Cuba. Also in 1991, Bangladesh elected its first parliamentary assembly in an orderly way, and in May of that year the people of Nepal voted for the first time in thirty-two years. Early in 1991, too, the leaders of Zaire, Zambia, and even Tanzania conceived of moving toward multiparty democracy. Unfortunately, only Zambia proceeded to do anything further, and Zaire came apart in violent convulsion in September of that year. On the other hand, in Congo, an African country heavily burdened by "real" socialism, a national conference of the ruling party removed from the president almost all of his dictatorial powers without recourse to violence. Nineteen ninety-one even saw the flowering in the Third World of self-criticism, an ingredient that is as necessary to democracy as it is to development. "The balance sheet of thirty-one years of independence is negative," Zaire's new prime minister dared to proclaim in the People's Palace at Kinshasa.

However, in this same year there was a coup d'état in Thailand. At the end of 1990 the legal government of Pakistan headed by Benazir Bhutto was forced to resign under unconstitutional pressure, only two years after it had put an end to a military dictatorship. The democratic renewal of the past few years is undeniable, but it should not mask the fact that there continue to be movements in the other direction. Moreover, Third World countries that have adopted political pluralism and universal suffrage are finding out, just like countries recently emerged from communism, that political democracy does not erase the original sin. History shows that over the long run democracy and development are complementary, but it should be clear that a few months or even a few years of democracy will not produce the kind of prosperity and well-being that it took centuries for the "older" countries of democratic capitalism to achieve. The advantage of democracy and the market is that they make room for individual enterprise; they cannot substitute for it. Political liberalization alone does not insure growth if it is not accompanied in short order by economic liberalization, which is far more painful and difficult.

Even in sub-Saharan Africa in the early nineties, democracy and liberalism advanced timidly. There were peaceful elections in Benin that did away with a Marxist-Leninist dictatorship; in Mali, a popular insurrection overthrew a dictator who had been there twenty years, paving the way, at least, to democratic possibilities. Tragically, France's support for the dictator in question, "President" Moussa Traore, had allowed him to stay in place as long as he had, up until his last grasp for power when he ordered that hundreds of peaceful demonstrators be shot and killed. It was, once again, an example of the astonishing preference of the Western democracies for the status quo, in the Third World no less than in the ex-communist countries. The relations between France and Vietnam between 1988 and 1992 provide another example. And yet, with anything but help from the old democracies, new democracies keep struggling to be born.

A 1989 World Bank report shows, moreover, that African countries (including Guinea, Malawi, Niger, Nigeria, Somalia, and Zaire) that did away with authoritarian price controls quickly witnessed increases in production. This has costs, however: it provoked food riots in cities, as consumers saw prices rise prior to readjustments downward in a normal market. In Somalia, in an all-too-well-known tragedy, a civil war undercut the benefits of economic liberalization and in 1992 brought on one of the worst famines in a continent well accustomed to them. Excessive illusions often lead people to think that a short, timid liberalization will suffice to repair decades of that modern economic despotism known as centralized planning, which is so much more destructive than traditional authoritarianism. The East Germans' belief that a few months without communism would suffice to bring them California-levels of prosperity is not an isolated case. But progress is possible, little by little; even Bulgaria, in its elections of October 1991, understood that the communists (renamed socialists) had to be booted out.

Paradoxically, democracy is good for everyone, but not all cultures are equally receptive to democracy. Haiti and the Philippines did not overcome their endemic anarchy after ridding themselves of their respective dictators in 1986. Why did the British political model "take" somewhat better in India than in Pakistan? And why, as V. S. Naipaul has shown so well, does India, despite the relative strength of its political institutions, find it so hard to enter the modern world mentally? If democracy ultimately fails in India it will be due to unexpurgable ethnic and religious conflicts, fueled by terrorism. Why, again, is Islamic culture evidently incompatible with democracy—or is it only Arab culture? Or only Shiite culture? There are no easy answers, as we will see in the next chapter, but we should remain, if I may put it this way, bitterly optimistic. For the fact is that humanity is doomed to democracy, and this is so because without democracy, it is doomed, period.

CHAPTER TWELVE

ISLAMIC DEMOCRACY OR ISLAMIC TERRORISM?

"Youssof-Cheribi, mufti of the holy ottoman empire by the grace of God, hereby forbid our loyal subjects to partake of the infernal invention recently brought back to us by our loyal ambassador to the miserable little kingdom of France, namely printing.

"And while we are at it, we forbid our loyal subjects to ever read any books whatsoever. Indeed, we forbid parents to teach their children reading, and we forbid anyone to pronounce more than four sentences that produce a clear and coherent thought."
— Voltaire, "Of the Dangers of Reading" (1765)

Outrageous as these satirical quotes may be, they show that for over two hundred years now Western writers have been confronted with the issue of whether there may not be something utterly incompatible between Islamic culture and democracy, tolerance, diversity, indeed rational discussion, without which there can be no cultural liberty. The question came to the fore again in February 1989 when the Ayatollah Khomeini ordered the assassination of Salman Rushdie, a British citizen of Indian background, guilty of a supposedly blasphemous novel, *The Satanic Verses*. The order applied to all Muslims, wherever they might be. The *fatwa* (sentence) calling for murder was aimed not only at the writer, but at anyone who took part, directly or indirectly, in the circulation of this book: publishers, printers, translators, booksellers, mailmen and delivery boys, literary reviewers. Faced with this threat, several publishers, throughout the world, canceled or postponed plans to bring out the book and thousands of bookstores in Europe and North America took it off their shelves, at least temporarily.

This event revealed the inability of Islam to adapt itself to democratic civilization, but it also demonstrated the inability of democratic civilization to find an appropriate response to totalitarian attacks upon itself, be they political, ideological, or religious—or, as in this case, politico-religious.

We should respect the beliefs of others? But not all beliefs are respectable. We should be sensitive to others' religious feelings? But these feelings do not give them a right to go and murder those who do not share them, or even those who offend them or mock them. If all convictions are equally valid or, to be more exact, have the same right to be expressed—and this seems to be the final wisdom at the end of the century—then it must be taken for granted that no violence can be used against anyone wishing to express a skeptical view. Tolerance must be the rule.

With regard to Christianity, tolerance has been the rule for a long time: much of the West's literature, theater, cinema, is anti-Christian, even blasphemous. The violent reaction to Martin Scorsese's *Last Temptation of Christ* was condemned by Church and lay authorities, even though they did not approve of the film. Of course, the Church was intolerant for a long time, but it is granted today that the modern world, the product of many centuries of evolution and founded in theory on the Universal Declaration of Human Rights, is incompatible with religious intolerance, or intolerance toward any beliefs and practices so long as they do not infringe on human rights.

Thus it seems, judging from its reaction to Rushdie's book, that Islam is not part of the modern world. It wants to enjoy its economic and political benefits, but it rejects its cultural, moral, and legal rules.

I have read a great deal of material by Muslim and Western specialists on the Koran to the effect that Islam is, in its essence, among the world's most tolerant religions. Well, it must be a well-hidden, secret essence, for I have rarely seen its concrete manifestation in practice. I am told the Koran counsels tolerance because there is no point in being impatient on this earth, for the wicked will be punished on Judgment Day. If this is the case, I am forced to remark that the impatient are legion in Islam. The Muslim religious authorities could have conformed to their job descriptions—although in so doing they would have violated modern-day principles regarding freedom of information—by forbidding the faithful to read *The Satanic Verses*. The Catholic Church's famous Index, proscribing certain books on doctrinal or moral grounds, remained in force, after all, until 1966. But the Index, which told Roman Catholics what books they must not read, did not require that books should be taken out of circulation or that their authors should be murdered. It did not affect the liberties of nonbelievers, or of members of other faiths.

What is original in the Rushdie Affair is the attempt to suppress a book the world over, even among non-Muslims. This represents a dictatorship of enormous dimensions, which even the Holy Inquisition in its worst periods would not have dreamed of, since its tribunals were constituted within Christendom only, to suppress Christian heresies. One can only imagine the wild mirth that would have been provoked by the idea, even in the blackest days of Catholic bigotries, that the Holy See should have tried to define orthodoxy in regions of the globe inhabited by Buddhists, or Hindus, or Muslims! In fact, quite a number of Catholic countries, including France and the Republic of Venice, refused to let the Inquisition operate on its territory.

Two factors were at play in fundamentalist Islam's offensive in 1989 against the freedom of the rest of humanity. There was, first, the sentence of death pronounced by a state, Iran, against a citizen, Salman Rushdie, of another state, Great Britain, and against all the citizens of all the countries where this book was published and distributed. Second, and in some ways even more disturbing, there was the spontaneous reaction to the book by the ordinary Muslim.

As to Iran's order, which was a clear violation of international law, it should have been automatically seen as a declaration of war by other countries, were habits of appeasement and cowardice not thoroughly entrenched. What, other than a casus belli, is a foreign state's incitement to kill our citizens on our territory? It is difficult to find a more glaring example of the incoherence of contemporary government, which busies itself with so many private matters that are none of its business, but which does not know how to react when the security of citizens, clearly its most elementary concern, is at stake. At first, the member states of the European Community had recalled

201

their ambassadors for consultations, the conventional way to signal disapproval. But within a month, most had sent their diplomats back to Teheran with the most stunning discretion, for nothing is more conspicuous than cowards who stay in the shadows. The imam Khomeini had a field day taunting Europe, whose ambassadors, he said ironically, "return humiliated, shameful, sorry for what they did." The "imam" was surely mistaken when he added that these diplomats "had not foreseen they would fall to such degradation," for nothing was more foreseeable. But he was right for the rest.

One of France's sharpest analysts of foreign affairs, Ambassador François de Rose, observed that, "Unfortunately, Khomeini's evaluation of the situation is correct. The EC countries are indeed 'humiliated and shameful,' since they are sending their ambassadors back only a month after announcing that the restoration of normal relations depended on Iran's renouncing violence and the threat of violence. The worst is not that we are ashamed and humiliated before the world for turning ourselves in thirty days from tough guys to wimps, but that the EC itself is responsible for this by reversing its position."

Moreover, the attitude quickly spread in the West that Rushdie was a pest who should not have made waves by writing novels. Speaking as a "Christian," Prime Minister Thatcher announced that *The Satanic Verses* is "profoundly offensive" to Islam. The wall of solidarity with the writer, in support of cultural freedom, began to crack. Douglas Hurd, the Home Secretary, stated that, "I sometimes feel that Mr. Rushdie has some difficulty in understanding the institutions of the country to which he belongs." Turning the matter around in this way took some nerve. Evidently it is not the million and a half Muslims living in the U.K. who have some difficulty understanding the country's institutions—all they are doing is burning books and screaming for blood, it is their target. This doubtless is why the United Nations refused to consider the matter, shamelessly deserting the field of battle which its own Universal Human Rights Declaration had defined. The Vatican, by way of the *Osservatore romano*, assailed the "irreverence and blasphemy" in Rushdie's novel, continuing incoherently: "If the work is not strictly speaking blasphemy, then it at least is a gratuitous distortion." Death for gratuitous distortion! Now here is an endearing point of canon law. "Who fails to see," the *Guardian* quoted Lord Shawcross (the British prosecutor at the Nuremberg Trials), "that Rushdie has caused inestimable harm to all?" Now Rushdie is the only guilty party! Not quite, according to Sir Immanuel Jakobovits, Chief Rabbi of the U.K.: "Mr Rushdie and the Ayatollah have both abused freedom of expression." This is a good example of what I referred to as moral equivalence in *How Democracies Perish*. To Sir Immanuel, Rushdie's opinion is in effect a murder, and the assassination order of the Ayatollah is an opinion. The French weekly *Evenement du Jeudi* wrote on 2 March 1989: "Whether or not he meant it, Salman Rushdie has turned himself into the objective ally of Khomeini." With the help of this old Stalinist notion, you could demonstrate that the Jews were the objective allies of Hitler. With communism on its way to the abyss, the democracies are falling back on Islamic fanaticism to indulge in their intellectual briar patches. Struck at their moral foundations, they hurriedly adopt the values of the enemy. And as with communism, their salvation in the last analysis will be due not to their own clearheadedness, but to the fact that the adversary's system is not viable.

Now as to the reaction of the Muslim-in-the-street, that is a cause for concern of a different order. Not only in Pakistan, but in countries where Islam is a minority, such as Britain, France, and India, crowds rioted, burned books, demanding that the novel be banned and its author executed. These Muslims claimed the right to enforce their own taboos in pluralistic societies whose intellectual and spiritual standards they wish to set down by violent means. It is obvious that this intolerance is in violation of contemporary civilized standards accepted around the world. Muslims understand this world so poorly that Pakistani rioters, on 12 February 1989, which is to say prior to Khomeini's *fatwa*, looted the American cultural center in Islamabad when they learned *The Satanic Verses* would be published in the U.S. Six persons died and over a hundred were wounded. How can one presume to participate in contemporary civilization without knowing that in democratic countries, and in the U.S. in particular, publishing houses are independent of the government and an official agency like the unfortunate American Cultural Center of Islamabad does not have even the most meagre responsibility for a book being brought out in New York.

In centuries past, intolerance and the totalitarian mind-set existed in a compartmentalized world. Evil spread slowly. Lately, humanity lives with much faster and more permanent interaction. In the sixteenth and seventeenth centuries, the Ottoman Empire, considered as threatening to Europe as the Soviet Union was during the Cold War, was at the gate: but it did not spread ideologically and politically into our very societies. Today, massive immigration and lax regulations for the acquisition of citizenship (of which I do not disapprove, so long as this does not threaten to undermine our societies founded on the rule of law), give intolerant Islam growing numbers of bases among us. In 1989 Islam was the second religion in France, and of French citizens.

In the United Kingdom, British Muslims organized book burnings of the *The Satanic Verses* and looted impious bookstores, again even before the ayatollah had fulminated his death sentence, which they proceeded to accept, as did a number of French Muslims, Muslim immigrants in France, and even French converts to Islam. The latter did not bring to their new religion the spirit of tolerance essential to their cultural tradition, but instead contracted the intolerant attitudes of their chosen faith. The most disturbing aspect of these homicidal shrieks is that they were emitted in countries where Muslims are in the minority and where, therefore, they can practice their religion only thanks to the tolerance of others. As early as October 1988, the Indian government forbade the sale of *The Satanic Verses* under Muslim pressure, even though Muslims constitute scarcely more than a tenth of the population. In Great Britain, on 14 January 1989 (exactly a month before the *fatwa*), the Muslims of the city of Bradford demonstrated noisily and angrily. They burned copies of the book, imitated in this, on the 20th, by London's Muslims. On February 16, the Islamic Organization Conference demanded of the publisher, Penguin, that it remove the book from sale throughout the world, including of course in countries that have nothing Islamic about them, or all Penguin books would be forbidden in the forty-five countries belonging to this organization. By the end of February and in March, screaming mobs called for Rushdie's death and, in the meantime, burned him in effigy in the U.S., Denmark, France, Greece, Switzerland, Holland, West Germany, Canada, Spain, Australia. On May 27, there was a violent confrontation between twenty thousand Muslims (some papers reported one hundred thousand) and Scotland Yard's anti-riot brigade. In one of the world's most tolerant countries, these orgies of intolerance continued relentlessly for the next two years. In Belgium, the aftereffects of these frenetic gestures took a graver and more barbaric turn. On March 29, the rector of the Bruxelles mosque, Abdullah Ahdel, a Saudi Arabian subject, and the librarian of the Islamic Cultural Center, Saleh El Behin, a Tunisian, were murdered. Their crime was to have taken a moderate position in the Rushdie controversy. The rector, in particular, had declined to approve Khomeini's order unconditionally. *Agence France-Presse* and *Reuters* commented that the murders were due to "disagreements" in the Belgian Muslim community regarding the novel. No matter how indulgent one wanted to be, how can anyone call a religion tolerant when disagreement is synonymous with execution? The murders were later attributed to a Beirut-based Islamic organization which called itself, no doubt with a rich sense of humor, "The Soldiers of the Law."

Apart from this small group of itinerant assassins, the most serious nuisance comes from Muslim minorities established in Christian and secular countries. Not only do they obtain the right to practice their religion (whereas this right is very rarely granted Christians and Jews in Muslim countries), but additionally they demand the exorbitant privilege of imposing their views on the majority. This is why it is difficult to grasp how the members of this religious culture will be able to build democracy some day in their own countries, in view of the fact that they have such a hard time understanding its principles and practice in the various countries that welcome them and where they can observe its concrete reality. These Muslim communities within non-Muslim societies can only, in the near future, increase, given demographic pressures in all the countries of the Mediterranean's southern littoral and the Muslim countries of Asia and in Indonesia. There is bound to be irrepressible population pressure from south to north, no matter what policies are adopted to control them (and these are not proving to be very efficient). Will these Muslims, whether or not they become citizens, claim a different law? Will we accept the idea that they can take orders, including assassination orders, from foreign capitals? My question is rhetorical: we have accepted it already. In France, demonstrators carrying signs proclaiming "Rushdie must die" were not prosecuted for incitement to murder, even though the Prime Minister declared firmly that "next time" he would seek indictments. While we are waiting for the next time, we have to admit the precedent was established: the law was broken with impunity. Queried on this by Europe One (radio station) on 6 March 1989, the Minister of the

Interior* declared that in the absence of indictments—and even more importantly than indictments—what was needed was "the moral condemnation of these fanatics by the immense majority of Muslims." Even if this so-called immense majority was anything other than the product of an optimistic imagination devoted to doing nothing, the implication here amounts to an astonishing special exception to the rule of law: it grants the French Muslim community the right to judge itself and to decide for itself what is fanatical and what is not, thereby escaping the responsibilities of following the rules of the Republic and acquiring its own jurisdiction.

It was quite an intellectual feat to profess such a thing in the year of the bicentennial of the French Revolution, the very event that had abolished the unfairness of separate judicial systems applying different laws in accordance with social and religious categories. Thus European Islam would acquire the privilege, which the Catholic Church has not had for centuries, of punishing unbelief outside the common law. Such capitulations on our part are seen as victories by Islam, as proof that it can demand of the West that it bow before its law or suffer terrorist attacks. It has learned to make fine use of these, with very nearly no reactions on our part. The volunteers of intolerance are never lacking in our countries. To say they are only a handful is an expression of ignorance and incompetence, for those who terrorize others are always but a handful. Great criminals, too, are but a handful. Should we leave them alone? Even if the majority is in disagreement with the "handful," the latter's influence will be decisive. A competent Interior Minister would have gone after the fanatical minority immediately, in order to show the supposedly peaceful majority that it can count on the full force of the law. By showing it the exact opposite, it is turned over to intimidation by the fanatics.

As in Great Britain for that matter. Going against her reputation, the Iron Lady spoke less clearly in this spiralling madness than the French Prime Minister Michel Rocard, and she opened the door to the legitimization of terror. To blame Rushdie by declaring that *The Satanic Verses* were "deeply offensive" to Muslims was to miss the point. The point is not whether or not Muslims have a right to be offended by a given book—of course they have such a right—but

---

* France's Minister of the Interior has many of the functions of the U.S. Attorney General; since the days when Georges Clemenceau held this post, he is known as "France's top cop."

whether they also have the right, in Great Britain, to prevent the distribution of this book and to kill its author. So long as the second point is not clear, the first one should not even concern us. I am as ready as the next man to sympathize with someone who feels he has been humiliated, to plead his case, to insist that his sensitivities be respected—but not if he pulls a gun out and starts shooting at random. In this case, the first order of business is to disarm him. Tolerance for all, yes; tolerance for intolerance, no.

It is this sort of confusion between the right to respect and the right to violence that led, for example, none other than Cardinal Decourtray, archbishop of Lyon, *"primat des Gaules"** and president of the French Episcopal Conference, to weigh in on the side of the fanatics. This is especially astonishing considering that official Catholicism would never presume to demand that blasphemy, even in print, be sanctioned, let alone be punished by murder.

The point here is that terror makes us think we need to be more sensitive to our enemies' feelings than the occasion demands; this in itself is a victory for them. This habit of mind was shown by the number of publishers who canceled plans to bring out *The Satanic Verses*. One can hardly blame them for not wanting to risk murder and arson when the state authorities themselves are backing off from their responsibility for the preservation of law and order, but it is truly alarming when publishers go even further and cancel contracts for books that contain critiques of Islamic culture, as happened in the case of two houses, Basic Books in New York and Collins in Great Britain, both belonging to Rupert Murdoch.

Even as I carefully differentiate between fanatical and tolerant Muslims, I must admit I found this distinction increasingly difficult to make as the Rushdie Affair proceeded. Could one be sure the fanatics were the minority, rather than the reverse? If there are moderate Muslims in the West, they were not much heard from. They staged no counter-demonstrations calling for tolerance. How significant, in terms of Muslim opinion, is the moving statement by the Moroccan novelist Tahar Ben Jelloun (4 March 1989 in *Le Monde*): "Eschewing tolerance and dialogue, some wish to keep people in a totalitarian environment, inside iron curtains. Islam is not revenge and hate. Its message is one of peace. This is the Islam I learned and believe in."

---

* The archbishop of Lyon is, hierarchically, the first of France's Catholic prelates, due to the history of the Christianization of France.

This is a noble creed, but I am afraid it is not widely shared. Consider the courageous position taken by the Nigerian novelist and Nobel prize winner Wole Soyinka, also a Muslim, who wrote in defense of Salman Rushdie in several newspapers. The consequence was that demonstrators demanded his death as well!

It was by no means a question of Shiite Islam, since violent demonstrations took place in countries where this sect is not present. Even so-called moderate Muslims demanded, in all innocence, that the democratic countries of the West change their laws, even if this meant contradicting the basis of their constitutional principles. In France a "Muslim Coordination Committee" bringing together the principal Islamic organizations, stated that it would do everything legally possible to prevent the distribution of Salman Rushdie's deeply offensive book. It was an improvement that they rejected violent methods, but the misunderstanding of democracy and the rule of law was stunning. It did not occur to them that the French Republic cannot pass laws contrary to its Constitution and the Declaration of the Rights of Man which serves as its preamble, nor is there any way to do anything, let alone everything "legally possible" to do what in effect would be illegal. The Republic is secular and favors no religion. It cannot determine what is sacrilegious and what is not. Since our society is a veritable magnet for immigrants, are we going to turn our legislators into theologians of every religion on the planet? The best and only thing the Republic can do is guarantee religious freedom and promote tolerance. It surely cannot grant to any religious community the right to incite its members to hatred against those who do not share its faith and who express their views, a right guaranteed by the Constitution. The Western democracies happen to be the only societies that grant to all immigrants and naturalized citizens protection against intolerance—they do not grant them the right to be themselves intolerant! To demand such a right even as they make ample use of the benefits of liberal civilization is a sign of egocentric chutzpah and a complete absence of education in the culture of modern democracy. If this is not corrected, Muslims will not be able to fit into liberal societies. Immigration will be a constant source of new tragedies. In effect, the "moderate" Muslims are asking for something we have not had for a long time: a state religion, only it should be Islam, not Catholicism. The latter is not protected from "blasphemy"; even in Britain, where the sovereign is also officially the head of the Church of England, religious pluralism and the right to attack Christianity are guaranteed.

The "moderates'" "legalism" thus does not suffice, I am afraid, to dispel my conviction, diametrically opposed to Tahar Ben Jelloun's—and I wish it were not so!—namely that Islam is a religion, more precisely a politico-religious system, that up until now at any rate has been essentially totalitarian by nature. In the Sudan, Muslims forcibly tried to impose the *Charia* (Islamic law) upon non-Muslims. This barbarism led to atrocious famines and frightful massacres. In democratic countries, the Islamic mind finds itself unable to adapt to the civilization of pluralism that it has taken us centuries to build, a civilization where religion is a private matter, where no religion enjoys special privileges, where no religion can demand that the law be brought to bear in defense of its doctrines—a civilization, in short, in which violence is controlled by ideas and not the other way around.

On 27 March 1989, British Foreign Secretary Sir Geoffrey Howe, visiting Islamabad, apologized to the Pakistani prime minister, Benazir Bhutto, for the publication in Britain of *The Satanic Verses*. He granted that the novel is offensive to Muslims and deplored its "blasphemy." Britain's minister of foreign affairs thereby capitulated on the essential point, for he admits to his government's indirect responsibility, or at least its moral involvement, in the book's publication. Otherwise, in what way is he qualified to offer apologies to those whom the book offends? His answer should have been: "Madam Prime Minister, in our societies, the writing and publishing of books are activities entirely independent of the political authorities, who merit neither congratulations nor scoldings from those who may like or dislike any given book published in their country." Moreover, in debasing himself the foreign secretary accepted the absurd notion that in order to have interstate relations, you have to praise the religious faith of the people whose country you are negotiating with—a notion utterly contrary to the conventions or practices of international relations in our times, or even in ancient times. At any rate Sir Geoffrey was soon rewarded for his obsequiousness: in the night of March 27–28, a bomb blew up the library of the Islamabad British Council, Britain's cultural agency which (need one say it?) had no more influence than the American USIA on Salman Rushdie's literary activities. Its function is to make English culture known abroad, not to direct it—but this is a difference the Islamic mind apparently cannot grasp.

The British foreign secretary's apologies to angry Pakistani readers of *The Satanic Verses* were all the more grotesque as there were no

Pakistani readers of *The Satanic Verses* to speak of. The mob's fury was not the result of their reading the book, but of incitements by hate-filled leaders, who would have invented Rushdie had he not existed. Out of one hundred million Pakistanis, less than one in four knows how to read. They do not avail themselves much of this skill. Three hundred books, in all categories, are produced each year; you can wander about for days in Karachi, Lahore, or Islamabad and never see a bookstore. Sir Geoffrey's sensitivity was therefore superfluous. It is eminently respectable to be sensitive to others' feelings; but to judge oneself on the basis of a value system founded on intolerance is not respectable. On the contrary, it is despicable, for it implies that one is incapable of defending one's own civilization. The Muslims merited the following reply: "Either you join a civilization founded on tolerance, or you stay outside it. In the former case, you gain the right to protest, verbally or by recourse to law, against incitements to hatred; but in the latter, you lose your right to participate in pluralistic civilizations and to demand of us that we grant you freedom of religion in our countries, since you wish to deny us our freedom of thought. You exclude yourselves from the world of tolerance. This forces us to reopen the question of Muslim minorities in our countries: for we cannot accept that they should tyrannize non-Muslims, or even tolerant Muslims." The only other dignified and logical attitude would have been to say: "You are right! I am converting to Islam and I will join you in persecuting all the infidels!" But no one took this position either. We caved in to intolerance even as we pretended to remain faithful to our own values.

Indulgence toward the enemies of the open society should not be confused with cultural relativism, the great advance of Western culture and exclusive to it. Third World countries accuse us of "Eurocentrism"; in fact, Europe, in the past four centuries especially, has been the only civilization that has taken a real interest in cultures, art, laws, faiths, ways of life other than its own. Europeans—I am generalizing of course and I do not mean literally "all" Europeans—were unique in accepting the idea that other civilizations might be, indeed were, in many respects superior to their own. In other respects they might be inferior and in still others they might be neither one nor the other, but the point is that they were worthy of esteem. This awareness of the diversity of human culture was by no means a denigration of our own civilization, but it implied a willingness to find in other customs and institutions solutions outside our own traditions to our problems. For this notion to become widespread, a double effort was required: first, against other cultures, which despised all that was different from themselves; and second, within our own cultures, against those (principally Catholics and more generally Christians) who believed the whole world should be converted to our views. To achieve cultural pluralism, it was first necessary to transform religion into a purely private affair, a matter of personal or family choice.

Since then, the systems of thought that have included in their very origins the idea of universal conquest have been: nazism, communism, and Islam. The first two were twentieth century inventions. Islam, of course, comes from the past. We cannot compromise with a system one of whose objectives is our destruction. As clearly shown by Alain Finkielkraut in *The Defeat of Thought* (1987), you must know how to distinguish between respect (which should not be uncritical) and servility in the face of systems whose internal logic implies the debasement or annihilation of our own. The former is an expression of curiosity, of wonder at the rich diversity of human cultures; the latter is a wish, conscious or not, for the restoration of some kind of totalitarian culture. And this morbid wish of the enemies of the open society finds support among politicians, too clever by half, who think they can come to terms with fanatics. They forget this rule: you can make deals with the interests of others, but not their prejudices, for the latter are never satisfied. If you give ground, you will get not gratitude but more hatred for not having given all. And if you give all, they cannot be grateful because morally you no longer exist.

Which is what Salman Rushdie himself found out when, in December 1990, tired of a life spent in hiding from Islamic killers, he thought a public repudiation of his book might guarantee his safety. In a solemn statement, he repudiated the sections in his book supposedly offensive to Mohammed and swore to forbid any further translation or a paperback edition. To give greater luster to his plea, he also announced a great spiritual event: his conversion, or rather reconversion, to Islam "following a long intellectual journey." By contrast, the journey of the ayatollahs was brief: it took twenty-four hours for the "guide" of the Islamic revolution, Ali Khamenei, to let it be known that he did not care for Rushdie's remorse and the "historic *fatwa*" promulgated the previous year by Khomeini (who had died in the meantime) against the "blasphemer" was "irrevocable."

211

To Khamenei, of course, Rushdie's retraction was not a gesture of conciliation but an admission of defeat not only by the guilty author but by the entire West; it was a sign of Islam's victory and an incitement to redouble the energy in the fight against impiety. Which is what the faithful did, since in 1991 they murdered the Japanese translator of *The Satanic Verses* and gravely wounded the Italian translator. Koranic tolerance spreads beyond religion into politics: in 1990–91, there were no less than thirteen Teheran-ordered assassinations of Iranian political refugees in France, including Chapour Bakhtiar, the Shah's last and most liberal prime minister. This murder (Bakhtiar's throat was slit near Paris in August 1991) was no doubt designed to thank the president of France for granting a parole the previous year to the killer who had tried to kill Bakhtiar in 1981, killing two of his neighbors in the attempt. This was but one more proof that totalitarian regimes always interpret our concessions as victories for themselves and encouragements to persevere in their methods.

French Muslim fundamentalists, likewise, felt they had scored a victory when at the conclusion of the so-called "Islamic veil" affair in the fall of 1989 the Minister of Education authorized Muslim girls to go to class wearing their veils. This was a violation of French law, which is strict on the issue of separation of church and state in the public schools. Where the crucifix had been removed in the name of freedom of conscience, another religion's vestments were now welcome. This symbolic capitulation stemmed, of course, from the fear of being accused of racism. Religious pluralism, essential to an open society, includes the right to establish private denominational schools, but it also gives to the state the right to prevent sectarian ostentation in the public schools. To call the desire to respect democratic principles racism is, in truth, to misunderstand democracy. Modern democracy authorizes and indeed organizes the coexistence of several moral codes within the same society, under the rule of the same, nonreligious, law. Islam by contrast allows for no independence of the state, the law, morality, society, intellectual life, or even art. Imam Khomeini himself made this clear: "The Koran has a hundred times more verses concerning social problems than religion. Take fifty books on the Muslim tradition, maybe three of four will be concerned with man's duties to God. The rest is concerned with society, economics, law, politics." This is why it is hard to see how contemporary Islam can be compatible with democracy, despite the undoubted efforts of some Muslims to reconcile tolerance with their faith.

Indeed, during the "veil" affair, French citizens of Algerian origin argued that five hundred fanatics had spoken for three million other Muslims. But, again, if the moderates were so overwhelmingly in the majority, why were they so utterly silent? Bernard Lewis has shown throughout his work that the Islamic countries' difficulties with modernity and development comes from the idea of secularism. In Islamic culture there is no distinction between what must be rendered unto Caesar and what must be rendered unto God, a distinction present from the very beginning in the Christian conception of society. Lewis explains that neither in classical Arabic nor in the languages that derived their political vocabulary from it basic distinctions familiar to us are absent, thus: "church and state," "spiritual and temporal," "sacred and profane," "religious and secular." In Christendom, even where there is, or was, a state religion, the latter never controlled or determined all the state's activities, nor those of individuals. If there is a founding principle of modern democracy, it is surely that the law is human and not divine, that it is not unchanging but can evolve when the majority of society agrees. Without a secular state and a neutral civil society, there can be neither democracy nor development. For among the conditions for development is intellectual creativity, impossible without liberty and without an education that, even when it is obtained through denominational schools, must in its essence be free of censorship and dogma. Otherwise, the result is sterility. Moncef Marzouki, an Arab intellectual, wrote in a 1987 book, *Arabs, Can You Speak?*: "Name one of this century's innovations, one school of thought, a single example in science or art that we created!"

Whether or not they are Arab, the Islamic revolutionaries who find their model in Khomeini's Islamic republic turn toward the past, toward the cradle of Islam, in refusing the democratic world—or at least its values and its institutions, if not its technology and other material products. In understanding the nature of the Islamic revival, it is important to bear in mind that revolutions are most popular when they restore traditional norms. In this regard, indeed, the Iranian revolution is a prototype. Some Westerners like Michel Foucault, who labeled the Khomeinists as "progressives" did not realize that the "revolutionary" Islamic states are in reality far more conservative, indeed "reactionary" than the so-called conservative states.

By contrast, the Turkish revolution and the republic it produced were inspired by the Western significance of these terms, in particular by the concept of separation between politics and religion, the civil code and the divine law. Lewis points out that since there was no word corresponding to the French *laicité* (secular) in Turkish, the Turks invented *layàk*. The history of modern Turkey proves that the development of a secular, and then a democratic, state in a Muslim society is indeed possible. Turkey is an exemplary case: the one Muslim country that, without giving up its religious traditions, chose Western political, economic, and civil (not the least important since this concerns matters like marriage and divorce) values. For many Turks, the significant change is less a matter of economics than the kind of civilization they want to live in.

The Western media were severe and rightly so concerning the Turkish army's repression after it seized power in 1980. The situation in the country had grown chaotic, with assassinations every day and the virtual disintegration of the state's authority. But it is worth noting that the soldiers returned peacefully to their barracks in 1983 when stability and democracy were restored. While democracy is not perfect in Turkey, it is the only country with a Muslim majority that has adopted and generally lived with political institutions comparable to ours in Western Europe. While human rights need to be defended vigilantly in Turkey, one cannot help but be struck by the contrasting indulgence, on the part of Western observers, with regard to such blood-soaked totalitarian regimes as Saddam Hussein's Iraq, Qaddafi's Libya, or Ben Bella and Boumedienne's Algeria. Turkey is the only Muslim country which is not moving in a literally "reactionary" direction.

Many specialists have asked themselves whether the recalcitrance in the face of democracy and development are not properly Arab problems, rather than Islamic. After all, a number of Muslim countries have made varying degrees of adaptation to the modern democratic world—Turkey in particular but also, intermittently, such countries as Senegal, Bangladesh, or Pakistan, which elected a woman to the post of prime minister in 1991. By contrast, most Arab countries go from socialism to fundamentalism without being able to stay on a course of liberal democracy. This is why they reject the three basic elements of modernity: economic pluralism (the market), political pluralism (they favor one-party states), and cultural pluralism (over which they choose either religious fundamentalism or dictatorships based on "philosophies of revolution," which boil down to grotesque personality cults).

Calling a state secular does not make it democratic, when only the state and not civil society, as in Turkey, benefits from this secularism. The Baath ("party of the Arab socialist renewal") parties were secular not because they were interested in individual freedom of opinion, but in opposition to the religious parties. This purely repressive secularism did not stop Saddam Hussein, a product of the Baath movement (whose strongest influence has been in Iraq and Syria), from having visions of Mohammed during the Gulf War (which apparently did not bring him much good advice). The West was mistaken in judging these secular states—Egypt under Nasser, Syria under Assad—to be more "progressive" than the traditional religious monarchies.

So, is the Islamic incompatibility with democracy something peculiarly Arab? This, supposedly, stems from the retreat of Arab power since the fifteenth century, source of "humiliations" by the West. But instead of overcoming this handicap by searching for its causes and by putting themselves to the hard task of development, the Arabs have substituted imagination and fantasy, medieval visions of power restored thanks to the Koran and the sword. Instead of using the proven tools of development, they throw themselves into the arms of megalomaniacs who lead them to fresh defeats and humiliations. Then, instead of seeking out their own mistakes, they blame their problems on foreign conspiracies against Islam. The Arab oil-producing nations wasted their fabulous income, from 1973 to 1980, in the financing of armaments, terrorism, and fundamentalism. They got rich, but they stayed underdeveloped. And they have not had the courage to face up to their own failure and seek out its real causes. There was no better demonstration of this failure than the Gulf War of 1990, instigated by Iraq.

The seven months of the Gulf War (August 1990–February 1991) provoked within the Arab world such passionate and contradictory reactions that one could not fail to be struck again by the old question of whether or not they have a fundamental resistance to rationality and thus to development, modernity, the state of law, democracy. I am referring of course to Arab civilization, not to its prisoners, who in conditions of freedom might build a quite different one. From the start, mobs in Jordan and the Maghreb grew feverish with mythical notions of what was going on. Fantastically, they imagined the crisis stemmed from Western imperialistic aggression against Saddam Hussein, and in consequence the entire Arab world ought to consider itself under attack. A refusal of the facts as elementary as this suggests a loss of contact with reality. Algeria's foreign minister, Sid Ahmed Ghozali (subsequently prime minister) declared to the *Figaro* (4 March 1991) that war came because the West "wished to destroy an Arab nation for the sake of Israel." With one line he thus blocked out three facts:

First of all, it was the West that had created Iraq's military might. Second, the war started because one Arab nation had invaded another one. And third, the first nations to condemn Iraqi aggression were Arab ones. Indeed, the division among the Arab nations exploded another oft-heard fable, namely that the disagreements between Saddam and his neighbors could be resolved "among Arabs," without any Western interference. In this way of thinking, the Arabs nations that appealed to the U.N. for protection against Iraq were "traitors." Unfortunately, if negotiations among Arabs had been possible, there would have been no invasion of Kuwait. The purely Arab solution failed twice: first, before the invasion of 2 August 1990, and then at the Arab summit in Cairo on August 10, which ended in fist fights. The participants hurled insults at one another, threw tableware, drew their sidearms, called one another liars. Two ministers struck each other, another had a heart attack. Col. Qadaffi was crying. In spite of all this, there was a vote. Twelve countries condemned Iraq's aggression, eight refused to (Tunisia was not present). Thus, the split in the "Arab nation" was the work of the Arabs themselves. Had they been willing to analyze the war's causes honestly, they would have admitted that it stemmed from internal antagonisms, rivalries, jealousies, and hatreds among Arabs, as well as from their antidemocratic political systems which allow brutal and vain despots to be carried away in warlike, repressive, and regressive intoxications.

The "Arab nation" is a pernicious fiction. The Arab "world" is a mosaic of disparate nations whose only common denominators are language and religion. Would one ask an Argentine or an Andalusian to support any Bolivian or Paraguayan dictator just because they belong to the Hispanic world, speak Spanish, and are Christians? Moreover, why should the Arabs get away with appeals to "pan-Islamism"? There are a billion Muslims in the world, of whom only two hundred million are Arabs. Why should an Indonesian accept the demented ambitions of a Saddam or a Qadaffi?

Even if we were to forgive the illiterate masses of Arab countries for falling for the delusions of their blowhard despots, what of the immigrants and their children in Europe? They have access to information provided by a free press—should they not come to a more sensible view of things? Why were the Arab intellectuals so impotent in this crisis? The role of intellectuals is to bring a critical judgment to bear on events, even if they must counter public opinion. But the intellectuals seemed to go even further than the general public in their delirium, encouraging xenophobia and incoherence with references to Western colonialism. Arab intellectuals did not have the courage to recognize that the colonial epoch is long over and the disasters that have befallen their countries are due not to outside intervention but, so to speak, to internal intervention.

I am still awaiting the book of an Algerian Voltaire or Solzhenitsyn, capable of denouncing the totalitarian, corrupt, incompetent regime responsible for misery and repression in Algeria. I am not aware that the West is responsible for the behavior of Qadaffi, who wastes his country's resources to pay for international terrorists, but I do not see Arab intellectuals saying so. In Sudan the Muslim northerners are exterminating the southerners because they refuse to accept conversion to Islam; is this the West's fault? When he attacked Iran, Saddam Hussein caused the death of hundreds of thousands of Muslims and the ruin of his country. Turning this man into a hero, Arab intellectuals did not exactly serve the Arab cause. I do not doubt the West made many mistakes with regard to Saddam; but Arab intellectuals, while they are welcome to criticize our failures, could make a contribution by examining those of their own countries. They could help them accept rationality and the fundamental insight of modernity, which is that it is founded on universal values whose key is democracy.

One of the most courageous and penetrating Muslim philosophers of today, the Egyptian Fouad Zakharya, points out that the difference between what Arab intellectuals say in public and what they say in private is often due to fear of being killed. The fact is that they are afraid to examine their own societies' failures, and in this they are no different from the political leaders whom they ought, as intellectuals, to stand apart from in a critical relationship. A conference on democracy bringing together over a hundred intellectuals from all across the Arab world was held in 1983 on Cyprus—which is itself significant: not a single Arab government allowed the conference to be held on its territory. Not a single orator, however, mentioned the violation of human rights and the absence of democracy in his own country.

Compare with the first summit of the Arab League after the Gulf War: meeting in Cairo on 30 March 1991, it specified right off that no mention should be made of the war or of the repression (against Shiites and Kurds) that was taking place at the very moment in Iraq.

In his *Islam and Secularism* (1981), Fouad Zakharya—who may some day be called the Tocqueville of the Muslim world—makes insightful observations that sum up what I have been saying about the difficult confrontation between Islam and the modern democratic world. He notes that Muslim societies will get out of their intellectual, material, and political underdevelopment only when they become secular. "Secular" does not mean atheistic or anti-religious; what it means is that political and religious ideas and ways of thinking must be kept separate. It does no good to seek arguments for democracy in the Koran, for here one remains the captive of religious references. Fundamentalism is the imagination's compensation for failure, but it leads to greater failures still. And finally, a modern civilization requires secular education, which of course does not mean children cannot also receive a religious education. When these conditions are met, Muslims will be liberated not from their faith—for the violation of their consciences is not the purpose—but from what Renan called (with reference to Islam) "this iron curtain that surrounds their minds." When these conditions are met, too, free intellectuals and honest politicians in the Islamic world will be able to speak up and give themselves the means of building democracy, without which Islam, and the Arab world especially, will continue to agitate vainly in violence and decadence.

Unfortunately, by some kind of backward march, a number of great Muslim countries are returning to theocracy instead of advancing toward secularism. Even Pakistan, which has been able to adopt a representative regime, albeit flawed, chose the last decade of the twentieth century to announce that it would impose the *Charia*, or Islamic law. In April 1991, Prime Minister Nawaz Sharif put through legislation that limits the country's judicial code to the Koran and the Sunna.

It is not true, as is sometimes said, that the West, too, went through a period in which religious law, applicable to private behavior, and public law were fused as they are in Islam. The Christian West has been no less fanatical and persecutive than Islam, but it remains a fact that it maintained a body of law and a system of justice separate from Christianity. Even during the religious wars of the sixteenth century, points out Emmanuel Le Roy Ladurie, "secular magistrates often had the last word on matters of heresy." It was this preeminence of the civil authorities that avoided even worse excesses of religious fanaticism, which to be sure was bad enough. Western secularism has roots in Athenian democracy and ancient Rome, but even within Western Christendom it also developed in the Middle Ages. In the twelfth century, the Church itself insisted on dividing spiritual and temporal competences with the sovereigns. Thence comes the notion of separating politics from religion. The remarkable creativity of the thirteenth century did not spring by accident; it followed this first secularization of the state, which would be followed by that of civil society.

Long perceived through Marxist concepts, the causes of underdevelopment appear today primarily human and psychological. They stem from customs, mentalities, the weight of ossified civilizations, inadequate education, family and tribal structures, religious fanaticism, interethnic violence and warfare, oppressive political authority that destroy potential and are incompatible with development. It did little good for the West to bring money and technological assistance to people oppressed by predatory states so long as fundamental changes did not take place in social, cultural, and political structures. These changes were never demanded by a West that was afraid of appearing to despise the "cultural identity" of the countries involved, so post-World War II development schemes for the most part failed. Even among Arab oil-producing countries, which had from 1973 on immense riches to make use of, autonomous development, truly rooted in society itself, did not take place.

All of this is true up to a point. However, the problem is not resolved if we limit it to an opposition between the old and the new. The key breakthrough of recent years is that democracy, which conditions and is conditioned by liberal economics, has been understood as the path to development. However, what I referred to as the "democratic euphoria" caused a critical and even annoyed reaction among certain observers. Against the optimistic view of democratic universalism, they see the ineluctable resistance of traditions—African, Muslim, Chinese, etc.—that are deeply foreign to the democratic spirit and that simply cannot be changed in just a few years. These traditions stick; next to them, democracy is not a priority. Moreover, societies that today are democratic—the argument continues—got that way little by little and never completely. Why should the countries of the Third World get democratic in the same way and with the same kinds of institutions as Europe? To be sure, massacres such as occurred at Tiananmen Square in 1989 must be condemned, but should one not doubt that the more than a billion Chinese, a majority of whom are illiterate peasants, are ready for democracy? Or again: it is necessary to fight Saddam Hussein, but it is unrealistic to want to replace him with multiparty democracy, a system that the Arabs do not understand and have not even expressed much desire for. As to black Africa, its connoisseurs are the most skeptical of rapid democratization, which will not overcome its ancestral structures and particular evolutionary rhythms.

The weakness of this argument resides in the fact that most of the societies of the Third World are governed by regimes that are not traditional systems, but rather modern systems superimposed upon traditional ones. China has been brutalized by one version of modernity, communism, which reduced it to a barely livable pulp. Against the notion that one should not transfer Western political models to the Third World, one must reply that, for better or for worse it has been done already. Unfortunately, they were the wrong ones. The Third World took the worst the West had to offer: the fascist and Stalinist models instead of liberal democracy. Few Third World societies today are the products of their own traditions, and those that are, such as India, seem to accept democracy better than those that imported from Europe so-called progressive models. Morocco's traditional monarchy is probably more apt to liberalize itself gradually than the single-party Islamic-socialist dictatorship that smashed neighboring Algeria to pieces. Saddam Hussein borrowed more from European nazism than from the Arab tradition—with his secret police, his torture chambers, his executions, his genocides, his racism, his personality cult, his propaganda orgies, his fascination with military power and total war. It is likely the West did more harm to the Third World with the bad ideas it gave it after independence than through the injustices of the colonial era. In Vietnam as in China, democracy is inhibited not by traditional civilization but by Stalinist totalitarianism. And it is also for this reason that democracy is indispensable, for it is the only way to overcome this power that crushes all human development. There are authoritarian societies that function—not necessarily well, but they function; socialistic and fascistic Third World societies do not belong to this group. They are simply machines to destroy material and human resources that civilized societies need. They may ally themselves to religious fanaticism, as in Khomeini's Iran, or to secular idolatry, as in Mao's China, or to the grayness of a sordid bureaucracy, as in Vietnam, or to the murderous buffoonery of a Latin caudillo, as in Cuba. The result is the same: they destroy all that is creative in society. So for them, democracy is not a choice, it is the only way to advance toward a situation where the real problems can be faced and, perhaps, resolved.

PART FOUR

DEMOCRACY IN THE DEMOCRACIES

CHAPTER THIRTEEN

ROTTING FROM THE HEAD

OR KLEPTOCRACY

At the close of the twentieth century, even as all people till now deprived of democracy are striving—or pretending to strive—to secure it, democracy seems to be falling apart and losing its meaning in the very countries where it has been long established and most profoundly rooted. Paradoxically, at the very moment that the inventors of liberty ought and could at last serve as models, guides, and champions of liberal democracy throughout the rest of the world, their system appears to be malfunctioning, lacking a sense of direction.

There seem to be four causes of this pernicious enervation of democracy in the democracies. There is corruption. There is the ever-growing role in politics of advertising men and media consultants ("directors of communication"), who, standing by the mighty and the powerful, have replaced astrologers, magicians, and prophets—though evidently without eliminating these entirely. There is the lack of interest by citizens in public affairs, apart from the defense of their special interests; hence the decline of political participation, beginning with voting. And finally there is the dissociation of liberty and law, which is to say the definition of liberty not as the process of making laws on the assumption that all will obey them, but as the unconditional and unrestricted right to accede to all individual and group demands and impulses, even the most savage ones.

Throughout the world, the state, that enormous money-pumping machine, robs and impoverishes people. This is well-understood as far as communist and fascist dictatorships are concerned. It is less well understood, and far more alarming, where democracies are concerned, for it is evidence of the decay of one of their basic mechanisms, indeed their reason for being, namely the control by the citizens themselves of the management of public finances and of the honesty of their leaders. How will mature democracies rid the young ones of corruption, which is so harmful to development, if they themselves import the customs of the Third World? To be sure, corruption is spread very unevenly among the democracies, their political parties and their leaders. The U.S., despite what is said about it in Europe to lessen guilt by means of comparison, and Great Britain are less corrupt than France, Greece, Spain, Italy, or Japan.

In Japan, corruption is so well-organized and fused into the system's extralegal mechanisms that the press refers to it as "structural corruption," which implies that without it the system could not function. The same excuse has been proffered often in France with reference to the so-called (and evidently endless) phony invoices affairs. But this is surely the most damning explanation—for what is the merit of democracy if it is viable only thanks to stolen money? At least in Japan, non-"structural" scandals are punished without pity; not so in France.

In Greece we learn that the former Socialist prime minister, Andreas Papandreou, received, in 1988, $6 million in kickbacks from the Bank of Crete. The former director of this institution, his friend Georges Koskotas, hightailed it and ended in a U.S. jail, but not before spreading around $500 (yes) million to various leaders of the PASOK, the Greek Socialist Party. According to Koskotas, Papandreou used political power to force nationalized firms to make deposits in the Bank of Crete, which was a cornered minotaur, and to wipe out the deficit that another one of his friends had run up, a hotel-chain owner.

In Italy, the most important of the nationalized banks, the Banca Nazionale del Lavoro, found itself close to bankruptcy after lending over $4 billion to Iraq by way of indirect and complicated routes—and no one, officially, had ever authorized the loans! In the end the taxpayers will foot the bill without having ever had a chance to control the transaction or even know it was taking place. Moreover, it is estimated by specialists that fully a third of Italy's parliamentarians, ministers, and government officials are either members of the Mafia or under its control.

In 1989, the Austrian Finance Minister was personally implicated in one of the greatest political scandals of the decade, the clandestine delivery to Iraq of arms, in exchange for oil. The most virtuous democracies, the ones that preach to the whole world, involve themselves with gusto in the arms business; the same year, Sweden was up to its eyeballs in the muck of the Bofors firm.

More: Bofors' ordnance exploded far from home, making craters in still another democracy, one of the few, and one of the oldest, in the Third World, India. Several ministers, including the premier himself, were reported to have received $70 million from the Swedish firm "under the table." In France the shells made less noise: those of the Luchaire firm, sent to Iraq illegally and secretly, but with official blessings, were "disarmed" or at least equipped with a "silencer," namely the power of the president, which in our country always succeeds when it needs to in shutting up the other branches of government. Development Corner, Vibrachoc, Société générale, Pechiney, phony invoices—all our scandals dissolve in the moving sands of public lethargy or the cleansing waters of the self-amnesties that our politicians grant themselves. After all, this is not Japan or Switzerland, where officials feel they have to resign just because they got caught!

For a long time, dishonesty was merely a sore that came along with democracy, in the few truly representative regimes. It was not at the center of the system, as it was in countries where political power controlled economic life, as in the communist countries or Third World dictatorships. Nowadays, corruption has moved dangerously close to the heart of the system in a number of well-established democracies. This is probably caused by the opportunities offered by the state-created "mixed economy."

One form of corruption is to make direct or indirect use of political or administrative power in ways for which it was not intended, obtaining monetary or in-kind advantages for oneself or one's friends or servants or relatives or supporters. When a minister grants a subsidy to an organization with an imaginary purpose, even if he follows the regulations, he is in the wrong, especially if the beneficiaries of the subsidy are his political or personal friends. A subsidy of a million francs, for example, in 1992 was a year's profits for a successful medium-sized firm. Take a few thousand such cases (and usually with substantially larger sums), and what you have is a tax on producers in favor of prebendaries. The more production is taxed this way, the less investment and job-creation there is. Even if regulations are formally followed in these maneuvers, democracy does not escape unscathed. The people's money is channeled into partisan or personal uses, while the economy as a whole is enervated. The good minister who helps out his cronies probably does not see anything wrong in his behavior—this makes it only more serious.

Even in an advanced democracy, it is possible to loot the people in a thousand underhanded ways. There are consultant firms whose only purpose is to write phony invoices. There are municipal boondoggles for party workers. In this regard, the decentralization of power in France, in itself praiseworthy, provides innumerable new opportunities for abuse. This has to be understood so that safeguards can be put in place.

Some cynics maintain that, anyway, illicit money going into the treasure chests of a political party or a minister is merely a tax on the private sector, which does not cost the taxpayers anything. This is an error. Irregularities such as rigged bids distort the economy and cost the public far more than do fake invoices. The costs are passed on to the consumers. Entrepreneurs grow discouraged and hire fewer workers, so unemployment increases. What is needed in France is a reform of the regulations controlling nonprofit associations. These are crucial in a free society, but we need to review the criteria that allow them to operate and receive grants without any sort of oversight. For there is a breach here into which public money has been flowing uncontrollably under all manners of humanitarian, social, or cultural prextexts. For example, in 1986 an Inspection des Finances* report on a certain "Club TF1," an organization created in 1985 by the executive of TF1 (which at the time was a public television channel) with a budget of between five and ten million francs (there evidently exists no exact accounting), touched only the tip of what seems to have been an iceberg of abuse of public funds. The same year in Spain there was a scandal involving the illicit franchising of salespoints for the national lottery to family members of Socialist Party officials.

Corruption comes about when underhanded deals are made between public authorities and elements in the private sector in order

---

* The Inspection des Finances is the elite corps of high-level functionaries of the Ministry of Finance, charged with oversight of all French finances.

to get special fiscal favors, contracts for public works, exemptions from regulations, and so forth. This tends to occur in liberal regimes but is likely to grow with the increase of state intervention in economic life. In economies that have been collectivized to a larger degree, for example where there has been a great deal of nationalization, there is another kind of corruption, wherein the regime confuses what belongs to the state and what belongs more generally to the nation. This leads to a generalized use by the state of the national treasure to reward friends of the ruling party. These two forms of corruption are not mutually exclusive. The best obstacle to corruption is democratic control, and, by corollary, corruption is one of the most pernicious ways of subverting democracy. To understand how easily the French Socialists (among others) have been involved chronically in financial scandals even as they have held as a basic axiom that money is inherently evil, it is necessary to enter into the psychically bizarre world where the Left meets money.

The influence of Marxist ideology and, earlier, of the Catholic ideology led to a search for the corrupting influence of money precisely where it was least noxious. The fact is that to both Catholics and Marxists, money is to be fought in its commercial manifestation, not in its political form. On the other hand, they see nothing wrong with money when it is under the control of the political authority. In this, they are in fact going back to the uses of money in the old French and Spanish monarchies. Modern socialist states use money the same way. Holland in the seventeenth century, a commercial civilization if any place ever was, was far less corrupt than France or Spain in the same period. Dutch merchants had no reason to want to buy the state, which was weak to the degree it existed at all and whose favors they did not need to pursue their lucrative occupations. By contrast, in France and Spain the state's favors were the main source of enrichment—beginning with that of the top ministers, who were the great thieves of the time: Richelieu, Olivares, Mazarin, Colbert. Yet this institutionalized corruption, which was massive, continuous, no less inherent to the system than that of the communist and socialist nomenklaturas of our own time, is generally viewed as being less sordid than the kickbacks that occasionally tarnish the capitalist system. These are, to be sure, serious transgressions, but this is the point: they are recognized and punished, as such, which is not the case with institutionalized corruption (except as a pretext for political vengeance or purges), which stems from the control of the economy by the state.

Similarily, the Catholic Church said it was sinful to lend at interest, but viewed it as normal and even virtuous for the state to grant it abbeys and bishoprics, which came complete with rich revenues from immense land holdings and the exploitation of peasants. In the twentieth century, many priests and pastors have preached anathemas against capitalism while sparing the criminal states that starved and enslaved their populations, because these states, having abolished the market, could by definition no longer sin. The giving of prebends (the origin of the word is ecclesiastical) shocks neither the clergy nor the Marxists, but they are scandalized when a broker earns a commission for performing a real service, or when an investor who took a real personal risk takes a profit. To this incomprehension of commercial civilization is added, in France and the Latin countries especially, a notion of equality according to which disapproval is reserved for inequalities of personal wealth.

Our French egalitarian passion has led us to hide higher incomes, rather than try to raise lower ones. The French are notorious for hiding their wealth. The modesty of the rich regarding their gains helps the poor accept the modesty of their means. Another odd thing is that those who earn much from their own efforts are despised, while those who get just as much from the state are not. There is here a double incomprehension, of economics and of democracy. A lucrative, unproductive position obtained through favoritism or nepotism shocks less than wealth accumulated through economic creativity (which enriches others as well). Unlike the American public, we hardly mind when a high public official uses the state's airplanes to go off on a vacation paid for by the taxpayers, but if a rich citizen pays for his own vacation with his own money we consider it a gross insult to social justice. The French egalitarian passion is focused entirely on wealth produced by economic activity. It never is aroused by the ridiculous, ostentatious, and wasteful protocol that surrounds everything our rulers do.

Many authors explain our "scorn of money" by referring to our Catholic and revolutionary roots both, religion and socialism. But where do they get the idea that we hate money? We hate it when others make money by capitalistic behavior and approve when we make it for ourselves in less burdensome ways. What is at work here is not hatred of money as such. French avarice and greed, the passion to hoard, the extreme reluctance to give, our inhospitable customs, the virtual absence of private philanthropy and of individual generosity contrast proverbially with other countries that are close to us in their civilization and level of affluence. When a museum in the U.S. is called the Smith Gallery, it usually means that Mr. Smith gave away part of his fortune to create it. When in France a museum is called Musée Dupont, it means that Monsieur Dupont, former minister, had it built at the taxpayers' expense. Catholic Italy has innumerable private foundations of the kind found in America. The fact is that pinning the blame for our sordid behavior on Christian or revolutionary morality is a poor excuse. The French despise money the same way the ancien régime nobility did—they think it is humiliating to work for it, but not to get it and spend it if it comes in the form of rents. When I hear that a certain head of state "despises money" and then uses for his personal enjoyment public funds that a billionaire would be ashamed to display even if they were his own, I am reminded of a sketch by the cartoonist Maurice Henry. On the terrace of a cafe, two high-class bimbos (as they used to be called) are chatting. "It is true," one of them says dreamily, "money is not the only thing in life; there's also jewelry, furs, cars . . ." Of course the world's *elites* despise money! They are quite satisfied with castles, villas, cars, clothes, medical care, vacations, free feasts. And around the *elites* there gravitate the clerks who are "close to power," upon whom their political patrons shower favors. They are to French society today what the court abbots were in the eighteenth century. Taking time off from their publicly supported idleness they write powerful books against the "money culture."

And beyond the mere enjoyment of public funds, the amassing of fortunes by illegal means does not trouble the French. They hate capitalist fortunes which imply national economic progress, but they tolerate political fortunes, which is to say in effect money stolen from them. This resembles nothing so much as the Latin American attitude, which forbids private entrepreneurs from enriching themselves and applauds political leaders for doing the same for themselves and their friends. Here is a glaring example of what I mean. In 1982, Alsthom, a subsidiary of CGE (Compagnie Générale d'Electricité), which had just been nationalized, bought a firm, Vibrachoc, belonging to a friend of President Mitterrand. This small company, with capital of 10 million francs, was bought by Alsthom and two nationalized banks for 110 million. As if this were not enough, six months later Vibrachoc's books revealed that it had been suffering losses to such an extent that in fact it was worth only two million. A man named Alain Boublil, at the time assistant to the President of the Republic for industrial affairs (and whom we will find again in 1988, when he was the staff director of the Minister of Finance, implicated in the Pechiney insider trading scandal), was responsible for ordering this purchase. To whom did he give the order? To Georges Pebereau, recently appointed CEO of CGE by Mitterrand and who will surface again also in 1988 though in connection with the Société Générale bank scandal. In short, the word is fraud. It was organized at the highest levels of government and it allowed a close friend of the President, Roger-Patrice Pelat (the owner of Vibrachoc) to in effect steal 108 million francs from the state, that is to say from the taxpayers, for do not forget that Alsthom was a nationalized firm. More, the Finance Ministry allowed said friend to transfer to Switzerland part of the benefits of his sale, at a time when all capital flight was forbidden. In this case, the fraud perpetrated at the country's expense was not caused by "corrupt money." No sensible capitalist would have spent money to buy Pelat's failing business. The cause of corruption in this case is political power, and in particular the nationalization policy, which gave the officials in power the tool with which to commit their crime. So there is some cause for hilarity when you hear diatribes against "dough" on top of praise for the "scorn for money" by the kinds of men who arrange or allow such fraudulent schemes. One wants to quote Sacha Guitry at them: "You say you do not like money? Well then, give it back!"

Another form of "scorn for money" can be observed among people in France who, while certainly less rapacious than the state's great birds of prey, are no less blind with respect to the economic principles that make a society, notably their own, viable. I am referring to those who are not evidently part of the texture of production and exchange. I say "evidently," for in reality a teacher—for example—is basic to future productivity. But he does not view himself as part of the economic machine, and he feels rejected by the industrial and service cultures. In 1988 and 1989 much was made of the poor and worsening conditions in the teaching professions—drop in social status, fall in purchasing power, lack of esteem—and two complaints, in particular, kept recurring. They complained that Raymond Barre, a former prime minister, had referred to them as "well off." And they complained that in the eighties, the business executive had become the model figure of the times. "If you do not start a business, you are despised," complained a young history teacher on television. He could not stand the idea that Bernard Tapie (a Donald Trump type) should have become a media star in this period, as well as a Socialist minister until he was forced to resign in a fraud scandal. Well, as regards, "well off," what the teachers thought was that Mr. Barre meant "rich" when in reality he meant that in a period of rising unemployment and inflation, their lifetime job security, assured and indexed pensions, and similar benefits were not to be gainsaid. As to the prominence of the entrepreneur as role model, where is the insult? Is it not time to applaud the end of a long-held prejudice in our civilization, wherein only nonproductive, or more exactly noneconomic, jobs are held in esteem? In a country where a full third of the active population belongs to the public sector, where personnel costs in the state represent more than half its budget and more than a tenth of GNP, where do they expect to find the money to pay everybody? Where does this young history professor think money will be found to increase his salary, if not through taxes on the activities of wealth-creating producers? He cannot, unless he is stupid, despise money earned by an industrialist while esteeming his own. It is true that incompetence in this area sometimes reaches astonishing dimensions. On a popular television show (29 September 1989), Regis Debray, a high-level adviser to President Mitterrand, and himself a pure product of the French education system as well as Che Guevara's erstwhile public relations man, emitted the following profundity: "When the stock market gains forty points, two should be awarded to teachers." He probably had never heard of capital gains taxes, far more onerous than the "two points" he referred to although it is not clear just what that was supposed to mean. Also, he did not say if "two points" should be taken from teachers' wages when the stock market went down.

If the only respectable incomes are the minimum wage, the benefits of public service employees, and the subsidies given to the proteges of the Minister of Culture, then surely what this means is that our society is no longer viable, or we have an entire class of clerks too sick in the head to admit that it is fed by those whom it despises: the men who work with money. But what is significant here is this: the state's proletarians, who work for small salaries, provide a screen, with their small ideas, for the high-flying profiteers who waste the taxpayers' money.

This rapacity cloaked in hypocrisy, this preference for parasitism over productive activities, this determination nonetheless to hide both—the former because it is dishonest, the second because it is unpopular, are the cause of one of the most sterilizing features of French society: they prohibit private wealth from serving the public interest, or more clearly: they prohibit the rich man from helping his fellow-citizens. When we speak of the "public interest," we understand "the state." But there are a thousand ways of serving society without having recourse to the state. At least this is so in societies where citizens have enough autonomy in relation to the political and administrative authorities to work together for the common good.

Consider, for example, American universities. Donations from private individuals and organizations are essential to their well-being—not only private institutions but state schools as well. Buying the land on which they are built, establishing labs and libraries—at every step there is recourse to private generosity rather than public funds, which is the only way the French can imagine getting anything paid for. Higher education will fail to meet international standards if this continues. The only way French society takes part in the educational system is destructive: when teachers strike, when students protest, when parents complain. Creative initiatives on the part of citizens are unheard of. America, more than Europe, has preserved the classical tradition, strong in classical Greece and Rome, whereby a private citizen felt it was his duty, when he achieved a certain degree of opulence, to make public improvements. The French scoff at rich men's donations, saying it is merely a way Americans avoid paying taxes—as if we had not turned fraudulent tax evasion into a national sport!

But in truth, why should the wealthy in France feel an impulse to public generosity, when society despises them for their achievements? If rich men are going to meet with public scorn and ridicule for displaying their wealth through philanthropy (except when it is used to sustain a soccer club), why should they be generous? Why should a man create a library or a hospital wing if all he will do thereby is call attention to the fact that he earned a lot of money through despicable capitalistic activities? The consequence of our "Christian and revolutionary" hatred of money thus produces a society that is not less unequal than others, but that is surely more avaricious, egotistical, and hypocritical.

And more: it produces a paralyzed society. A cultural project initiated by the state is necessarily constricted, uninspired, undermined by favoritism and cost overuns, biased in favor of what is spectacular (due to the need for political propaganda) rather than serious. The abuses of this form of financing never stop those who profit from it from denigrating either the society of "show" or that of "money," even as they never suspect that they are talking about themselves. For example, what chance does François Mitterrand have of creating "the largest library in the world," plans for which he announced in the summer of 1988? (His sycophants later claimed he never used so bold a superlative, but the transcript of the interview in which he described, what since then has been reduced to "very big," leave no doubt as to his original wording.) The libraries of two American universities, Harvard and Michigan, with eleven and six million volumes respectively, have more books than our National Library, which has between eleven and twelve million. I will not be so cruel as to compare this to the collections in the Library of Congress or the British Library. But I would like to point to an example taken from the American average, for that gives one a better sense of what a culture can produce. The French section alone of a second-rank American university, Indiana, has more books in our language than the library at the Sorbonne. And its French collection ranked only seventeenth among American universities, at least when I visited it in 1983. Moreover, at the time it was already computerized. Our National Library still was not in 1987 when Emmanuel Le Roy Ladurie became its director, it was then done in a matter of months after years of procrastination. In twenty years we have established only one new library, the one at the Centre Pompidou; and it has a mere five hundred thousand volumes, not a very impressive number set against international, and even national, criteria. In a country where the state, with a monopoly on culture, has allowed its libraries to fall into such sorry shape, it is grotesquely funny to observe Mitterrand with his plans for the "greatest library in the world." Even if we had the resources to build it, we could not afford to fill it up with books, a majority of which are no longer in print.

The "triumphalist" library plans are typical of statist deformation. Unable to take care of what we have and to develop it in a reasonable way, we run away from our failure with a utopian and pretentious slogan, a project with "show" written all over it, though it will cost a great deal just to try it out and watch it fail. To be sure, it has the advantages of providing jobs for a few of the president's friends and it will bring him lots of publicity. We saw this already in the Bastille Opera project. Here you had a megalomaniacal delirium in the very conception of the thing, to which was added ignorance of the constraints of the lyric arts, and then the whole undertaking was capped by naming as the head of the Operas of Paris—all the operas, if you please—a dilettante jack-of-all-trades who could take the job only on a part-time basis, since he also runs a major couture firm* and whose only qualification for the post was that he had initiated, in 1988, a petition of intellectuals calling for the reelection of François Mitterrand. You might say that his appointment was the gift of designer socialism to lyric art. The lack of concern for the cost to the taxpayers, all in the name of the "democratization of culture," are the self-satisfied characteristics of the opera and library projects. "Scorn for money" in reality is scorn for other people's money, ordinary citizens'. But it is all done for their higher interests, of course. Perhaps this is what we now call the "republican spirit." In the name of morality, we say we have an "aversion for a system based on money" to cover up our cynical and underhanded squandering of public funds that are then used to glorify the leader by sycophants more interested in celebrating him than the world of art.

It is childish to think greed is only found in the worlds of industry and commerce. On the contrary, it is here that it is least unhealthy, because financial gain is the avowed purpose. Greed is far more dangerous when it hides behind supposedly disinterested activities. Far from having sullied itself in the "system of money," the problem with French society is that it has not got into this world enough. We French continue to have morbid relations with money instead of just getting in and acknowledging that you can have a rational attitude toward money and understand it for what it is, a tool and a measure. To see in money, as we do, an autonomous reality with its own dark forces, independent of the human beings who work for it, use it, spend it, is to exist in a prelogical universe of magic and prejudice. It is astounding that one of our major political parties was able to carry on for years on the subject of "corrupt money" and thought this amounted to a political program. Money does not corrupt a man: other men do, if not with money then with something else. You surely will not eliminate corruption by eliminating money. The greatest source of corruption in the world is not private property but public property.

---

* The reference is to Pierre Berger, one of the principal owners of Saint-Laurent, one of France's premier fashion firms.

François Mitterrand, appearing on television in February 1989, engaged in a clever obfuscation when he blamed on private capitalism the responsibility for recent financial scandals, since every one of them had its source in the political world, in the state bureaucracy, or in schemes between the latter and nationalized firms. The world of capital, the stock markets have their share of dishonest individuals, as do all sectors of all societies; and the law exists to deal with these people. But what had led Mitterrand to make a televised address was not ordinary criminality; it was a whole series of scandals in which political power was implicated in financial fraud. Most of the world's corruption stems from the mingling of politics and finance. For at its most basic, corruption is the use of political power for financial gain, or the use of financial power to buy political favors. The financial scandals of 1988 all had their source in the state. The Pechiney insider trading scandal involved a nationalized firm which, under the Finance Minister's control was buying an American firm. In the Société Générale affair, the minister himself launched a hostile takeover of another bank, using a front company organized for this purpose by, coincidence, a squad of the president's friends, who pocketed a tidy and ill-gained profit. Then when the deal soured, the minister took funds out of the Caisse des Depots* to bail it out, that is to say a savings institution guaranteed for small savers. Where was private capitalism? Nowhere. Mitterrand grabbed some television prime time to blur the real issues. Referring to the "gangsterism" of the the Paris stock exchange not only was an attack on his own country's credibility; it also happened to be a lie, since the transgressions here had nothing to do with the stock exchange and everything to do with the Finance Ministry and the presidential palace. In the indictment that came down in 1991, it was shown that Roger-Patrice Pelat, one of Mitterrand's oldest friends, had secretly bought, through a front, stock in the targeted company, Triangle, the majority shareholder in American National Can.

More economics and politics mix, more corruption grows. Even liberal (i.e., free-market) Switzerland got a taste of this in the Kopp affair, wherein the federal justice minister used financial information obtained through her political position. There have been major political-financial scandals in Germany, Australia, and especially Japan,

---

* The Caisse des Depots is the public office charged with responsibility for public funds and private savings—somewhat like savings and loans institutions in the U.S.

and they all have the same cause: namely, the opportunity of political office holders to grant favors to business firms to obtain, through them, confidential information.

So there was a certain amount of irony when some French Socialists suggested that the way to fight corruption was to renationalize some of the firms privatized by the liberals during their government in 1986–1987. It was as if to prevent alcoholism you handed out free Beaujolais at highway toll booths.

Excessive state interference in the economy is one of the major causes of corruption throughout the world. The more influence the political authorities have on economic decision making, the more it is tempting—and easy—to use political power to get rich. The well-known doctrine of separation of powers, which is fundamental to democracy, applies to economic power, too. The corruption resulting from the confusion of political and economic power is one of the plagues of the Third World, as it had been of the communist world. But now it seems to be undermining the established democracies as well—just when these ought to be serving as models for the new ones that are in the process of development.

Insider trading—the illegal use of confidential information to make profits in the stock market—is serious indeed when private operators engage in it, stealing, in effect, from other private investors. But it is far more serious when those involved are political officials, or their nominees, for here they are stealing from all the taxpayers. The blame then falls on the state, and the cost falls on the citizenry. When the U.S. SEC (Securities and Exchange Commission) sends a corrupt financier to prison, as was shown in the film *Wall Street* (based on a true story), it is punishing a dishonest individual, not the state. The latter is doing its job. But who will punish the state when it engages in fraud?

François Mitterrand's televised defense of his friend Pelat was beside the point. The issue was not whether Pelat merited esteem for his courage during the Resistance, nor whether he had a right, subsequently, to make a fortune. Obviously the answer is yes. The only issue was whether part of this fortune was a consequence of Mitterrand being president of the Republic, and whether it was obtained dishonestly. On this issue, Mitterrand did not utter a word, even though he monopolized a program that normally runs fifty minutes for two-and-a-half hours.

In Italy, democracy is perverted by the infiltration of the state and the political party organizations by the Sicilian Mafia, the Neapolitan Camorra, and the Calabrian N'dranghetta. But it is perverted, too, by the way the parties are modeled on business conglomerates. They own, control, and manage immense economic interests, in industry, banking, real estate, retailing, and services. But if parties are indispensable to democracy, since they provide the channels through which opinions can be expressed and perchance be turned into legislation, they go beyond their role when they become economic players. An entrepreneurial party is no longer simply a political party, if its freedom of action and opinion are constrained by its activities (and interests) in the economic realm. At the same time it is not a true entrepreneur, competing fairly with ordinary businessmen, since it has, thanks to politics, secret channels that allow it to cheat. In other words, it becomes a source of economic corruption instead of economic creativity. The mix damages the economy no less than it harms democracy.

The same sort of pattern is seen in Spain, in an even more overt and cynical way. Alfonso Guerra, number two in the Gonzalez government, installed his businessman brother, Juan, in an office in a government building in Seville. This office was used for years as a center of influence peddling thanks to which the Guerra family prospered. After six years the racket had ballooned to such a degree that the Socialists could no longer stonewall about it and the authorities had to shut it down. Juan Guerra was prosecuted, and over a year later Alfonso was forced to resign from the government, even though he remained in his position at the head of the Socialist Party. In spite of all, the Guerra affair did show Spanish democracy and justice at work, in stark contrast with the situation in France in the same period, where the Socialists were passing a law granting themselves a blanket amnesty for their many illegal activities.

The French presidential system, nearly absolute compared to the limited American presidency, has led to the creation of a political market of the sort we knew during the monarchy. More like the South American presidential systems than the U.S. (and no Latin American president has the power to dissolve parliament), what we have in France is a plebiscitary democracy in which the constitutional checks on executive power have been continually eroded. Until Mitterrand, we had to deal with straightforward autocracy. Since his election in 1981, we have seen the development of a vast system of corruption emanating from the very top and pervading the democratic institutions, in particular the judiciary. Under Mitterrand we have come to resemble Latin American regimes, complete with the covering up of the crimes of the regimes partisans and their relatives, interference with prosecutions, nepotism and favoritism, appointments and nominations to official positions and the leadership of nationalized firms on the basis of political criteria.

Not only is the national wealth looted when this happens, but when professionalism is the last concern of the master in selecting his nominees to high positions, the state's administrative competence soon begins to suffer. La Bruyère in the seventeenth century already observed that certain government jobs seemed to have been created simply to enrich individuals at the expense of the general population. Democracy was supposed to free us of this abuse, but it did not, and what is more, we find that jobs created to serve the public are turned into rewards for incompetent partisans. The economic chronicler of *Le Point*, Yves Guihannec, pointed out that when you get down to it nationalizing firms had little to do with Marx and the idea of collectivizing the means of production. It had to do with Saint-Simon, rather, the shrewd observer of court life under Louis XIV. Firms are nationalized to create lucrative positions for the monarch's favorites; forget about their qualifications!

Another form of corruption, or perversion of democracy, consists of creating useless jobs in the public and parapublic sectors to reward political loyalists. For example, in addition to its embezzling of public funds and other criminal activities, the PASOK (Greek Socialist Party) in 1989 tried to broaden its electoral base by creating, at a single stroke, fully 42 percent more state jobs! In the month preceding the legislative elections of 1989, Prime Minister Papandreou nominated seventy-two thousand redundant high officials for whom the next government had no use as well as no funds with which to pay them. Vote buying of this kind takes place in France too, particularly by way of statist intervention in cultural affairs. This results in the corruption of culture, the rotting of the spirit. Arts and letters then become instruments of propaganda for the president and the government. The Ministry of Culture and the Elysée (presidential palace) distribute jobs, decorations, subsidies, favors, invitations. They pay for moral slavery and flatter the vanity of cultural sycophants.

Thus, in a disturbing number of democratic countries, power transforms itself, as in dictatorships, into a means not of governing for the common good but of enriching oneself or, at least, of living well beyond the requirements of one's position; a means, I would say, of spreading prebends, at taxpayers' expense, among one's loyal supporters, of working up dubious financial schemes—in short, of looting the nation without risk.

In addition to being in and of itself a subversion of democracy, corruption leads to the deterioration of the judicial and parliamentary institutions, for the executive branch must reduce them to silence, and even more to impotence, if its own criminality is not to become known. Moreover, by its immorality, the state has a perverse influence on the rest of society. The rot spreads in the civil service even in countries like France where the state's bureaucrats traditionally have been, and for the most part still are, of exceptional integrity. But prosecutors and ranking civil servants find that in order to survive they must become, ever more, the accomplices of their masters. Finally, corruption in the advanced democracies has the effect of stimulating corruption in the Third World, thereby retarding the development of the poor countries, which the leaders of the rich countries claim virtuously they want to help. The venality of the political classes in the underdeveloped world in many cases can satisfy its needs only thanks to the venality of the leaders of the developed world. The "fight against hunger" has its advantages for the well-nourished, too. Classic examples of this sort of thing are the African summit at Bujumbura (Burundi) in 1982 or, the following year, the Luchaire affair (involving the illegal sale of ordnance to Iran), both of which events turned out to be profitable for the local political class and for the French Socialist Party. Some of the blame for the persistence of poverty in certain parts of the Third World needs to be sought among the politicians of the developed countries. Our corruption is conducive to their chronic underdevelopment, and the connecting thread consists of illicit operations organized with the connivance of their leaders and carried out due to our complicity with them. Moreover, this complicity prevents us from denouncing the defrauding that the populations in these countries suffer from at the hands of their leaders.

Gunnar Myrdal, who won the Nobel prize in economics in 1974 and was both a great economist specializing in the Third World and a mentor of the Swedish Socialist Party, wrote of Southeast Asia in 1968: "As a research subject, corruption is virtually taboo. It is rarely mentioned in scientific debates on political strategy or economic planning. Even Western experts have a marked bias which amounts to subordinating research to diplomacy. Whether they are of left or right, sociologists avoid these embarrassing questions."

For the fact is that neither the experts nor the officials of international organizations would keep their jobs very long if they factored corruption into their analyses of the Third World's persistent poverty. The political leaders who deserve indictment are the very same who command the majorities in these organizations. Why should there be any surprise when U.N. officials meekly approved atrocities taking place in Cambodia or Ethiopia? How much indulgence was shown to the authorities of Addis Ababa, who embezzled part of the international aid and transferred populations in conditions that caused hundreds of thousands of deaths! Around 1988 it was noted that African governments suddenly began to complain indignantly because NGOs (nongovernmental organizations) were proposing to furnish in-kind aid directly to the people who needed it. Imagine that! Aid must be turned over in cash to the relevant ministers.

Corruption complements corruption in developed and developing countries. It is pernicious for developed democracy no less than for embryonic democracy. Each has a snowballing effect on the other. On both sides, decision-makers and political parties get kickbacks through their fronts on the huge contracts for armaments, public works, food exports, sales of automobiles, jet liners, pharmaceutical products. Such a complicity prevents democracy from being introduced, even while weakening it where it already exists, if only because it forces the government to resort to lies and cover-ups and obstructions of justice.

The transnational strangulation of democracy by way of larceny received a great deal of attention in March 1991 when it was learned that for a dozen years Saddam Hussein had been embezzling public funds and sequestering them abroad. There was something grotesquely comic at play here, in addition to the purely technical side of the theft. Until then, it was possible to celebrate in Saddam the hero of the Arab world, or view him as a bloody megalomaniac who mistook himself for the reincarnation of Saladin. One could admire his crude cult of force or disapprove of the tyrant for whom crime was the principal instrument of power. It was possible to view him as a shrewd and persistant nut, or as a vain and stupid braggart whose interest was to cover his country with giant portraits of himself, even as he did everything wrong. Hero or devil, fox or idiot, he had at least one undeniable virtue, namely: he believed in his mission and was sincere in his conviction, even if he was delirious and fanatical about it—that he had a historic role to play in unifying the Arabs. And now we find that the hero is a seedy crook who slyly stole, every year, 5 percent of the oil revenues of his country (the world's second largest exporter) and, through secret fronts, hid it abroad. Behind the killer, in short, there was a con man and a swindler. And it was not a case, as usually happens with cornered despots, of stuffing a suitcase full of bills in preparation for his getaway; no, a money-laundering firm by the name of Montana had been incorporated in Panama as early as 1979 by his half-brother, soon to be the head of his secret police—and 1979 happens to be the year Saddam consolidated his rule in Iraq. In other words, even in an unassailable position, he had no faith in the future of his country or the mystique of the "pan-Arabism" that he trumpeted. So little faith indeed that he spirited $10 *billion out* of the country that was supposed to save the "Arab Nation." What would the Palestinians and the Maghrebians and the Jordanians think of their Joan of Arc after that? Joan of Arc had visions and heard voices too; but she did not stash her boodle in Switzerland.

Even on his own, Saddam would have looted his people. But the gigantic frauds that he pulled off were made possible by the West's cooperation—and this cooperation depended on dishonesty in the West no less than in Iraq. It was widely known as early as 1987 or 1988 that Iraq, despite its vast resources, was insolvent. This did not stop many Western firms from signing contracts with Saddam, even though they knew they would not be paid by their client, but rather by official agencies such as the French Insurance Company for Foreign Trade,* which the state guaranteed, not without a number of political favors in exchange. The bill was paid in the end by Western taxpayers, swindled by their governments to permit Saddam to swindle the people of Iraq.

According to the IMF, in the ten years from 1975 to 1985, developing countries placed in the West no less than $250 billion fraudulently gained. One hundred and fifty billion of these (three fifths) were for the rulers of these countries. In their programs and policies, "kleptocracy" has replaced democracy.

---

* This is the French Insurance Company for Foreign Trade, which functions rather like the U.S. Export-Import Bank.

Corruption is subverting most the world's states, eroding established democracies, blocking new ones. At a time when humanity requires nothing so much as democracy, the very model that we speak of spreading around the globe is becoming corrupt, perverting itself, changing for the worse in the very countries that the rest of the world should be looking to.

One consequence of corruption, and the requirement that it be kept quiet, is that political communication is increasingly turning into a technique of cover-up. As a general rule, politicians no longer win elections by telling the truth; indeed, they scarcely try to find out what it is. A successful electoral campaign nowadays is one that severs the links between the voters' common sense and reality, connecting it instead to the faked representations of the propagandist. By a peculiar perversion, this is taken to its furthest extreme in the advanced democracies. The "media advisors" and "communications directors" are now kings.

Nothing, perhaps, better illustrates this decline of democracy than what happened in France in May 1991. For the first time ever in the world, the president's personal public relations man, Jacques Séguéla, announced on television, ahead of his own boss and the day before it officially happened, the sacking of the prime minister, Michel Rocard, and his replacement by a woman (which may have been his idea, since nominating Edith Cresson as France's first head of government was expected to stir up support).

Now this may have been a good idea, but it had strictly nothing to do with the issues before the French government at the time. The whole purpose of media experts is to take the public mind off the real problems and get it focused on images. The idea is to replace thinking with feeling. It would be a mistake, however, to call them charlatans. They are, rather, like plastic surgeons, breast implant manufacturers. The charlatans, here, are their employers—the politicians. Modern public relations has brought about a situation where the voters make their decisions on the basis of appearances more than reality. As I noted earlier in this book, people's judgment is pretty reliable where choices are straightforward, for example when the issue is getting out of a dictatorship or a manifestly disastrous economic experience. But the more democratic societies become, the more complex become the issues and the more difficult the choices among desired but incompatible solutions. In this confusion, conducive to demagoguery, to say that democracy is a good regime because the sovereign people cannot err is a poor argument. The people err often enough and are easily led into error. It is *despite* this sorry reality that democracy is the least bad regime. But then tricks must not become the ultimate element in the arsenals of campaigns—in a grotesque dance of mutual alienation between the voters and the candidates, wherein the latter grow ever more manipulative and at the same time enslaved by public opinion, which they themselves deform.

This is an additional cause of the disappearance of democracy in those places where it should be strongest. The improvement of the means of persuasion, obsession with public relations, the appeal to feelings instead of critical reflection, the supremacy of affirmative instead of demonstrative statements, all the tricks of "communication"—which is the art whereby a leader gets himself judged on the basis of the impression he puts across rather than his record or his proposed programs—lead the voters to forget the facts, to lose sight of the real issues and their contexts. They then have a persistently growing difficulty in expressing, through their ballots, a choice based on real results or real reflection on the future. There is no doubt that this is partly a consequence of television. But we should beware of our tendency to blame on technology itself the way we use it; the responsibility for that is more likely to be found in ourselves than in our inventions. The art of seducing people by creating illusions or by hiding the truth is as old as politics itself. It goes all the way back to antiquity where, without sound equipment and cameras, there were orators just as good at this as politicians of our own time. They learned rhetorical techniques in special schools and had communications directors—they were called sophists—who were shrewd professionals and the most skilled of whom received fees that would make today's drool with envy. Eloquence was an obsession in antiquity and our own classical period, just as television obsesses us today, and it could be used and abused.

After the problem of corruption, and maybe because of corruption, there is a serious question in mature democracies as to whether the art of getting elected bears any connection to the ability to govern. Getting elected consists, increasingly, of getting votes on the basis of promises. It does not guarantee that one will govern in accordance with said promises, or even that one will govern with any sort of competence. As politics enters the age of advertising, dominated by communications directors and image experts, it is not, as Guy Hermet put it so well, the people who choose their representatives as much as it is the latter who get themselves elected by the former. Another slide into the decay of democracy occurs when election strategists take over the political high command, even if they have neither the competence nor the honesty to exercise it. This charlatanism is the fruit of corruption and adds to it, both before and after elections. After, the principle of incompetence and profit seeking that motivated the conquest of power will also motivate appointments to nonelected positions. Thus in Spain, not one of the 15,608 government job openings between October 1984 and April 1986 was filled on the basis of a competitive exam, as the law required. In France in the 1980s, the number of boondoggles at the highest levels and in cultural and diplomatic services reached proportions of shamelessness and ridicule comparable to the worst practices in banana republics—which is precisely the term that certain observers began applying to France. But they should be referring to a banana monarchy, for rulers who engage in these kinds of practices at the taxpayers' expense and in defiance of the laws are no longer democrats, even if they are elected.

Advertising strategies damage democracies before elections too, because high costs require that politicians seek unlawful ways of financing their campaigns. Indeed, we are now hearing the argument that corruption can be justified on the grounds that the high costs of campaigning render it necessary—otherwise there will be no democracy. It is worth saying the obvious: if a democracy is possible only on condition that it authorizes larceny, then it is a bad regime. Fortunately, what we have here is not democracy but a degradation of democracy due to its imitation of commercial advertising. It is interesting to note that the Socialists, who hate retailing and advertising in economic life—which is precisely where they belong—should copy its most vulgar techniques where they do not belong, namely in politics. The intellectual phoniness of democracy by advertising has a close causal relationship with corruption, firstly, in a purely financial sense, and then by eroding all sincerity from declared convictions.

We know what happens when the mutual contempt that eventually develops between voters and politicians sets in as a result of these practices: what happens is that people do not vote. Europeans often make fun of America's low voter turnouts, which in some elections reach half those eligible. Just so, but they forget or do not know that in the U.S., abstention is calculated on the basis of the total eligible population as determined by the last census. In Europe, it is calculat-

246

ed on the basis of those who are actually registered. If abstention were calculated the same way in Europe as it is in the U.S., we would have to add to our nonvoters many who are not even registered, and then we would find that our rates are quite comparable. For example, in the June 1988 legislative elections in France, of nearly 38 million registered voters, over 13 million abstained, or a little over 34 percent. If you add those who were not registered, you get a 40 percent abstention rate. With under eight and a half million votes, the "majority" party which would form the next government (i.e., the Socialists) had barely two thirds as many votes as there were abstentions. They had a third of the votes cast, less than a quarter of the registered voters, and about a fifth of the population that was eligible to vote. At this level, can one speak of a representative regime, even granting the conventional wisdom that the winning party represents the national will? Some "winners" look too much like losers. How can the European Parliament be representative when it is elected by less than half of registered voters and even less than 40 percent in many countries? Western observers were quite right to deplore the 60 percent abstention rate in Poland's legislative elections in October 1991, with all the scorn for the newly won democracy that this suggested. Even if the voters' disgust was motivated in part by the grotesque proliferation of caricatural parties that the proportional system encouraged, the Polish turnout in fact was respectable by comparison with many turnouts in established democracies.

The depth of democratic apathy seems to have been reached in the country that was the incubator of democracy in Europe, Switzerland. On 21 April 1991, the Administrative Council of the city of Geneva, the well-beloved home of the author of *The Social Contract*, was elected in a turnout with a 78 percent abstention rate! The "majority" that emerged from the 22 percent of votes cast formed a coalition government including one Communist, a Socialist and an ecologist! No doubt, even when elected by a fraction of the population, a government chosen according to the rules is legal and legitimate. Citizens who abstain from voting do so on their own volition and they are free the next time to stop doing so. The fact remains that it becomes difficult to speak of "universal suffrage" when participation is so low, and you have to question whether it expresses the general will. The relation between universal suffrage and the sovereignty of the people begins to ring false. Political leaders elected with such meagre support begin to look like trade union leaderships that are more oligarchic than representative inasmuch as they keep their positions through control of the union bureaucracy and the disinterest of the majority of their members.

Eminent historians such as Guy Hermet and Giovanni Sartori point out it is well to bear in mind that abstention was massive among the working classes during the early decades of universal suffrage. They recall that there are old traditions, even in the oldest democracies, of patronage voting in various forms. There is a passage in Tocqueville's memoirs that recounts the 1848 elections in Normandy when everyone in his village voted for him. These practices are still common in the Third World.

True, but I would answer that abstention, voting in accordance with what your ward leader tells you, submitting to the dictates of neighborhood racketeers, accepting corruption and vote buying, all these may indeed be viewed as democracy's growing pains, but they represent failure in democracies with two centuries of experience. Democracy in developed countries, long accustomed to representative regimes, is supposed to be the model for the stammering democracies of the Third World and the former communist countries, the goal they are aiming for. If the proposed model is nothing but a larger version of the embryo's vices, if the sought-after goal is capable of puerile regression or senile rot, then how can it be offered as a solution for the future? What must be kept in mind is that democracy allows the majority to express its choice; it does not guarantee the choice will always be a good one. There must be a clear distinction between freedom of choice and the assurance of the right choice. The former is a judicial and political concept; the second a mystical one in which "the people" are held to be infallible. As long as there are self-correcting mechanisms in the system, over the long run it is empirically demonstrable that popular votes will be the least unsatisfactory way of making choices. But to maintain that it is always right amounts to a pernicious sort of democratic bigotry. Peoples shedding dictatorships, totalitarian bureaucracies, oppressive systems, are sometimes those that display the greatest common sense because based on their own experiences the choice is straightforward. I have given several examples of such cases, which, however, need to be balanced by other examples.

Nepal's first elections based on universal suffrage almost produced a communist victory—in 1991! Putting aside the hypothesis that the charming and gentle people of Nepal are suicidal, we find quite understandable and ordinary causes here. First, since communications are not at the cutting edge in Nepal, there was little or no information available on the breakdown of the Communist regimes elsewhere. Indeed, Nepal was one of the last havens of ignorance in the world, one of these islands of credulity where even Beijing's propaganda services, discredited everywhere else, could peddle their "revolutionary" tracts. Second, in this primitive place it was not difficult for Communist politicians to simply go back to the crudest of their primitive slogans: we will distribute everything equally, land, houses, cars. As a matter of fact, prior to the elections crowds gathered to examine the properties, apartments, and vehicles that presumably were going to be parcelled out. Quite a few residents of the capital, Katmandu, went home to their villages to make plans with members of their families for dividing up the national wealth. Since, nevertheless, the Congress Party pulled off the election by a small margin over the Communist Party, Nepal did not become the first Hindu-Buddhist-Marxist monarchy in history.

European voters too have been led astray by lack of preparation. Even as they rejected their experience of communism they had deplorably naive illusions about the prosperity that was bound to follow in a matter of months. Without going over ground already covered, let us not forget that even well-informed people, with rich democratic experiences, can fall from time to time for primitive temptations. Was not the city of Geneva the last place in the world, apart from Nepal, where a Communist Party could make some headway in 1991? Alas, the Swiss Workers Party, too, became depressed following the failed August coup in Moscow and, in September, it announced that it was taking the word "communist" out of its bylaws and no longer accepted the designation. In fact there was a epidemic of this sort of thing. Soon after this, overcome by the suicidal madness, Guadeloupe's Communist Party announced its self-dissolution.

However, as citizens see modern democracy degenerating into political racketeering, as they increasingly feel that the way to get things done is to hustle the system rather than play by the rules, and as they see the system itself hijacked by special interests, you move toward a condition that I would call democratic apathy. This feeds an opportunistic skepticism regarding the virtue of legality. When in a state that calls itself democratic you can no longer expect it to provide basic services effectively through the application of the rule of law, not even security, indeed when it becomes apparent that the state itself—not to mention those who benefit from privileged relations with it—operates outside the law, why should anyone feel a duty to respect it? Moreover, by now everyone knows that to insist on one's rights often leads to nothing other than a long, exhausting, and useless struggle. Nowadays, the authorities in democratic states are not frightened and motivated by citizens taking their grievances to court, but rather by press scandals, demonstrations, and protests, violent actions that draw the attention of the media and provoke the appearance of disorder. Experience teaches members of society that it is easier to get attention from the authorities by burning down a public building, or looting a department store, or blocking traffic on the highway, than by going through the competent and designated channels. Add to this the senile romanticism of the notion that engaging in violent rebellion is to some degree justified because it implies that one was victimized somewhere along the line, and the state of law is taken less and less for granted. It is absurd to think of democracy as if it were dictatorship, but doing so expresses a profound malfunctioning of democracy. Violence is used either to protect unfair privileges or to obtain rightful ones, but the idea spreads that neither can be obtained through legal channels, and that whether or not you hold the law in respect, it does not pay to have recourse to it. Pressure rather than reason is what will influence the authorities. This is quite different from the arguments of Marx and Lenin against "formal liberty." Indeed it is the opposite. They said that "bourgeois" democracy was a fraud precisely because it is exercised. Here, we are talking about citizens who perceive a fraud because it is *not* exercised. In Marxism-Leninism, the legalistic illusion of democracy cannot be corrected, it is inherent to the system. Here, we are in the presence of the system's vices—which, I submit, can be extirpated.

We must not forget that even within the open society there are, and there always will be, those who want to do away with it. Communism nearly destroyed man, but man invented communism. The totalitarian systems of the twentieth century are discredited, but only after having reached the limits of their wickedness. However, the psychic needs that they somehow fulfilled have not disappeared. The hatred of liberty, disguised in "progressivism," will always motivate certain sectors of humanity. It cannot express itself in its Marxist form for the latter has been shamed and ridiculed everywhere except American universities. The totalitarian mind can reappear in some new and unexpected and seemingly innocuous and indeed virtuous form.

Naturally, we do not yet know under what doctrinal rationale the future danger will present itself, though its premises are probably already among us. It is likely that, in imitation of socialism, it will put itself forward under the cover of a generous doctrine, humanitarian, inspired by a concern for giving the disadvantaged their fair share, against corruption, and pollution, and "exclusion." Utopias are shrewd seducers, that propose the opposite of what they are really aiming for. Socialism concentrated all the wealth in the hands of an oligarchy in the name of social justice, reduced peoples to misery in the name of the sharing of resources, to ignorance in the name of science. It created the modern world's most inegalitarian societies in the name of equality, the most vast network of concentration camps ever built in the name of the defense of liberty. But such is the energy, talent, and terror marshalled by utopians to make the case that they should be judged by their intentions rather than their actions that a large part of humanity, watching communism from the outside, thought for a long time that it was natural or acceptable that the socialist ideal should be so radically negated by the real thing. Let us observe the behavior and the slogans and the movements that are inspired by these old utopias and we will get a sense of where the future threats are coming from.

There is another criterion for spotting an embryonic totalitarianism: it will almost surely, again, be anticapitalist. The utopians want to mobilize humanity in order to reform it. They hate economic liberty for they see clearly that the disappearance of private property leads to the end of political and cultural freedom. Totalitarianism's success is not only a matter of power relations. It is based on a permanent flaw in human nature and it expresses an ancient current of thought, which is all the more dangerous in that it depicts itself in the grandest colors. You cannot understand totalitarianism, let alone fight it, unless you first detect its intellectual roots. As Karl Popper showed in his classic *The Open Society and Its Enemies*, totalitarian thought is characterized by, among other things, "social engineering" or "social technology." This means that social reality can and must be entirely contructed in accordance with a blueprint. It is what socialists call a "program for society" (projet de société). This obsession must not be confused with "planning for society," (prospective sociale) which involves attempting to foresee the possible directions in which society might go and trying to plan accordingly, without trying to determine the direction in advance. The utopian project seeks a total remolding of the social organism in each of its parts, in the detailed manner that Plato designs his republic, from the foundations to the roof. This cannot be done outside a meticulous despotism.

This despotism is foreseen even at the theoretical level by the supporters of the closed society. Ordinarily we think of utopian philosophers as harmless dreamers, the only flaw of whose generous idealism is that it is unrealistic. When utopia comes to power, in Russia or China or elsewhere, this flaw leads it—we think—away from its overly ambitious humanitarian goals; in trying to reach them, it suppresses liberty. But this is not it. All the utopian authors factor repressive totalitarianism into their blueprints for society. Tyranny is the very essence of their thinking, not a consequence of the difficulty of putting it in practice.

It is the case in the *Republic* and the *Laws* of Plato, in Thomas More's *Utopia*, in Campanella's *City of Sun*, or in the *Manifesto of the Equals* that was inspired by Babeuf during the French Revolution. Forcible conformity, spying, constant supervision of work and private life, restrictions in the right to travel, similar houses and clothes for everyone, death sentences at nocturnal tribunals where no one can see the judges, as in Plato, for those who do not want to submit— these are some of the charms of utopias, as Igor Chafarevitch observes ironically in *The Socialist Phenomenon*. Both the *Communist Manifesto* and *Mein Kampf* provide for obligatory work for all, including the setting up of labor armies trained, organized, and led on the model of any other army.

These writings show that totalitarian plans continually have occupied an important part of men's intellectual efforts. They provide a catalog of symptoms that can help one identify the totalitarian or antidemocratic tendencies of currents of thought that may seem innocuous or even strongly philanthropic.

Maybe, in the last analysis, liberalism is nothing more than the confused sum of humanity's ways of resisting the persistant obsession with the idea that it can be purified by being enslaved. What is the open society other than a society where the organization and management of public affairs begins and ends in private liberty, where all citizens are equal before the law and have individual rights that no political power, even democratic and majoritarian, can take away from them. The annihilation of the private sphere and of the rule of law can be the consequence of the monopoly of power by the state, or a single party, or a religion. It is not religion as such, in truth, that threatens democracy, it is religion when it claims for itself the right to set down ideas and laws, in other words theocracy.

As we know, the establishment of the *Charia* (Islamic law) as the source of political, civil, and penal law, regulating public, private, and cultural life in Muslim countries is an obstacle on the road to democracy, development, science, and technology. But it is not the Muslim faith as such that deserves blame; it is the folly of wanting to confuse it with the state, with the law, with society. This kind of folly is even more astonishing when it emerges in a society that is a well-established democracy—Israel. Fortunately, here it is still only a temptation, not a reality. It is analyzed with depth and erudition by the Israeli philosopher and historian Gershon Weiler in a book of fundamental importance, called, as it happens, *The Theocratic Temptation.* Weiler vehemently—and knowingly—attacks the demands of Israeli religious fundamentalists "who are calling for the transformation of Israel into a Halachic-run state,* in opposition to the present theory and practice that make it a state of law." Should the fundamentalists win, Israel would resemble the Iran of Khomeini, whose laws "though more severe than those of the *Halacha*, nonetheless present a remarkable structural affinity with the *Halachic* system." It would be the revenge over Baruch Spinoza of Isaac Abravanel. This extravagant Jewish thinker (1437–1508), after a shrewd career in international politics as a leading diplomat, during which, like Talleyrand three centuries later, he rendered services to several sovereigns and several regimes without ever subordinating himself to them—all the while amassing a sensational personal fortune—proclaimed the dissolution of all forms of human government and the beginning of the kingdom of God. Against this, a century and a half later, Spinoza offered the *Theological-Political Treatise*, the unequivocal and straightforward founding statement of the idea of separation of state and religion. For Spinoza, God is not political nonbeing. The state cannot be sacred, since it can only be the emanation of human will, and it cannot obey two rival authorities simultaneously, i.e., base itself on two antithetical sources of legitimacy.

The idea of a secular state is still, even in our own time, far more than a matter of historical curiosity. Secularism means neutrality, for

---

* Halacha is the Jewish religious law.

253

the secularists too. However, many secularists think of secularism in terms of anticlericalism: which is to say, in terms of transferring to a secular authority the monopoly on ideas that previously had been held by the clerical authorities. This was the idea motivating the French teachers' unions when, in 1984, they tried to corner the market on education by establishing a single educational agency under their control. No one believes that the millions of French people who demonstrated peacefully to oppose this proposed legislation spend their lives at confession and at mass. The Catholic faith alone could not have sufficed to mobilize so many people in defense of private schools. The alarm was provoked by the perception that intellectual control over young people was going to be exercised by a new clergy: the Socialist and Communist members of the National Education Federation, whose political and cultural characteristics were not representative of French society. The theocratic threat, as we see, can take unexpected forms and, as the fable says, the shepherd may be the wolf in disguise.

This is not the only situation in which there is such a subterfuge. Democracy would be easy to practice if all the causes that are defended in its name were really democratic. The whole world requires democracy in order to survive or to be reborn. But this need will not be fulfilled, democracy will not spread, if the peoples who have had the good fortune of enjoying it longer than others do not rid their states of the two diseases which subvert it: falsehood and greed. How will the train roll if the locomotive breaks down? The world will be neither viable not livable unless it adopts democratic capitalism. But democratic capitalism will be neither acceptable nor will it be accepted if it does not become moral.

PART FIVE

TOWARD WORLDWIDE DEMOCRACY

CHAPTER FOURTEEN

DEMOCRATS ALL, IN SPITE OF OURSELVES

Ibant obscuri sola sub nocte per umbram

—Virgil

(They advance, alone, under cover of darkness)
We've been struck by an incurable good

—Philip Murray

"Few today hope to see the establishment of democracy on an international scale," wrote Hugh Thomas in his 1981 book, *An Unfinished History of the World*, expressing a perception that was amply supported by the progression of totalitarian and ordinary dictatorships on most continents. Ten years later, those who did not hope for a rapid spread of democracy on an international scale were the ones whose pessimism was blamed. I have explained earlier my doubts about the excesses of the recent "democratic euphoria." Yet, without leaping from anguish to ecstasy instead of going through the hard work of reflection and action, is it naive to acknowledge that in the end the fittest survived and it is possible to conceive, for the first time in history, the democratization of the world?

It is not. Democracy is not only conceivable, it is inevitable. It has been indispensable, but until now it was not inevitable. The best doctor, says Marcel Proust, is disease, which alone can force us to take care of ourselves when the time comes to make a choice between getting cured and dying. For humanity, this time has arrived. If democracy imposes itself, it is because it is the only doctor available. All other remedies failed, from Machiavelli to Marx, from Mohammed to Hitler. Worse than failed: They caused irreparable disasters, for even if they are fixed, that which could have been will never be replaced; the lost opportunities will never come back.

Democracy must be viewed soberly. It is not a luxury palace; rather, it is a night shelter for the homeless, a place to begin. Democracy is self-government, taking charge of oneself. Every time people say "them" when they refer to leaders, it is a bad sign. Democracy, too, is a kind of insurance against going beyond the tolerable level of mistakes, which is why, like Proust's doctor, it is needed even more by societies that are not well. Even in societies where customs seem to render democracy impractical, it brings about less destruction than the miracles with which so many in the twentieth century tried to replace it.

There have been natural cataclysms in history, epidemics, droughts, earthquakes, and cyclones, and they have killed millions, destroyed cities and crops, annihilated artistic and intellectual treasures, devastated the infrastructures of nations. Yet these plagues are nothing compared to those that have been caused by human action. The most destructive catastrophes are man-made, and above all statesman-made. They come from his appetite for conquest and domination, from the dead-end political systems he thinks up, his uncountable religious or ideological fanaticisms, and, especially, his obsessive need to reform societies instead of letting them change at their own pace. Democracy blocks, or at least slows down, this disastrous—and wicked—human propensity.

Twentieth-century history is clear on two points: only capitalism engenders economic development; only democracy can correct the worst political abuses and errors. This is why humanity faces a stark choice: democratic capitalism or extinction. I would revise Michael Novak's term to read: democratic and liberal capitalism. For capitalism can be illiberal—protectionist and closely associated to the state. In this case, it is not as much of an obstacle to development and individual liberty as is socialism, but it hinders them and creates incentives for the corruption of political leaders. Liberal democratic capitalism is not the best system: it is the only one [that works]. The parrots who keep telling us about its imperfections are right, it is imperfect. But the only prohibitive vice for a system, is not

258

for it to be without vices, but to be without qualities. And what we know about all the tested alternatives to liberal democratic capitalism is that they are without qualities. It deserves plenty of criticism, but these should not lead to the temptation of returning to collectivism or even milder forms of state control. Of course democratic capitalism has its share of sins; but as Robert Nozick put it, socialism does seem to be an excessively heavy punishment for them. And anyway it has been tried already.

Moreover—must it be repeated?—it would be a useless punishment. The leaders of underdeveloped or ex-communist countries (often the same) argue that economic take-off must come before democracy. For this read: they want the West's money but they do not want democracy. In the West, too, in "development" circles, the idea persists that take-off requires direct aid. The point is always the same: It is up to Western Europe and North America, the regions of the world that have attained a certain level of prosperity thanks to economic liberalism and democracy, to repair the disastrous and vain mistakes that ruined so many other countries on the planet. They must do it in two ways: by financing their economic reconstruction and by welcoming their emigrants. Most of humankind is circling around fifteen developed countries, calling upon them to open their coffers and their borders. Which confuses two issues. On one side are normal programs of humanitarian aid, the acceptance of real political refugees, economic and technological cooperation, rational investments. On the other side there is a fantasy whereby these devastated countries have a right to expect from us a permanent allowance even as they send us the mouths they cannot feed. According to the current cliche, they have a right to ask for their share of the cake. Apart from everything else this is a travesty of economic thinking. One tenth of humanity cannot bake a cake for the other nine. The only solution is for the other nine tenth to adopt the systems that worked in the West. A large part of the Third World committed suicide by copying the Soviet model or some other bureaucratic-authoritarian model. To repair the damage it is not enough to preach the new liberal gospel; it must be applied. And then there are the civil and foreign wars that add to the damage or bring poverty back. It is no solution to transfer all of the Third World's populations to the West and all of the West's wealth to the Third World. There soon would be nothing left of either. The levers of development are known. Success depends on the political will to use them.

An advantage of democracy is that it allows people to do well despite the poor quality of their governments. The looser the links between government and society, the more people can be productive despite the mistakes and the greed of their leaders. This is why *political* democracy is the absolute priority compared to *all* other goals of development, social justice, or anything else. "This is why," writes Giovanni Sartori, "when you speak of democracy without qualifying it, you naturally mean *political* democracy." But, he adds, "What democracy *is* cannot be separated from what democracy should be."

In short, democracy is not the disappearance of problems, it is only the least of them. It is not perfection, it is merely the best way to meliorate things. Above all, democracy is not totalitarian—if I may employ a truism—in the sense that it is not an "all or nothing" system. It is a system of "something," even of "just a little"—of "better than nothing." Liberalism is not the opposite of socialism. I have insisted on this throughout this book: in many regimes that are at many levels antidemocratic, there can exist beginnings of democratic institutions on which others can be built (and there can exist totalitarian elements in democratic societies that queer them).

These nuances must be kept in mind to guard against another misunderstanding that until now has confused the discussion about the spread of democracy, namely, the confusion between the idea of global democracy and global government. Global democracy does not mean some kind of utopian planetary government that would flatten the diverse nations and civilizations and cultures, annihilating the heritage of the past and the future diversity of humankind. To favor the democratization of the largest possible number of human societies is not to desire their homogeneity. Democracy begins with diversification since it gives to each people and each individual the right to differentiate themselves from others. Thus it favors the assertion of original cultures—which does not prevent, as a matter of practice, the organization of multinational communities with economic, political, or strategic objectives. Empires, not democracies (despite Tocqueville's worries) have been the cause of uniformity, especially totalitarian empires that are founded on a religious or secular religion. All empires that are founded by violence tend to make uniform the peoples subjected to the central authority. But ideological totalitarianism goes further: it crushes the center as well. This is the suicidal characteristic of communism. As Alain Besancon pointed out in 1977, "The Soviet Empire is not like others, a center surrounded by colonies. Solzhenitsyn and other Russian dissidents have no problem in demonstrating that the Russian people suffered from the Soviet regime as much, probably more, than the Armenians or the Georgians." To claim that democracy will force the peoples of the Third World to give up their cultural identities in order to conform to the Western model is to blame on liberty the effects of tyranny.

Actually, the problems that are likely to arise as democracy spreads in the world will be due less to growing similarities among different places as to a return of national, local, and individual particularities. Indeed this is what the Western governments, conservative as ever, feared so much (and still do) as the communist empire disintegrated. Unlike the totalitarians, we must not aim for some mad "perfection," and we must not blame democracy if it does not solve all problems at once; that is neither its aim nor its function.

"We are heading toward a time," wrote Jacob Burckhardt in the middle of the nineteenth century, "when the alternatives will be between complete democracy and absolute despotism. Despotism will no longer be practiced by dynasties, which are too compassionate. The new tyrannies will be run by military leaders who will call themselves republicans." They called themselves revolutionaries, the most prestigious word in the twentieth century. It was a century of coups d'état that were called revolutions. The misfortunes of this century are due to the fact that great criminals realized that the best racket they could come up with was to seize control of the state. And one thing is certain about this century: the more society submitted to statist power, the less well it was governed. What is needed is less state and more government. The democratic renewal stems from nothing so much as the practical necessity of diminishing statist omnipotence and impunity while enhancing governmental competence and responsibility—for humanity cannot persist in self-destruction. To put an end to this, democracy is not a goal, it is a minimal starting point, the only one possible. The entire planet cannot be hostage all the time to a series of local nuts. With some bad luck we would have been the century of Qaddafi. Better it be that of Jean Monnet.

This is what, during the decade of renewal, led to the revision of the notion of the sovereign state, in favor of democratic legitimacy and international solidarity. In the first place, it will be necessary to make of democratic legitimacy the sole and only criterion that could justify the recognition of one state by others; second, it will be necessary to lay the groundwork for a legitimate coordinating authority among states, replacing the interdependence that exists anyway but that is chaotic and irresponsible, with a coordinated and deliberate interdependence. Less pernicious management implies the elimination of illegitimate regimes and the breaking up of closed societies that are manipulated like grenades by dictators who are concerned neither with their own peoples' rights nor with those of the rest of the world. The distinction between foreign and domestic affairs will become to some extent blurred, leading, paradoxically, to a sort of Brezhnev doctrine of limited sovereignty, but in the service of democracy rather than totalitarianism. This is a logical evolution of international law: Countries that request economic aid, on the pretext that it reinforces the chances for democracy, ought to understand that the donor countries can taken an interest in their internal affairs.

Our era is aware that it is becoming impossible to perpetuate the absolutism of the sovereign state, particularly from the angle of human rights. Seeing the persecution of the Kurds at the hands of Saddam Hussein and the Turkish government, Jean-François Deniau, one of the most intelligent and courageous figures on the French political scene, suggested in 1991 that France draft an international statute for the protection of minorities. The idea was not taken up by the French president, but sooner or later it will be accepted. The fact that it can be enunciated shows how our notions of state sovereignty are evolving. Here again, democracy provides the ultimate solution, for the more a state is democratic the more it is likely to protect minority rights.

Nonetheless, relinquishing sovereignty is not merely a matter of human and minority rights. In June 1991 the international community called on Bulgaria to close down a nuclear reactor due to the risk of another Chernobyl. The Bulgarians said they would not do it unless a replacement were built for them. Interdependence is accepted when there are gains to be had, but not yet when there are responsibilities! In a case like this, it was, precisely, outside control over Bulgaria's nuclear program that was needed. The same will happen, or ought to, in such areas as arms proliferation, the spread of diseases such as AIDS, agrarian reform, destructive fishing practices, acid rain—the list can go on. The only way to control these cancers that affect all of humanity is to establish the right to intervene in order to disband regimes that promote them. It is clear that the cost of non-democracy is prohibitive.

An interesting sign of the times is the evolution of the idea of the "duty of intervention," which was popularized in 1987 by the founder of Doctors without Borders and Doctors of the World, the future French Minister for Humanitarian Affairs, Bernard Kouchner. Kouchner advanced this idea, which had been mentioned in one of my editorials in *L'Express* in 1971, to the point where it is being viewed as a right and not only a duty, and the U.N.—which for so many years ignored violations of human rights—has begun to be more aggressive in this area. The charter of the U.N., to be sure, may need some further elaboration. Peace and justice, to the men who founded the U.N. and had been engaged in the war against nazism, were part of the same effort. Democracy is not explicitly stated as a mission of the U.N. in its charter; perhaps it ought to be. Why expel Saddam Hussein from Kuwait, if within his borders he remains free to exterminate his own people?

Self-determination is not the same thing as the right to democracy. The history of the postcolonial era shows this: independence is not synonymous with democracy, on the contrary. The right of people to self-determination must be recognized as applying to foreign powers, but also to their own states. In other words, the principle of the independence of the nation-state cannot be separated from another principle: the legitimacy of this state. The latter must come first. Which implies a right to ask the following question, and a right to demand a satisfactory answer: Under what conditions did the authorities in any given state come to power?

The ideal legitimacy today is democratic. It alone would establish a clear legal basis for refusing intervention, since the policies pursued by a democracy express the choices of a whole people. But there are regimes that are legitimate without being democratic—regimes that have not yet advanced beyond their traditional political customs. They will advance toward democracy gradually. But regimes in which power has been seized violently do not deserve this sort of indulgence. Which is why human rights policies should not be thought of as being synonymous with pacifist policies. On the contrary; as Michael Novak showed in his 1986 book, *Human Rights and the New Realism*, human rights policies are as likely as not to be conflictual and subversive.

Saddam Hussein should not have been legitimate, precisely so that Iraq could get a legitimate state. The notion that he was needed to maintain stability is nonsense. It was grotesque to watch the world-wide coalition organized against him, whose power had been rendered possible by the democracies, defeat him in war and then let him off scot-free. It is clear that international law must evolve, even if it will be difficult to find the new and appropriate notions to allow it to do so.

The past two centuries can be viewed from the angle of the progress of democracy, or the progress of totalitarianism, or as a race between the two. At any rate the debate is now closed. Enough madness: we are condemned to be governed under liberal democratic regimes.

Men are able to conceive and build political institutions that are more rational than they are, and to freely place themselves under their rule. However, it is unlikely that we will ever be capable of building a world that is qualitatively better than we ourselves are. There is within us an unchanged impulse which prefers failure to success, misfortune to happiness, might over right, violence over justice. To attenuate this fatal flaw, our primary political goal ought to be able to stop thinking about it.

In other words, politics ought to rid man of politics, which is to say: it should teach him to be himself without depending on the collectivity. This is where we see that it is a mistake to fault liberal society for "lacking an ideal." On the contrary, this is what renders it noble. An individual needs a society-given ideal when he is incapable of giving himself one. But then he is not adult—not even adolescent. Yet the whole evolution of the West has been to make an individual who is free and even obliged to become the author of his own destiny, and who is capable of doing this. The tragedy is that until our own times, so many individuals have shirked before this prospect, fearing mediocrity, anguish, loneliness. So they invented collective madnesses to avoid their personal responsibilities, on the threshold of free and liberal civilization. Totalitarianism is a deadly substitute for man's self-improvement.

Democracy depends, to function well, on citizens being autonomous individuals. This means that culture is understood to provide a capacity to sustain oneself, escaping from the emptiness and loneliness by the resources of one's own mind. Education is ever more important as societies grow more democratic. The purpose of education is not to prepare for a job; it is, far more, a preparation for understanding and giving meaning to the civilization in which one lives. Only the cultural maturity of the majority will allow democracy to last. Otherwise fanaticism and violence will motivate people. They will be their only way of filling the spiritual void of their existence, by replacing individual liberty with collective exhaltation.

It is therefore not at all true that the triumph of liberalism will create a dull society. This mediocrity has been feared ever since Tocqueville. Political society may become dull, but civil society will be exciting. For when public life is banal, private life becomes original. Only professional politicians would make us believe in the greater importance of collective affairs, for they fear the loss of their field of action. When societies are shaken by tempests and utopias, man becomes an impersonal atom, tossed about by forces that drown him in anonymity, crush him, determine his destiny and his place in life. And what could be more dull than these grand melodramas in which people are brutalized together? Where else do we see more uniformity and conformism, people who resemble one another chanting identical nonsense written by others? There is no lasting democracy without the cultural autonomy of each person. Democracy allows free men to be born, but free men enable democracy to last.

INDEX

DATE			